The Legend of
the Golden Boat

ANTHROPOLOGY OF ASIA SERIES

Series Editor: Grant Evans, *University of Hong Kong*

Asia today is one of the most dynamic regions of the world. The previously predominant image of 'timeless peasants' has given way to the image of fast-paced business people, mass consumerism and high-rise urban conglomerations. Yet much discourse remains entrenched in the polarities of 'East vs. West', 'Tradition vs Change'. This series hopes to provide a forum for anthropological studies which break with such polarities. It will publish titles dealing with cosmopolitanism, cultural identity, representations, arts and performance. The complexities of urban Asia, its elites, its political rituals, and its families will also be explored.

Dangerous Blood, Refined Souls
Death Rituals among the Chinese in Singapore
Tong Chee Kiong

Folk Art Potters of Japan
Beyond an Anthropology of Aesthetics
Brian Moeran

Hong Kong
The Anthropology of a Chinese Metropolis
Edited by Grant Evans and Maria Tam

Anthropology and Colonialism in Asia and Oceania
Jan van Bremen and Akitoshi Shimizu

Japanese Bosses, Chinese Workers
Power and Control in a Hong Kong Megastore
Wong Heung Wah

The Legend of the Golden Boat
Regulation, Trade and Traders in the Borderlands of Laos, Thailand, China and Burma
Andrew Walker

The Legend of
the Golden Boat

Regulation, Trade and Traders in the Borderlands
of Laos, Thailand, China and Burma

Andrew Walker

UNIVERSITY OF HAWAI'I PRESS
HONOLULU

© 1999 Andrew Walker

Published in North America by
University of Hawai'i Press
2840 Kolowalu Street
Honolulu, Hawai'i 96822

First published in the United Kingdom by
Curzon Press
15 The Quadrant, Richmond
Surrey, TW9 1BP
England

Printed in Great Britain

Library of Congress Cataloguing-in-Publication Data

Walker, Andrew.
    The legend of the golden boat : regulation, trade and traders in
the borderlands of Laos, Thailand, China, and Burma / Andrew Walker.
        p.   cm. – (Anthropology of Asia series)
    Includes bibliographical references and index.
    ISBN 0–8248–2255–2 (cloth : alk. paper). – ISBN 0–8248–2256–0
(pbk. : alk. paper)
    1. Mekong River Region–Commerce.   2. Boundaries–Mekong River
Region.   3. Ethnology–Mekong River Region.   4. Inland water
transportation–Mekong River.   5. Trade regulation–Laos.   6. Trade
regulation–Thailand.   7. Trade regulation–China.   8. Trade
regulation–Burma.   I. Title.   II. Series.
HF3790.8.Z5W35   1999
382'.09597–dc21   99-28886
                                                                          CIP

Contents

List of tables

List of maps

List of plates

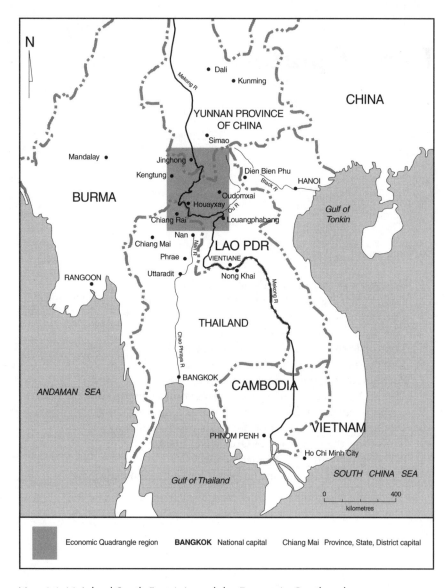

Map 1.1 Mainland South-East Asia and the Economic Quadrangle

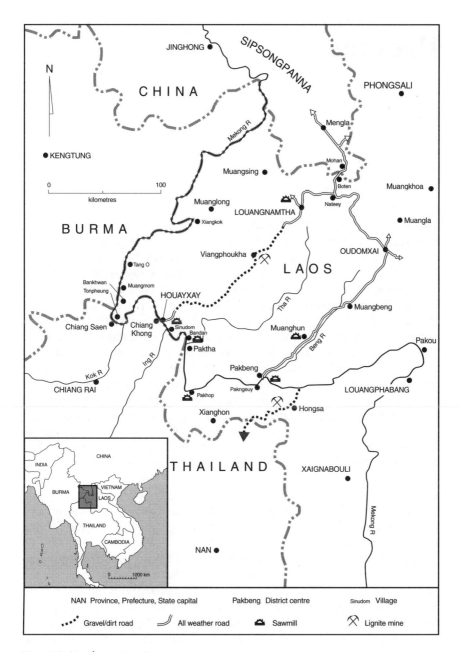

Map 1.2 North-western Laos

Preface

This is a book about places in the upper-Mekong borderlands (Maps 1.1 and 1.2) and about the people who create and regulate commercial linkages between those places. My journeys through these places started – and finished – in the northern Thai town of Chiang Khong, a busy trading centre on the Mekong River border with Laos. In 1994 and part of 1995 I lived in a house which overlooked the town's river cargo port and lay directly opposite the official residences of the Chiang Khong customs officers. It was an ideal location to observe the regulation of trade and cross-border passage. Most days I would make the short walk past the customs house and the local temple, and down the concrete ramp to the cargo port, a non-descript stretch of mud where traders loaded their purchases onto boats at the start of their downstream journeys to the Lao towns of Pakbeng and Louangphabang. The port is exposed and hot and I often squatted in the shade of piles of boxes or stacks of Lao timber chatting to traders and boat operators about their commercial ventures. The port is "managed" by the Chiang Khong cross-river boat operators who, after initial caution, welcomed my presence at the port and provided me with a wealth of information, not only on their own activities, but also on trading conditions across the border. My evening drinks and discussions with them, overlooking the mellow Mekong, provided some of the highlights of my life in Chiang Khong.

Several times a week I travelled across the Mekong border to the cargo port at Houayxay, passing hours talking with traders as they waited patiently for their customs formalities to be completed. A small shop above the port provided welcome shade and refreshments and numerous conversations with boat owners, local officials and the ubiquitous three-wheel taxi drivers who were always full of snippets of information and scandal. Less regularly I travelled downstream to the dramatic port at Pakbeng, where rows of trucks wait for cargo to arrive from Chiang Khong or Louangphabang and where crowds of wild-eyed port labourers sometimes gathered around to watch me as I scrawled notes in my pocket note-books. This was the most "heterotopic" port of all – Lao traders unloading their tinned fish and orange juice; cautious Chinese drivers (with girls in high-heels) squatting by their trucks sipping on jars of tea; tiny Hmong boys scrabbling in the riverside rubbish for plastic bottles; Thai sawmilling entrepreneurs with useless mobile phones worrying over the food in the *Bunmi Restaurant*; and Dutch tourists causing shock (and delight!) by bathing naked in the scantily partitioned bathroom of the *Sarika Hotel*. It was an ethnographer's dream.

During the time I spent at the ports, I formed close relationships with several groups of Lao traders who welcomed me into their boats, trucks and homes, often overwhelming me with their hospitality. In the course of my fieldwork, I travelled with these traders on about ten trading journeys to Pakbeng, Oudomxai – where the large market is a popular trading destination – and even to Mengla in southern China. These journeys provided invaluable information on their trading activities, on the operations of long-distance trucks and boats and on the complex and ever-present regimes of transport and trading regulation. The presence of a questioning and note-taking foreigner can hardly assist when conducting delicate trading negotiations with customers and officials and I am indebted to them for their constant and good-humored tolerance of my presence.

During my travels in northern Laos, I became aware of the importance of the export trade in Lao timber. In the latter period of my fieldwork, this became an important focus of research. There are powerful vested interests involved in this trade and collection of quality information was difficult. I visited all but one of the sawmills in the north-west and, in some cases, owners or local managers were happy to talk about some aspects of their business. I also visited all of the timber trading companies with offices in Chiang Khong and, once again, a number provided me with valuable information. However, due to the general reticence to discuss the timber trade, I relied heavily on collating fragmentary pieces of information collected in the course of my general research. At a late stage in my fieldwork, two key informants provided invaluable information. As far as possible, all information on the timber trade was cross-checked against government decrees, reports and statistics.

My work in Thailand was made possible by the *National Research Council of Thailand* and by the cooperation of provincial and district authorities in Chiang Rai and Chiang Khong. In Laos, research was made possible by the support of the *Ministry of Communication, Transport, Post and Construction*. Knowing little about myself or my research project, officials from this *Ministry* generously met my requests for assistance and arranged an invaluable multiple-entry courtesy visa. Provincial and district officials in both Laos and Thailand also assisted me in the collection of data, even when my requests were not directed through the appropriate channels.

This book is a revised version of my doctoral thesis which was undertaken in the Department of Anthropology, Research School of Pacific and Asian Studies (RSPAS), The Australian National University (ANU). My thanks are extended to the Department for providing the environment in which this challenging work could be undertaken. Professor Peter Rimmer (Department of Human Geography, RSPAS, ANU) provided invaluable advice on clarifying and refining the structure and argument. Dr Peter Hinton (Department of Anthropology, University of Sydney) and Ted Chapman (Department of Asian Studies, ANU) introduced me to the fascinating research possibilities of the upper-Mekong region. Professor James Fox and Dr Andrea Whittaker (Department of Anthropology, RSPAS, ANU) read drafts of the book and provided valuable comments. The comments of my doctoral examiners – Dr Paul Alexander, Dr Grant Evans and Dr Andrew Turton – also assisted in focussing and clarifying the argument. Preecha Juntanamalaga (Faculty of Asian Studies, ANU) provided me with an excellent introduction to the Thai language. Ian Faulkner and Neville Minch (Cartography Unit, RSPAS, ANU) produced the maps. My doctoral research was funded by an Australian Commonwealth Government Post-Graduate Research Award and by a Commonwealth Government Award for Research in Asia. It would have been impossible to undertake this work without the Australian government's financial support.

My partner, Diane Podlich, accompanied me for most of the time I spent in Thailand and Laos. I doubt I could have done this without her consistent support, advice, companionship and encouragement. In her perceptiveness of human relationships and her good memory for faces and events she is a much better anthropologist than I. Our daughter, Mali, born soon after our return from Thailand in 1995, has been a constant source of joy during the sometimes difficult period of writing this book. My thanks for moral and practical support must also go to Jean Podlich (child-minding), Lynette and Kevin Robin (endless practical support and accommodation), John Walker (proof-reading) and Marion Walker (juggling funds).

Finally, and most importantly, I must thank my parents, Elsie and John Walker, who taught me to read and write. It is more than appropriate that I dedicate this book to them.

Languages, names and currency

Languages

Lao words have been transcribed according to the system used in Kerr (1979) in his *Lao-English Dictionary*. However, where Kerr uses "ɨ", I use "y". For example, the Lao word for "boat" is transcribed as "*hya*" rather than "*hɨa*." Also, where Kerr uses a colon to indicate a long vowel, I repeat the vowel – "*paak*" rather than "*pa:k*" for "mouth." The one exception is that the Lao currency has been transcribed as *kip* – following common usage – rather than *kiip* (Kerr 1979: 98). Thai words are transcribed according to the system used by Haas (1964) in her *Thai-English Students Dictionary*. The one exception is that the Thai currency has been transcribed as *baht* – following common usage – rather than *baad* (Haas 1964: 288). For both Lao and Thai words, tone markers have been deleted. All transcriptions are written in italics. In the interests of readability, I have minimised the number of transcribed words. For other foreign words, I have used the English language spelling that occurs most commonly in the literature. I have translated quotations from French language sources, though the original spellings of place names in quotations have been retained.

Place names and ethnic groups

Place names in Laos are written according to the English language spelling used in official Lao maps issued by the *Service Géographique Nationale*. Where there are inconsistencies in the spellings in the official maps, I have followed the most common usage. Where places do not appear on the official maps, I have followed the conventions established by them or, where necessary, followed spellings in other official publications. However, there are a number of important exceptions where the names I have used differ somewhat from those in official maps or documents. First, the capital of Oudomxai province is indicated in official maps as Xai, or Muang Xai. However, by far the most common usage I encountered was Oudomxai. I have followed this popular usage and, where necessary, indicated if I am referring to the province or the town. Second, all of the province and district level towns in official maps have the prefix "Muang" (town) written as "M.". In popular usage, some of these towns are referred to with the prefix Muang while others rarely are. Once again, I have followed this popular usage and used the prefix with, for example, Muangsing and Muanghun but not with Pakbeng and Hongsa. Finally, for villages I have used the official prefix "Ban" where it is popularly used – such as Bandan – but deleted it where it is not. If alternative prefixes such as "Pak" (mouth) or "Muang" are commonly used, I have also used them.

Place names in Thailand are written according to the official English language spellings set out in the Prime Minister's proclamation on the writing of place names (GOT 1977). For small towns and villages that are not included in this list, I have used English language spellings provided by provincial and district authorities. For place names in Burma, China, Vietnam and elsewhere I have used the English language spellings that appear most commonly in the literature. I have used "Burma" rather than the official "Myanmar" for reasons of personal and political preference. For all place names I have used modern designations – with the exception of Siam/Thailand – even where such usage is anachronistic. In some cases this has involved some simplification: for example, northern Vietnam is used to refer to the French colonial territory of Tonkin. Of course, I have maintained original designations and spellings in quotations, with a clarification placed in square brackets if necessary.

For spellings of the names of ethnic groups, I have followed the main English language spellings used in LeBar (1964). Where other designations or spellings are used in quotations, I have inserted a clarification if necessary.

Personal and company names

To protect confidentiality, all personal names have been changed, except in the case of public figures. For all personal names, I have used the English language spellings that most commonly occur in the media and other literature. Business names have not been changed, though the source of confidential or controversial information provided by businesses has been disguised where necessary. For all business names, I have used the English language spellings used by the businesses themselves, even if these spellings conflict with the various conventions outlined above.

Currency

The Lao currency is the *kip*; the Thai currency is the *baht*; and the Chinese currency is the *yuan*. The predominant wholesale trading currency in the region is the Thai *baht*, though *kip*, *yuan* and American dollars are also used. When referring to prices and charges, I have used the currency that is most commonly used, usually *baht*. Within the Lao trading community, all the currencies are relatively interchangeable but *baht* are not readily accepted across the border in China and neither *kip* nor *yuan* are accepted by the wholesale shopkeepers in Thailand. At the time of fieldwork (1994–1995), one American dollar converted into approximately 25 *baht*, 700 *kip* and 8 *yuan*.

Abbreviations

ADB	Asian Development Bank
AFD	Agricultural and Forestry Development Company
ASEAN	Association of South-East Asian Nations
BP	Bangkok Post
DAFI	Integrated Agriculture Forestry Development Company
EQJDC	Economic Quadrangle Joint Development Corporation
FAO	Food and Agriculture Organisation of the United Nations
FEER	Far Eastern Economic Review
GLPDR	Government of Lao People's Democratic Republic
GOT	Government of Thailand
IBRD	International Bank for Reconstruction and Development
IMC	Interim Mekong Committee
LPDR	Lao People's Democratic Republic
MAD	Mountainous Area Development Company
NEM	New Economic Mechanism
NVA	North Vietnamese Army
PL	Pathet Lao
RLG	Royal Lao Government
RT	Reuters Textline
SWB	BBC Summary of World Broadcasts
TFAP	Tropical Forest Action Plan
TN	The Nation
UNDP	United Nations Development Program
USAID	United States Agency for International Development
VT	Vientiane Times

The Legend of the Golden Boat

Long ago, thousands of years perhaps, two brothers – Malawar and Malawor – came to the banks of the upper-Mekong, a short distance downstream from the site of modern-day Houayxay. They were the sons of a famous chief who ruled in a distant kingdom and they had come to find a suitable location for a new settlement. Preparing to camp for the night, they climbed a small hill that had magnificent views of the Mekong and the mountains and plains on the opposite bank. As they approached their chosen resting place, they met a wandering monk who had also travelled long distances in the sparsely settled upper-Mekong lands. Eager to make merit, they asked the monk to stay with them, promising that they would prepare food and present it to him the next morning (monks, of course, cannot eat after mid-day). The wandering monk agreed.

As evening approached, the monk told the brothers that he wanted to go down to the river to bathe. They went with him, scrambling down the steep slope to the river-bank below. He asked them to wash his robes, a request to which they readily agreed. When they had completed their meritorious task, he told them to spread the yellow robes out on a large rock where they would quickly dry in the remaining sunlight. The brothers then bathed themselves, careful not to venture too far from the bank into the brown and treacherous water. When they had finished, the monk told them to retrieve his robe. To their shock and delight, they found that it had turned to gold.

The old monk who recounted this story read it out of an exercise book. I had gone to his tiny temple, just a few kilometres south of Houayxay, with friends from the local tour company to visit a small stupa, which I had seen many times as I travelled up and down the Mekong by boat. Climbing up the steps to his rustic quarters, Mali – keen to play her part as a tour guide

1

– explained that I wanted to hear the story of the stupa. He was happy to recount it, slowly putting out his cigarette and sorting through a small pile of papers to find the book. As the story proceeded, the old monk became more animated and his digressions and clarifications made the story hard to follow. It was not clear, for example, what the itinerant monk wore once his robes had been turned to gold. Nevertheless, later that afternoon – over bottles of Lao beer and fried cashews – my "guides" helped me to piece the story together.

Malawar and Malawor made a bed for the monk and the three of them slept on that hill above the Mekong. The next morning, after the brothers had prepared food and presented it to the monk, he had more requests to make of them. Running his hand across his head, he produced three golden strands of hair which he presented to the brothers, telling them to use the strands and the golden robe to make a small boat. The brothers followed his instructions, using the golden hairs for the framework and the robe for the outer shell. The monk then told them to place the boat on the ground and build a stone stupa above it to protect it from theft and to remind people of his miraculous powers. He installed dangerous angels to guard over the stupa – anyone trying to steal the boat would bleed to death from the nose, mouth and other bodily openings. A little later, the monk and the brothers continued their separate travels. Where they went is not known, but the stupa has remained as their monument. Through millennia of invasion, settlement, devastation and depopulation, the golden boat has remained safe on its small hill above the Mekong.

CHAPTER ONE

Introduction

The Economic Quadrangle

> "The Economic Quadrangle" is now the focus of Asia ... as the economic place for consumers who demand more choices for shopping and excursion. Also investors, businessmen and manufacturers who are intent to expand their trading, and investment can aim at increasing their benefits. ... We are ready for those investors, who are aiming for success, and profits, by cooperating with the Lao People's Democratic Republic. This is a golden opportunity in doing business, in the area full of natural resources and labour with lower wages. Therefore we can assure you of stability and achievement in business. (*The Economic Quadrangle Joint Development Corporation* promotional brochure, 1996)

In the first half of the 1990s, the Economic Quadrangle emerged as a popular motif in discussions of South-East Asia's northern borderlands (Map 1.1). For its proponents in international development organisations, national governments and regional chambers of commerce, the Quadrangle was an ambitious vision of liberalised economic integration across national borders and rugged terrain. Creation of transport linkages between the expanding economies of northern Thailand and southern China via the hinterlands of Burma and Laos was promoted as a sure path to regional development and prosperity. In the tawdry tourist stalls where the borders of Thailand, Burma and Laos meet on the upper-Mekong, Economic Quadrangle tee-shirts (four flags and a river of blue) were sold alongside the opium memorabilia and Golden Triangle kitsch (three flags and a poppy) of an earlier socio-geometric era. A new frontier, we were told, was opening up: a deregulated upper-Mekong corridor; a new era for the borderlands.

3

The Economic Quadrangle Joint Development Corporation (EQJDC) – a joint venture between the Lao government and a northern Thai construction firm – was one of the most ambitious and optimistic proponents of this new era. As recently as 1996 it marketed an extraordinary future for north-western Laos, one of the "quarters" of the Quadrangle and the focus of this book (Map 1.2). The company's promotional brochure featured a glowing, golden map of north-western Laos, flanked by glossy pictures of investment opportunities, laid out to tempt the Thai entrepreneur. Service stations, warehouses, chemical plants and shopping centres mingled with charming thatched-roofed villages, nestled in verdant highland valleys. Artists' impressions of cruise-boats, trains, tour-buses and airlines were arrayed in formation, ready for the transport infrastructure that would dissect and liberalise the region. And a resort hotel, complete with a glistening swimming pool, glowed in the setting sun against the backdrop of a blood-red sea. As even the most cursory cartographic inspection will show, for north-western Laos this was a formidable vision indeed.

But in the Thai Mekong River town of Chiang Khong (Map 1.2) – the main trading point between northern Thailand and north-western Laos – an undercurrent of weariness about the Quadrangle hype provided a sobering counterpoint to this glossy bravado. Visiting in late 1996, I heard endless stories of the problems of doing business across the Mekong in Laos. These ranged from the trivial – the cross-border petty traders who were regularly harassed by the Lao immigration police as they sat and waited for orders from tardy customers – to the more significant – the summoning of Thai timber traders to a meeting in Louangnamtha (Map 1.2) where Lao military brokers demanded a multi-million *baht* payment in return for timber price stability in the coming year. In Chiang Khong itself the arrival of a Thai river navy unit – with machine-gun mountings on metal speedboats and allegedly overactive libidos – hardly encouraged a sense of borderlands liberalisation. And, at the southern end of town, Chiang Khong's 40 million *baht* cargo port – jutting out into the Mekong on a forest of concrete pylons – was busiest at night when small mobile restaurants moved in to sell hot food, cool beer and whisky. No doubt, it was a pleasant view looking across the Mekong towards the Lao provincial capital of Houayxay – lit up like never before, courtesy of a new power line running from Chiang Khong. But, when the frequent blackouts came, it was very dark. "That's the Economic Quadrangle," one customs officer told me. "When there's a blackout in Chiang Khong, the lights go out in Laos."

This book seeks to unravel and explore some of these ambiguous borderlands images. It focuses on transport and trading networks in north-western Laos. These networks branch out from Chiang Khong to the Lao towns of Houayxay, Oudomxai, Hongsa and Louangnamtha (Map 1.2).

The *historical focus* of the book (chapters 2–3) is on the long-term development of these networks, while the *ethnographic focus* (chapters 4–7) is on the truck and boat operators, traders and entrepreneurs that are contributing to the 1990s surge in borderlands trade. The aim of the book is to come to a more detailed understanding of the social and spatial processes in this sector of the Economic Quadrangle. While recognising the importance of contemporary transformation, it seeks to look beyond the hyperbole of promotional brochures and *Asian Development Bank* wish-lists (ADB 1993; 1996a; 1996b; 1996c) to explore the Quadrangle's ambiguous and contradictory terrain. In doing so, it provides a new approach to the study of the borderlands.

Beyond "The Periphery": Analysing the Borderlands

How are we to approach these contemporary processes in the borderlands? The central argument of this book is that the Economic Quadrangle is the latest in a series of regimes of upper-Mekong *regulation*. The essential paradox of the region – which goes a long way to explaining the contradictory images outlined above – is that *as trading and transport conditions become more liberalised, opportunities and incentives for regulation flourish*. This ongoing regulation, while generating frequent complaint and disillusionment, also provides (unevenly distributed) benefits and opportunities for the transport operators, traders and entrepreneurs who are the agents of cross-border exchange. In fact, these mobile border-landers are often active collaborators in processes of upper-Mekong regulation. Placing a focus on regulation provides important insights into the socio-spatial processes that are now unfolding in north-western Laos. These insights complement those gained from some of the more popular socio-spatial approaches used by anthropologists, geographers, historians and international relations theorists. Before examining the concept of regulation, two of these more popular approaches – the centre-periphery model and the globalisation model – warrant some detailed discussion.

Centres and peripheries

The concept of hierarchical, asymmetric and often exploitative relations between centres and peripheries has been enormously popular in the "mapping" of socio-spatial systems. It underlies the influential world systems theory developed by Wallerstein (1974); it is a central concept in seminal geographic analyses of locational behaviour developed by Christaller (1966) and Thünen (1966) – which have also inspired forms of "regional analysis" developed by Skinner (1964) and Smith (1976b; 1976c) – and is often implicit in anthropological pre-occupations with a peripheral and relatively less powerful "other" (Friedman 1994: 5). In mainland South-East Asia, centre-periphery models have had a compelling – though often unconscious – appeal in a region where a primary sociological motif has been the relationship between economic, administrative and religious centres in the densely settled lowlands, and less powerful settlements in the forested and mountainous hinterlands (Burling 1965; Leach 1977; Walker 1992). In modern times, the national and regional pre-eminence of Bangkok – its population is more than ten times that of any other city in Thailand and greater than the population of Laos – has given centre-oriented models a certain inevitability.

Centre-periphery models have been particularly prominent in analyses of pre-colonial social formations in South-East Asia. Writing of what he calls the pre-colonial "galactic polity," Tambiah (1985: 260) argues that it was based on a "conception of territory as a variable space, control over which diminished as royal power radiated from a centre." The royal centre, he argues "ideologically represents the totality" and "there is a faithful reproduction on a reduced scale of the center in its outlying components" (Tambiah 1985: 266, 261). In relation to Laos, Taillard (1989: 44) writes of the pre-colonial city surrounded by a series of "satellites, more or less distant and autonomous, but maintained within the centre's zone of influence" and Stuart-Fox (1997: 7) of the segmentary *mandala* in which "larger power centres extract[ed] tribute from similarly organized smaller ones." In northern Thailand and Laos, the key element of these socio-spatial structures was the *myaŋ* (as in Muangsing, Muanghun and Muangbeng in north-western Laos), a polity focused on a rice growing river-plain with dependant villages in more remote areas of the river valley and in the mountainous areas of the surrounding watershed (Penth 1994: 16–17; Stott 1991: 145–146; Wijeyewardene 1991: 162–170). In return for military protection, the outlying villages contributed labour, tribute, taxes and marriage partners thus "sustaining respectively the religio-symbolic, economic, and military bases of the central power" (Stuart-Fox 1993: 107).

In these studies of pre-colonial social formations, a common and influential theme is the weakness of central control in peripheral areas. Power, which *radiated* "like a candle's light" (Thongchai 1994: 100) from a central point, diminished with distance. In the jungles, mountains and "blank space" (Thongchai 1994: 75) of the borderlands, it was exhausted altogether or overlapped with the dim radiances of other remote centres. Some borderlanders, like the "[t]ribal people wandering in the mountain forests [who] were subjects of no power" seemed to escape central authority and regulation altogether (Thongchai 1994: 73). Even the townships in the borderlands were "more or less independent and neglected" and "generously given away [by the regional powers] for the sake of friendship" (Thongchai 1994: 99–100, 79; see also Ramsay 1976: 19–21; Stuart-Fox 1993: 107 and 1997: 11). According to these centre-oriented models, pre-colonial polities had no clearly defined boundaries or borders in their peripheral zones (Thongchai 1994: 74–80, Stuart-Fox 1997: 11). The borderlands, it seems, were the zone of ambiguity, flexibility and nonchalance, well outside the historical trajectories of the region's main powers.

In most historical accounts, centre-periphery relations were dramatically transformed by the bounding and demarcating pressures of colonialism and modern statehood (Hirshfield 1968; Keyes 1993: 11; Ramsay 1976; Thongchai 1994). As British and French colonial interests clashed – as they did on the upper-Mekong – it became necessary to create unambiguous and clearly demarcated systems of territorial administration. Thailand, fearing colonial penetration into its central heartland, actively participated in the demarcation of the borderlands and, to give the new boundaries some substance, developed administrative and military control over its own peripheral zones. Whereas the analytical centre-periphery motif of the pre-colonial era is *"radiance,"* that of the modern era is *"penetration."* In wide-ranging analyses of Thailand's frontier century, a series of writers have drawn attention to the centre's penetration and incorporation of the periphery through administrative development (Chaiyan 1994; Kemp 1991; Ramsay 1976; Turton 1989b); agricultural expansion (Pasuk and Baker 1995: 3–88); cultural and linguistic domination (Davis 1984: 24–27; Keyes 1993: 12–18; Tapp 1989); military conquest (Mayoury and Pheuiphanh 1989; 1994); development projects (Hirsch 1990); and even medical practice (Whittaker 1996). The socio-spatial relationships formed by this penetration seem more problematic than those of the past and in these accounts there is a frequent emphasis on conflict between national elites in the centre and resistant communities in the periphery (see also Chai-Anan 1995; Cohen 1987: 210; Grundy-Warr 1993; Rumley 1991). In Laos, where state structures appear to be much less developed, some have argued that traditional centre-periphery relations persist. "Provincial administrations today," writes Stuart-Fox, "are the modern *muang*" (Stuart-Fox 1993: 115; see also Taillard 1989: 63). However, Evans has argued that there is a "qualitative difference" between pre-colonial and modern structures in Laos and that "[t]he difference between deploying soldiers on elephants against wayward lords and being able to send MiG jets against refractory provincial governors should not be sneezed at" (Evans 1991b: 158–159; see also Gunn 1990).

From a centre-periphery perspective, the Economic Quadrangle can be seen as the latest stage in central penetration of an increasingly international periphery. This is reflected in a number of recent contributions. Rigg (1995), for example, is one writer who has written of the dangers of Thai domination of Lao economic and cultural life, reflecting what are said to be widespread concerns in Lao official circles. "It is Vientiane's historically subordinate position to Bangkok," he writes, "which provides an important background 'text' to current economic and political development" (Rigg 1995: 160). From this perspective, the Economic Quadrangle danger for Laos is that it may be crushed in the enthusiastic Thai embrace. Examining developments to the north, Evans (1996) has written of central Chinese domination of ethnic minorities in the Mekong borderlands of China. His study of the township of Jinghong (Map 1.2) is replete with foreboding images of local villagers trapped in a developmental "*cul-de-sac,*" feeling "powerless" in the face of the central Chinese onslaught that will eventually submerge them (Evans 1996: 25, 15). Feingold (1996), has also highlighted growing socio-economic pressures on peripheral populations, painting a grim picture of highland minorities in the Mekong hinterland confronting government resettlement programs, rampant commercialisation, infrastructural penetration, a burgeoning trade in women and girls, and an explosion in HIV/AIDS. Finally, at the most general level, the notion of unequal centre-periphery relationships underlies Hirsch's (1995) analysis of the "regional resource economy" which, he argues, is dominated by the resource demands of Thai industrialisation.

There is no denying that these various analyses have identified important social, cultural and economic processes in the Mekong region. However, this book argues that their prognosis is altogether too stark and pessimistic. The fundamental division they implicitly draw between dominating centres and dominated peripheries does not do justice to the complex and contradictory processes unfolding in the Mekong border-lands. If a more subtle understanding of the Economic Quadrangle's development is to be achieved, some of the underlying weaknesses of this hierarchical mapping of space need to be explored (Agnew 1993: 256–261; Grewal and Kaplan 1994: 9–11).

Of most concern is that centre-periphery approaches tend to over-simplify power relations, whereby power inevitably flows from the centre outward or, as if by gravity, from the "top" down (Abou-el-Haj 1991: 140). This is most evident in the common preoccupation with the extension of central state power into peripheral areas but, of course, it also has an international dimension. For Laos, geographically peripheral and inter-nationally insubstantial, centre-periphery models inform a discourse of vulnerability and disempowerment that is reminiscent of the paternalistic fantasies of the colonial era (Stuart-Fox 1997: 3–4, 41). Current concerns about Thai domination seem to have largely replaced previous claims about Vietnamese control, though in some recent formulations a submissive Laos faces de-facto dismemberment with Thailand, Vietnam *and* China dividing the spoils between them (Nguyen 1996; Stuart-Fox 1995b: 180).[1] Of course, there is no denying that different places, and

---

1 For a critique of earlier claims of Vietnamese domination, see Evans and Rowley (1990: 59–66).

nations, have different degrees of power, but these images of peripheral passivity may cast less light on complex relationships – between *and* within nations – than a more dispersed and fragmented notion of power. A growing body of research in Thailand, for example, is showing that power is often more complex and contested than previous models of central domination may suggest. The increasingly political role of business associations (Anek 1992); the emergence of provincial power bases (Hewison 1995: 156–157); the embeddedness of local officials in village and district power relations (Hirsch 1989; Turton 1989a); and the proliferation of corruption as a socio-economic strategy (Pasuk and Sungsidh 1994) all suggest that a "centre-centric" view of power may be misleading. In developing a deeper understanding of the Economic Quadrangle, there is a need to recognise the contours of "peripheral power" that are not always accounted for by the presence *or* absence of central power. What Massey (1993b: 148) calls the "happenstance juxtapositions which occur in place" – and what better place for juxtapositions than the borderlands – create ragged contours (and scattered nodes) of power (sometimes in the most unlikely places) that cut across the centre-periphery relationships privileged in many socio-spatial models.

A more general concern – that is particularly relevant to the study of the upper-Mekong borderlands – is that centre-periphery models often privilege the practices and ideologies of the centre. In the various centre-oriented models, peripheral areas tend to be characterised in terms of their *absences*, whether they be central power, civilisation, infrastructure, loyalty or even culture itself. In a not-so-subtle intertwining of elite ideology and spatial analysis, the peripheral borderlands come to be mapped as "frontier zones" characterised by "rebelliousness, lawlessness and/or an absence of laws" (Kristof 1959: 281). These images of the untamed frontier – packaged to perfection in the Mekong's "Golden Triangle" motif – often have more to do with the anxieties (and fantasies) of the "centre" than with the social and cultural realities of the "periphery."[2] Where peripheral social structures are taken seriously, they are sometimes presented as replicas of the centre – albeit on a smaller scale – providing so-called "structural continuities" (spatially and historically) that must be the dream of central administrators (Stuart-Fox 1993: 113). Similarly, where local histories are acknowledged, they are often written selectively, in terms of the locality's contribution to the "national narrative" (Thongchai 1995: 113). Even those theoreticians who attempt to give due credit to the socio-spatial

---

2 In a recent paper, Porter (1997: 217) expresses strong reservations about the imposition of "externally derived identities" in development practices in the eastern Shan states of Burma. Yet, at the same time, he maintains the central motif of the "Golden Triangle." Similarly, Watts (1992: 117) writes that "frontiers are characteristically savage, primitive, and unregulated. At the margins of state power, they create their own territorial form of law and (dis)order." See also McVey (1984: 18–20) and Sukhumband and Chai-Anan (1984).

processes in the borderlands seem to provide a mirror-image of centrist ideologies in their preoccupation with marginality, liminality and hybridity (Bhabha 1994).[3] For Gupta and Ferguson (1992: 18) the borderlands may well be an "interstitial zone of displacement and deterritorialisation that shapes the identity of the hybridized subject" but in the upper-Mekong borderlands many people lead quite regular lives – earning a living, sending their children to school and watching the six-thirty news at night. We need forms of analysis which are not preoccupied (negatively or positively) with their marginal status.

Globalisation

For some, the more open and flexible concept of "globalisation" is a theoretically attractive alternative to binary centre-periphery models. It is a "qualitative step forward," writes Abou-el-Haj (1991: 143). "It suggests no charged hierarchical divisions, is less concordant with spatial boundaries or geographical regions, [and] is capable of encompassing unequal distribution *within* as well as between national and regional entities." In the same volume, King (1991: 11) comments favourably on the "neutrality" of the term, carrying with it much less "cultural, religious, [and] historical baggage" than other socio-spatial constructs. The concept of globalisation, in its flexibility, is said to be more sensitive to the chaotic and disjunctive nature of contemporary inter-relationships; less *Euro*centric in its recognition of the intersecting and *multi*centric condition of late modern experience; more appreciative of the post-colonial displacement and diaspora that have mixed and confused "centre" and "periphery;" and more focused on the multiple and shifting identifies of an increasingly mobile global population.[4]

The central concept of globalisation theories is *connectedness*: not the one-dimensional connectedness of centre-periphery models, but the multiple, disjunctive overlapping and compressed connectedness that late modern changes in technology, production and consumption have bought about (Appadurai 1990; Harvey 1989; Robertson 1992). There is no doubt that the intense and intricate interconnectedness of the late-modern era has encouraged *homogenising* processes – as *Coca Cola*, for example, penetrates further into the cultural and commercial niches of the international market – but the predominant preoccupation of globalisation theory has been on the simultaneous production and maintenance of

---

3 Mitchell's (1997) discussion of the "limits of the liminal" covers these issues well.
4 Appadurai (1990; 1991); Abou-el-Haj (1991); S. Hall (1991; 1996b); Hannerz (1991; 1992); King (1991); Barth (1992); Gupta and Ferguson (1992); McDowell (1996); Robertson (1992); Grewal and Kaplan (1994); Fardon (1995); C. Hall (1996a); and Chambers and Curti (1996).

difference.[5] At one level, the proliferation of difference is reflected in Western pre-occupation with *non-Western* art, ritual practices, music, dance and theatre (Howell 1995: 165–174). A profound "cultural revolution" has occurred, according to Hall (1991: 34), as the hitherto margins have come into representation. At another level, difference is produced through processes of creolisation as cultural products are appropriated, dissected and repackaged in a bewildering display of global multiculturalism (Hannerz 1991). Don't be fooled by superficial homogenisation, we are warned; the *Coca Cola* bottle on the southern Japanese altar represents, in fact, "the torso of a pregnant woman" (Howell 1995: 177).

The "cultural optimism" of globalisation theory is reflected in a number of more up-beat assessments of the Economic Quadrangle. The Thai scholar, Chai-Anan (1995), has placed great emphasis on the opportunities that arise for borderland communities when cross-border connections proliferate. He applauds the erosion of the artificial and homogenising constraints that have been set down by centralising states and colonial powers. The re-emergence of "traditional" cross-border relationships, he argues, has enabled towns and villages in the borderlands to socially and economically "bypass the state." Cohen's (1996) analysis of a major ritual in the north-western Lao town of Muangsing is a vivid case-study of this re-emergence of trans-border cultural communities. While some may bemoan the homogenising presence of Chinese and Thai *karaoke* bars in northern Lao towns, the regionally important religious festivals in Muangsing suggest that "peripheral" creativity is flourishing as restrictions on cross-border passage have declined. Reynolds (1998) has also identified these cultural and economic processes in the upper-Mekong region but goes beyond this to suggest that the "gaze from Bangkok to the north" has implications for cultural and national identity in the Thai heartland itself. In brief, the Economic Quadrangle can be seen as creating opportunities for reclamation, renewal, and innovation.

This more benign approach to the Economic Quadrangle is an important influence on this book. It seeks to analyse the active involvement of local communities in creating and maintaining trans-border connections. My particular focus, however, is on the ways in which connections and flows are *managed* and *controlled*. The issue of power is crucial here. While centre-periphery models may too willingly and uncritically locate power and influence in central places, there is a real danger that the reality of power may be lost in the "[e]conomically and politically neutral, technologically-transformed space of 'the global'" (King 1991: 9; see also Hyndman 1997: 151–153; Mitchell 1997: 109). Theorisation about

---

5 For a discussion of some of the processes of homogenisation, see Hall (1991: 27–28); Hannerz (1991: 107–108); Appadurai (1995: 217–219); Harvey (1993: 12); and Gupta (1992: 19).

deterritorialisation, placelessness and diaspora may obscure the extent to which global interconnections are created and controlled by people living in, and moving between, places. As Massey has written:

> Different social groups and different individuals are placed in very distinct ways in relation to these flows and interconnections. This point concerns not merely the issue of who moves and who doesn't, although that is an important element of it; it is also about power in relation *to* the flows and the movement. Different social groups have distinct relationships to . . . mobility: some are more in charge of it than others; some initiate flows and movement, others don't; some are more on the receiving end of it than others; some are effectively imprisoned by it (Massey 1993a: 61; see also Massey 1993b: 145).

The issue then, is less one of homogenisation versus difference – with its centre-periphery echoes of penetration and resistance – than one of examining the complex ways in which people, in places, manage the interconnected nature of those places (Grewal and Kaplan 1994: 13). This management – what I call regulation – is the central theoretical concern of this book.

Regulating flows

Connections and flows – of goods, information and people – between places are problematic. They generate advantage and disadvantage; they are often the subject of dispute; and they are regularly the subject of intervention. They are an important sphere for the exercise of power. Following Massey (1993a: 62), this book attempts to develop a "politics of mobility" that goes beyond a celebration or condemnation of interconnectedness to an understanding of its "dimensions of control and initiation." It seeks to explore the strategies people living in places use to manage their connections with other places and, in doing so, participate in non-local processes. A concern with regulation lies at the heart of this analysis.

In this book the concept of regulation has a very specific focus. It is defined, quite simply, as *the practices people employ to initiate and control mobility and interconnection*. Specifically, my primary concern is with the social, economic and cultural practices that are used to encourage, restrict, direct, supervise and tax *transport* and *trading* systems. My emphasis on mobility draws on the time geography of Hägerstrand (1970; 1978) whose key interest was to analyse the spatial and temporal paths that interacting people follow in the short cycles of their daily activities and in the longer, often more linear, trajectories of their lives. Both Giddens (1985) and Pred (1985; 1990) have developed this approach, extending Hägerstrand's discussion of "infrastructural constraints" into a more sophisticated analysis of social power. In particular, Giddens' (1985) concept of "regionalisation," whereby social practices are "zoned" or "channelled" into particular spaces and times, has contributed to my discussion of regulation. Massey's (1993a) discussion of "power geometry" – referred to above – which draws attention to the unevenness of peoples' power to influence and manipulate the flows and connections of the late modern era has also been influential. In brief, while I draw heavily on the concepts of interconnection and flow in recent globalisation literature, I wish to emphasis the extent to which these connections are a focus for the exercise of power: they are *regulated* connections.

In the extensive economics and political science literature on regulation, the state – as "administrative rule mak[er]" (Boyer 1990: 21) – looms large. In one influential account the "central meaning" of regulation is taken to refer to a "sustained and focused control exercised by a *public agency*" (in Ogus 1994: 1, my emphasis) and an array of studies have been undertaken by historians, political scientists and economists on the regulatory intervention of the state in social and commercial affairs (High 1991). My use of the term certainly draws on this strong tradition and, in the pages that follow, emphasis is placed on the role of the Lao and Thai state in upper-Mekong regulation. In the sphere of transport and trade, some of these state regulatory practices are well known and immediately apparent: tariffs, tolls, visas, trading quotas and restrictions on border passage. Their physical manifestations are evident throughout the upper-Mekong region: customs stations, police posts, gates, flags, uniforms, guns, thick and grubby ledgers and endless forms. Expanding somewhat on the usual analysis of state regulation, I also seek to draw attention to the regulatory role of more dramatic space-transforming practices in which the state often plays a key role. Large-scale infrastructure projects – road building, navigation improvements, port and warehouse construction – are all attempts to entice trade flows along particular routes, attempts by provincial and national governments to capture the benefits of taxes, tolls and commercial profit. In brief, as lawmaker, administrator *and* development entrepreneur the state plays a key role in initiating, managing and directing the interconnections of the borderlands.

While embracing the notion of *state as regulator*, I am also concerned to demonstrate that *the state does not monopolise regulatory practice*. It is widely recognised in economic and political theory that state regulation, especially commercial regulation, often benefits "private interest groups" that are external to the state (High 1991; Ogus 1994: 71–75). Once again, I am influenced by this approach and, in the chapters that follow, I examine a range of ways in which social and spatial advantage is generated by government regulation. In some cases this does appear to amount to the partial "capture" of the state by powerful commercial interests, a scenario well documented by political scientists and economists (Ogus 1994: 57–58). However, more commonly, it takes the form of an intricate and spatially dispersed network of regulatory collaborations in which local institutions, ritual practices, cautionary tales and cultural precepts are intricately intertwined with the more formalised practices of the state. The importance of these localised regulatory practices must temper an approach which places primary emphasis on the state as the locus of regulation. Following Foucault (as interpreted by Hindess 1996: 134), I seek to identify the ways in which "government of societies takes place in a variety of state and non-state contexts." This more dispersed view of regulatory power calls for careful analysis of the active – rather than just beneficiary – role of non-state actors in regulatory activities (Regini 1995: 4–6).

Related to this issue is the popular distinction drawn between the "power of the state" and the "power of the market" (see, for example, Brumfiel 1994: 2; Ogus 1994: 1–2). Following on from the widespread association of regulation with the state, regulatory practices are typically portrayed as an *intervention* into the functioning of the market. Assessments of this intervention vary enormously, from those who see regulation as a legitimate response to market failure, to those who condemn the activities of "rent-seeking" bureaucrats who use political power to earn illegitimate revenue. However, what most assessments along this spectrum share is a view that the market is an entity that, analytically at least, can be separated from external social and political forces. My approach fundamentally departs from this point of view. I embrace a long tradition in political economy and economic anthropology that emphasises the embeddedness of economic action in political and social relations. As Polanyi's (1944: 68) classic work argued, "[r]egulation and markets, in effect grew up together."[6] In the pages that follow I argue that state (and non-state) regulation is intrinsically involved in the creation of the contexts in which markets flourish. Regulatory action is involved in the creation of market towns, trade routes and marketing infrastructure. The actions of national and provincial governments create market niches, generate unevenness in supply that can be profitably exploited, and provide social and political opportunities for local market power. In the upper-Mekong region long-standing regulatory action has helped to create the conditions in which traders, transport operators and entrepreneurs are now making very good livings indeed. My argument parallels that developed by Regini (1995: 2) in his analysis of contemporary economic developments in Europe:

---

6 Where I part company with Polanyi (1944) is in his claim that the modern market has become "self-regulating." I agree with Prattis (1987: 18, 29) who argues that Polanyi and his "substantivist" followers draw an overly rigid distinction between non-market and market economies.

> By structuring the options available to market participants, social
> and political institutions induce them – sometimes explicitly and
> deliberately, sometimes as an unintended consequence of their
> action – to pursue some goals rather than others. By doing so, they
> help the market to produce outcomes which its participants ...
> would be unable to achieve on their own.

The implication of this argument is that the parallel distinction between
regulation and market liberalisation must be subject to critical scrutiny.
If markets are, to a certain extent, an artefact of regulation then it seems
likely that liberalising initiatives aimed at encouraging the market, may in
fact, represent new and revised forms of regulation. Once again, Polanyi's
(1944: 67) comments are insightful: "[t]he 'freeing' of trade performed by
mercantilism merely liberated trade from particularism, but at the same
time extended the scope of regulation." This is a subtle and paradoxical
point that lies at the heart of much of the work that follows. *I argue that
many liberalising initiatives, rather than representing a reduction of regulatory
action, create the conditions for a new "mix" of regulatory practice* (see also
Regini 1995: 5). Liberalising initiatives which encourage mobility and
passage – the opening of border crossings; the reduction of tariffs; the
eradication of quotas – should not be assumed to be initiatives which
undermine regulatory power. As Foucault, (paraphrased by Hindess 1996:
101) argued, "the exercise of power requires a degree of freedom on the
part of its subjects." For this reason, when I refer to liberalising initiatives
in this book, I am referring to initiatives which encourage trade and passage
but I am *not* suggesting that these initiatives necessarily involve a reduction
in levels of state and non-state regulation. *Liberalisation, then, does not
necessarily amount to de-regulation.*

To summarise: regulatory practices, as defined in this book, are used to
initiate and control mobility and interconnection. This is an activity in
which the state is an important actor, but non-state actors are also active
beneficiaries and participants. Regulation is not seen as being external to
the market but as part of the process by which markets are created.
Liberalising initiatives, in encouraging flow and passage, can provide
regulators with more opportunities for action.

Regulation in the borderlands

This focus on regulation provides several important insights into the
situation of South-East Asia's northern borderlands. First, a focus on
regulation contributes to a recovery of the *history* of the borderlands,
undermining the historical caricature of centre-periphery analysis. In the
dominant historical narratives of mainland southeast Asia, the nineteenth
century borderlands are assigned to an ambiguous and unbounded

15

periphery, marginal to the interests of pre-colonial powers. The twentieth century borderlands are similarly stripped of their relevance with an over-emphasis on the bounding and excluding practices of modern states. By focusing on the *regulation of interconnection and passage*, the longstanding historical importance of borderlands trade and the changing role of local communities in its control and initiation are highlighted. With this historical perspective, the Economic Quadrangle can be seen as the latest in a series of "regimes" of upper-Mekong regulation, rather than the opening up of a previously marginal or closed-off periphery.[7]

Second, an analysis of regulation provides important insights into the role of the *state at the borderline*. While centre-periphery analysis often highlights the bounding and excluding practices of the state at the borderline – "borders themselves are seen as places of containment" (Mitchell 1997: 102) – this book argues that state power is more often concerned with *regulating* trans-border flows than with *preventing* them. The borders of nation states are typically places of passage – albeit regulated passage – rather than places of exclusion.[8] This accounts for one of the most important paradoxes of contemporary borders: as trade and passage becomes more liberalised, the opportunities and incentives for regulation flourish. Specifically, "open" borders, characterised by flow and passage, usually provide *more* opportunities for regulation than "closed" borders. Those who forecast the post-modern demise or erosion of nation-state borders with the rapid growth in trans-border flows fail to appreciate these subtleties of borderline regulation.

Third, a focus on regulation provides for a more sophisticated analysis of the *experiences of borderland residents*. Typically, relations between the state and borderlanders are portrayed in oppositional terms: penetration, incorporation, and homogenisation *versus* resistance, rebellion and difference. The outer-oriented practices of the borderlanders are seen as being at odds with the inner-oriented practices of the state (Kristof 1959: 271–272). As noted above, globalisation is sometimes seen as assisting borderlanders in their *struggle* against central authorities, creating "liberatory spaces that deconstruct the old regimes of the nation-state" (Grewal and Kaplan 1994: 9; see also Reynolds 1998). Once again, this book challenges these stereotypes. No doubt, officialdom in the border-lands creates constraints but it also creates important opportunities which often underlie the viability of commercial and social activities. Appadurai's

---

7 This historical perspective draws on the work of Wolf (1982); Hall (1991: 20); Hannerz (1991: 110); Gupta and Ferguson (1992: 8); Massey (1993b: 149; 1994: 165); and Grewal and Kaplan (1994: 10).

8 "Sovereignty not only depends on the protection of spatial borders, but it is above all the ability of state elites to regulate activities that flow across those borders, such as the crossing of commodities and surpluses, the passage of people in the form of labour, tourists et cetera, and the movement of cultural products and ideas." (Gupta 1992: 71)

(1995: 220) perspective on the "largely negative" context production of the modern state seems altogether too pessimistic. Given the "productive and positive" aspects of state power (Jessop 1990: 226), it is no surprise, then, that state regulatory practices are intertwined with those of local communities to the extent that borderlanders are often collaborators and active participants in regulatory activities. Frustrated international agencies and national business groups who deplore the persistence of financial and non-financial barriers to trade (ADB 1993: 35–39; GLPDR 1994e: 70–74) need to recognise the extent to which the residents of the borderlands have vested interests in their maintenance.

Finally, an analysis of regulation highlights processes of competition within the borderlands. Regulatory practices distribute benefits unevenly in space, favouring some locations over others through the placement of border-crossings, roads and river ports and through spatial variation in the imposition of tariffs and charges (Walker 1996). As mobility is enhanced, places must become even more active in their use and manipulation of regulation to attract the custom of increasingly footloose traders and transport operators (Harvey 1989: 295–296). Social benefits are also unevenly distributed as particular social groups are able to consolidate transport and trading careers while others are excluded or sidelined. Gender, ethnicity and neighbourhood are all caught up in this "power geometry" of borderlands regulation. It is well known that the borderlands are a "zone of contest" (Porter 1997: 229), but traditional analysis of centre-periphery conflict need to be supplemented with an understanding of the social and spatial divisions *within* and *between* borderland communities. The so-called periphery is far from homogenous.

North-Western Laos: An Overview

The geographic focus for this book is the north-western region of Laos, a wedge of territory strategically placed between Thailand, Burma and China, with Vietnam only a short distance to the east (Map 1.3). Three of the 16 Lao provinces – Bokeo, Oudomxai and Louangnamtha – lie wholly within this area, as do the northern districts of Xaignabouli province (Map 1.3). The study also incorporates neighbouring districts in Thailand – Chiang Khong district in particular – and, to a lesser extent, the Chinese district of Mengla (Map 1.2).[9]

Physically, the region is dominated by mountains and rivers. Over 70 per cent of north-western Laos is mountainous, with a series of ranges forming part of the extensive Himalaya "foothills." Many of the mountain areas are heavily forested though there has been widespread forest destruction as a result of both shifting cultivation and commercial logging.

---

9 Cross-border research in Burma was virtually impossible.

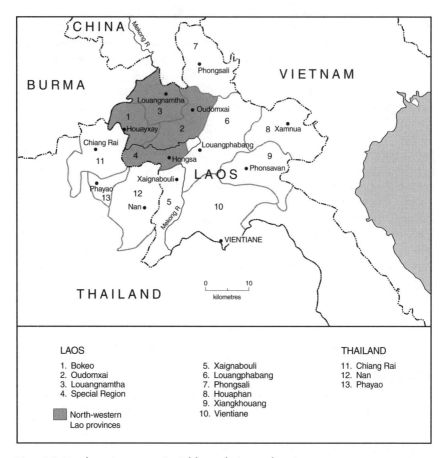

Map 1.3 Northern Laos: provincial boundaries and main towns

The mountainous terrain is one of the main factors accounting for the very rudimentary road transport infrastructure in the region. At present, the only road trafficable during the wet season is the Chinese-built road that runs from the Mekong at Pakbeng to Oudomxai, Louangnamtha and to Mengla in southern China (Map 1.2).

The dominant river is, of course, the Mekong. Rising in Tibet, it rushes south through the Chinese province of Yunnan before forming a 230 kilometre border between north-western Laos and Burma. Shortly after the famous Golden Triangle, where the border of Thailand replaces that of Burma, the river curves north and then south again. Soon after the Lao provincial capital of Houayxay it turns east – no longer forming the border between Thailand and Laos – and heads towards the main northern

Lao town of Louangphabang. There are numerous rapids, sandbanks and rocky shoals along the river and it has never lived up to ambitious hopes for large-scale navigation. Nevertheless, the section between Houayxay and Louangphabang is navigable year-round for vessels of up to about 120 tonnes.

A series of tributaries drain from north-western Laos into the Mekong (Map 1.2). The Tha River rises close to the Chinese border near Louangnamtha, and meanders south-west before entering the Mekong about 30 kilometres downstream from Houayxay. It is navigable by small boats for most of its length. The rocky and impenetrable Beng River runs through the heart of Oudomxai province, creating a series of lowland plains that enable the Beng River valley to support the highest population densities in the north-west (Taillard 1989: 193). Further east, the north-western region of Laos is bounded by the Ou River, a longstanding route of trade, migration and invasion in northern Laos (Map 1.1). There are many other minor tributaries. The places where these streams meet the Mekong – strategic places for the control of trade and ideal locations for fishing – have long been popular sites of settlement and numerous villages are identified by the word *paak* (mouth): Paktha, Pakkhop, Pakngeuy, Pakbeng and Pakou.

However, it is the intermontane rice plains in the upper reaches of the tributaries that have formed the main focus for settlement in the region. In the north-west, the major rice plains are located at Louangnamtha, Muangsing, Oudomxai, Xianghon and Hongsa (Map 1.2). Smaller rice plains are located at Viangphoukha, Muangbeng, Muanghun and Muanglong. There are also strips of rice-growing land along the Mekong near Houayxay and Tonpheung and numerous small pockets of lowland paddy along the tributaries. As well as being centres of rice production, many of these towns have also served as trading entrepôts, for both regional trade and trade between highlanders and lowlanders. Most of these towns, and the rice plains around them, have long histories of settlement, conquest, abandonment and repopulation, with the most recent mass-movements caused by bombing of communist-held towns in the 1960s and the post-war resettlement that continues until the present day.

There is enormous ethnic diversity in the region. Ethnic groups categorised by the Lao government as *laao lum* (lowland Lao) are congregated mainly in the lowland wet-rice areas that surround most of the towns and larger villages.[10] Ethnic groups within this category include the Lao themselves, northern Thai, Shan and Black Tai. All speak versions of the Tai family of languages and, for the most part, are Buddhists (LeBar, Hickey, and Musgrave 1964: 206–223). The largest north-

10 For a summary of this contentious system of ethnic classification, see Stuart-Fox (1986: 44–48).

19

western upland group is the Khmu who preceded *laao lum* groups in the settlement of the region. Most Khmu villages cultivate dry-rice in hill swiddens, though some have moved into lowland paddy areas and adopted many lowland cultural and social traits (LeBar, Hickey, and Musgrave 1964: 112–117). The Khmu have a long history of trading relations with the lowland *laao lum* (Halpern 1959). According to Lao government classification, Khmu form part of the *laao thəng* (Lao of the mountain slopes) which, in the north-west, also includes the Lamet (Izikowitz 1979; LeBar, Hickey, and Musgrave 1964: 117–119). Most *lao thəng* speak Mon-Khmer languages – together with Lao – and are animists, though those who have moved into lowland areas are likely to have adopted Buddhism. The final ethnic category is the *laao suung* (Lao of the mountain tops). This category includes a range of Sino-Tibetan animist groups which have migrated into the region over the last two centuries. The largest group in the north-west is the Hmong, with smaller communities of Yao, Akha, Lahu and Lantien (LeBar, Hickey, and Musgrave 1964: 30–38, 63–93). Most practice shifting cultivation in upland areas but they are also involved in regular trading relations with lowland communities. Currently in Laos there is a concerted effort being made to resettle upland communities in lowland areas, so as to reduce their impact on forests and fragile watersheds. An oft-quoted goal is that all upland shifting cultivation will cease by 2000 (Fisher 1996: 24). Finally, there is also a substantial Chinese community in the north-west, especially in the northern towns of Louangnamtha and Oudomxai. Many Chinese fled Laos during and after the civil war of the 1960s and 1970s, but now their numbers are being replenished with new groups of entrepreneurs, labourers and prostitutes.

Politically, the region is divided into provinces (Map 1.3). Under French colonial rule, which began in 1893, Houayxay and Louangnamtha lay within the province of Huakhong, while Oudomxai and the Beng valley fell within the domain of Louangphabang (which remained under the administration of its royal court). This provincial arrangement was maintained during the first decade of independence but, during the civil war in the 1960s, the communist Pathet Lao detached the western areas of Louangphabang province and established the new province of Oudomxai (Whitaker et al. 1972 158–159). After the Pathet Lao victory in 1975, Huakhong was renamed Louangnamtha and, in 1982, the new province of Bokeo was created around Houayxay.

The "Special Region" districts of Hongsa and Xianghon (Map 1.3) have had a confused administrative history, being incorporated into French Laos – along with the rest of Xaignabouli province – in 1907. In 1941, they were retaken by Thailand in a brief conflict with French forces, but returned to the French in the post-World War Two settlement. Up until the 1980s, they formed part of Xaignabouli province but were then transferred to Oudomxai. In the early 1990s, they were detached and formed into a "Special Region" under military administration, as part of an ambitious natural resource-led development plan. In 1995, they were transferred back to Xaignabouli province. In this book I will continue to refer to the Hongsa-Xianghon districts as the Special Region given that this was the arrangement during the period most of the research was undertaken. Table 1.1 summarises a number of socio-economic statistics for these various north-western provinces.

Provincial government in north-western Laos

Provincial governments are the key locus of state regulation in north-western Laos. Following the establishment of the Lao People's Democratic Republic in 1975 provincial affairs became the responsibility of "people's administrative committees." According to Stuart-Fox (1986: 78) these committees were "responsible for the implementation of [Lao People's Revolutionary] Party policy as this is interpreted by, or in the case of provincial matters, formulated by the provincial Party committee." However, in the 1991 constitution there was no mention of these committees and their substantial powers have now passed to the position of provincial Governor – directly appointed by the Lao President – and to an increasingly active provincial bureaucracy. The Governors are now the primary focus for central government intervention in the provinces, this

Table 1.1 North-western Lao provinces: key data

	Population	Cultivated Land (hectares)	Paddy (hectares)	Ethnic groups
Bokeo	106,000	13,628	4,000	Lao, Lü, Shan (50%) Khmu, Lamet (40%) Lahu, Hmong, Lantien (10%)
Oudomxai	193,000	38,000	10,500	Khmu (55%) Lao, Lü, (30%) Hmong (15%)
Louangnamtha	128,000	33,380	4,600	Khmu (40%) Lao, Lü, Black Tai (35%) Akha, Hmong, Yao (25%)
Special Region	74,000	6,034	n.a.	Lao, Lü (n.a.) Khmu (n.a.) Hmong (n.a.)

Source: Lemoine (1972: 26); Lok (1989); Chazee (1900; 1991); and GLPDR (1993).

role symbolised by their regular attendance of the Prime Minister's Council meetings in the national capital at which key strategic and policy issues are discussed. Most day-to-day administration is managed by government departments whose provincial presence broadly parallels the government structure at a national level. Major departments involved in the regulation of transport and trade are the Department of Post, Communications, Transport and Construction; Department of Trade; Customs Department; Department of Forestry; and Department of Immigration. All of these Departments have offices in the provincial capitals and some also have an administrative presence at district level. With the provincial bureaucrats answering to both the provincial Governor and their head office in Vientiane divided loyalties can arise and there is, to quote Evans (1990: 184), "considerable room for institutional friction."

During the 1980s provincial governments had a high degree of autonomy and there was a great deal of provincial variation in the way central government policy was applied. Stuart-Fox (1986: 79) suggests that this autonomy dates from the war years – when regional Pathet Lao commanders had substantial independence – and from the early years of the new regime when central administrative structures were poorly developed. One feature of this has been substantial provincial autonomy in the regulation of trading connections. Even during the years of the relatively strict "command economy" (see chapter 2) provincial administrators were actively involved in negotiating cross-border deals with Thai entrepreneurs, successfully avoiding the official trading channels in the national capital. Since the introduction of the liberalising New Economic Mechanism (see chapter 3) economic autonomy has been strengthened both by direct provincial involvement in trading activities and in the collection of a range of official and unofficial trading taxes and charges. In the north-west, a combination of commercial enthusiasm and relative independence has seen provincial officials become actively involved in negotiating cross-border cooperation agreements with officials in both Thailand and China.

Recent attempts to strengthen the power of the national administration appear to have had limited success. In 1992 control over provincial budgets was centralised with provincial tax collections paid into a central fund and expenditures forwarded to the provinces through departmental channels. This loss of fiscal autonomy has been vigorously resisted by the provinces and it is likely that a considerable percentage of local taxes and charges never pass through national accounting systems. The vast majority of provincial bureaucrats are very poorly paid and rely on the diversion of some state revenue to supplement meagre incomes. On a larger scale, the sale of state property, manipulation of state contracts and kick-backs for the favourable allocation of commercial quotas have undoubtedly contributed to the enrichment of some provincial families. In 1994 it was reported that at least US$30 million of state assets, in various forms, had been "embezzled" (RT 28 September 1994). Large-scale funding of transport and communications infrastructure appears to be motivated, in part, by a central government desire to cement control in the provinces but it is also likely that the commercial stimulus generated by these projects will create new entrepreneurial opportunities for provincial administrators and tax-collectors (see chapter 3).

Thailand, Burma, China and Vietnam

The relevant districts of the surrounding countries can be dealt with more briefly. The most important neighbouring districts in Thailand are Chiang Khong and Chiang Saen (Map 1.2). Lying at the head of a long narrow rice plain formed by the Ing River, the Mekong River settlement of Chiang Khong is Thailand's main trading point with north-western Laos. Its socio-economic fortunes have long been determined by its relationship with the Lao territories on the opposite bank. Further upstream, the ancient town of Chiang Saen lies on the edge of the large rice plain of the Kok River. In the past, it was the centre of a great kingdom, but now it plays a relatively small role in upper-Mekong trade. Both districts are predominantly settled by northern Thai, though there are also a number of Hmong, Yao and Lahu communities. Chiang Khong and Chiang Saen are both districts of Chiang Rai province, one of only two northern Thai provinces lying within the Mekong watershed. The city of Chiang Rai is a major northern administrative, marketing, retail and tourist centre. Chiang Rai's provincial population is slightly more than double the population of the four provinces making up north-western Laos and its population density is almost seven times as high. To the south-east, Thailand's Nan and Phayao provinces also have borders with Laos, though the rugged and remote nature of these borders has limited cross-border trading and transport links. Nevertheless, new links are being developed, especially from Nan province, which have important implications for north-western trading systems (see page 80).

To the north, Laos is bordered by the Sipsongpanna Autonomous Prefecture, which is part of China's Yunnan province. Traditionally the homeland of the Tai-speaking Lü, Sipsongpanna has been increasingly incorporated into the modern Chinese state with central Chinese settlers now outnumbering the Lü and other ethnic minorities. Jinghong, the capital of Sipsongpanna, was an important upper-Mekong power in the nineteenth century, and trading towns in the region have had longstanding relations with north-western Laos. Now, most Lao trade is focused on the town of Mengla (Map 1.2), some 60 kilometres north of the Lao border. To the west, north-western Laos borders on the Shan states of Burma. In the past, trans-Mekong trading relations with the Shan states, especially

23

the "capital" of Kengtung (Map 1.2), were very important but now they are much less so. Finally, some distance to the east, lies northern Vietnam. The key corridor running to north-western Laos from Hanoi runs through the famous town of Dien Bien Phu (Map 1.1).

CHAPTER TWO

Regimes of Regulation

1800–1988

Introduction: The Myth of Lao Isolation

> ... instead of assuming the autonomy of the primeval community, we need to examine how it was formed ... out of the interconnected space that always already existed. Colonialism, then, represents the [attempted] displacement of one form of interconnection by another. (Gupta and Ferguson 1992: 8)

It is easy to be dazzled by contemporary developments. With the construction of the trans-Mekong Friendship Bridge linking Thailand with the Lao capital of Vientiane, the image producers went into overdrive. "Laos," the newspaper headlines announced, is "open for business" (TN 24 April 1994), stirring from its slumber and "ris[ing] to the challenge of modern life" (TN 27 March 1994). As bulldozers shuddered into action on roads heading north and east, journalists and academics alike declared that Laos – landlocked, under-developed and culturally fragile – was finally embracing "friendship and cooperation" (TN 3 January 1994), "open[ing] up ... as never before" and striding "towards subregional integration" (Stuart-Fox 1995b: 180, 177). Some 700 kilometres upstream from the Friendship Bridge, a more modest development – the opening of an international border-crossing between Chiang Khong and Houayxay – was hailed as the dawning of a "bright new era ... for Thai-Lao bilateral relations" (BP 20 January 1994). In the morning mist at Houayxay's cargo port, the Governor of Chiang Rai and his inevitable entourage were presented with flowers by elaborately dressed Lao girls. With the Governor of Bokeo, he sat on a vinyl couch – set up on the port's concrete ramp – while a small Lao orchestra played for the assembled crowd. Bundles of gas-filled balloons floated off down river. A month or so later, a late-night fireworks display was held to mark the arrival of a Chinese cruise boat in Chiang Khong. As rockets raced skyward and exploded above the shimmering Mekong, an excited Thai official proudly announced – without a hint of irony – "our friends in Laos have never seen anything like it."

There is no denying the significance of contemporary events in the upper-Mekong borderlands, but it is important to recognise that Lao communities have a long history of regulating their connections with other places. This recognition is not helped by some recent analysis that has too readily adopted journalistic and popular rhetoric. Nguyen (1996), for example, in his recent assessment for *Southeast Asian Affairs*, places isolation at the (now vulnerable) heart of Lao national sovereignty. Laos, he argues "has been greatly marginalized for most of the twentieth century, almost intentionally, as it settled into its fateful position as a complacent junction of mainland Southeast Asia" (Nguyen 1996: 197). He writes that recent developments show that Laos is "awakening from its state of isolation, both through intentional stirring and rude awakening by its neighbours" a dangerous situation in which regional economic integration may compromise national sovereignty (Nguyen 1996: 199, 212–213). Thalemann's (1997: 99–101) recent assessment in the *Journal of Contemporary Asia* also takes up the linked themes of isolation and innocence, referring to the "sudden vulnerability shock" and "pervasive" fear of "anarchy" that Laos is experiencing as its subsistence economy is newly exposed to international market forces: "the concept of markets may not be easy to explain to peasants whose contact with the outside world is so limited that they often cannot imagine anything different from their present situation." And, in their analysis of national forestry administration, Rigg and Jerndal (1996: 145, 160–162,) attribute a similar spatial innocence to the Lao national government itself, writing of its administrative impotence now that the country is "[n]o longer an isolated backwater."[1]

The aim of this chapter is to provide a more balanced and detailed context for contemporary developments than that provided by these linked motifs of isolation and vulnerability. The regional transport and trading systems of the Lao borderlands have long had strategic importance, and the struggles to control and reshape them warrant more sustained historical attention. In the following sections I trace the changing patterns of borderlands regulation from the early nineteenth century until the eve of the Economic Quadrangle in the mid-1980s. I suggest that this period can be roughly divided into four "regimes of regulation" (Map 2.1). In the nineteenth century both of the major states with interests in north-western Laos – Nan and Louangphabang – were actively involved in the regulation of local and long-distance trade, though Louangphabang's interest was more critical given its limited local resource base (Map 2.1A). For the French – keen to secure colonial markets and

---

1 Of course, these images are not confined to Laos as Vatikiotis' (1996b: 170) discussion of Southeast Asia's "parochial traditions" indicates.

raw materials for manufacturers – the ultimately insurmountable regulatory challenge was to integrate north-western Laos into the trading and transport systems of Indochina (Map 2.1B). In the post-colonial period of civil war, both the communist and royalist regimes were heavily dependent on foreign assistance and regulatory practices strongly consolidated the trading and transport connections between Laos and its neighbours (Map 2.1C). After the communist victory in 1975, the new Lao state faced a crucial dilemma: internal and external regulatory forces encouraged economic autarky, but the strict regime of regulation compromised domestic surplus production. Not surprisingly, the restrictions were soon diluted and subverted (Map 2.1D). In brief, the Economic Quadrangle is the latest in a series of regimes of regulation in which Laos' external connections have been managed in ways that are shaped by changing political and economic constraints.

Nan and Louangphabang: 1800–1893

The social formation of pre-colonial Laos has been characterised as a "tributary mode of production ... a form of social organization in which surpluses are extracted from the subordinate population by *political* rather than *economic* mechanisms" (Evans 1990: 30, my emphasis; see also Gunn 1990: 66–69). In the upper-Mekong region the major tributary overlords were located in the northern Siamese town of Nan and the Lao town of Louangphabang. Their "non-economic" means of surplus extraction from lowland peasant and upland tribal producers included tax and rent in kind, corvee labour, and slavery. The tribute extracted by the elites in the major centres was usually collected by an administrative network of subordinate chiefs in towns and villages throughout the region. The power of the supreme and tributary chiefs was backed by military force and by an array of political and religious ideologies enacted in state rituals.

Given the emphasis on political – that is, non-commercial – means of surplus extraction, the role of trade in these tributary formations tends to be down-played. Theoreticians of the tributary mode of production have made it clear that the main locus of power was the politico-religious sphere and *not* the market (Amin 1976: 13–22; Wittfogel 1957: 297; Wolf 1982: 80). Of course, varying degrees of commercial activity and trade are acknowledged, but it is widely held that these spheres of economic activity are subordinate to the predominate tributary form and that they have relatively little impact on the naturally self-sufficient economy of peasant producers. Emphasis is placed on long-distance trade in luxuries – supporting the conspicuous consumption of the elites – rather than on internal trade in subsistence goods (see also Polanyi 1944: 58–61). This theoretical tradition has been influential in some prominent studies of Lao society. "Market transactions" Evans (1990: 31) writes, "were peripheral

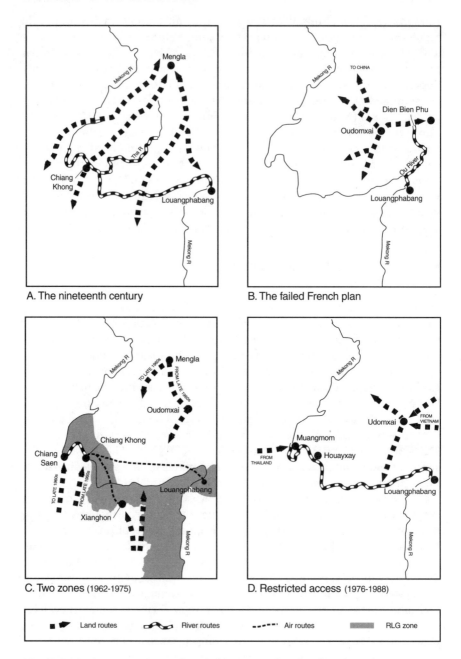

Map 2.1 North-western Laos: changing patterns of regional trade and transport

to the [pre-colonial Lao] peasant economy." Gunn (1990: 69, 72) adopts a similar position, suggesting that in nineteenth century Laos "centrality must be given to the non-economic structures, notably at the political and ideological levels" and that "the essentially 'static' subsistence economy had not yet been transformed into a mercantilist economy." Ireson's (1996) recent review of the "invisible walls" surrounding Lao villages is concerned with more recent times but a similar view of autonomous, subsistence-oriented village history is strongly implied in his work.[2]

Of course, it would be absurd to argue that pre-colonial Laos was characterised by a well developed market economy. However, historical evidence – albeit fragmentary – does suggest that pre-colonial social formations of north-western Laos where characterised by more multi-faceted internal and external trading linkages than the "tributary model" – with its implications of relatively self-sufficient isolation – may suggest. The pre-colonial states of Nan and Louangphabang were indeed involved in the direct extraction of surplus from peasant producers but they were also involved in the profitable *regulation* of luxury *and* subsistence commodity trade. Regulatory strategies encouraged and supervised trade both with subordinate villages within the region and with external trading centres in the surrounding states. Theorists of the tributary mode of production often present state regulation as being anti-mercantile in its orientation – a defensive, or even predatory reaction against a rival merchant class (Amin 1976: 30–36; Wolf 1982: 83–85). By contrast, my argument is that the pre-colonial states of northern Laos actively and enthusiastically supplemented their tributary income with direct and indirect revenue from trade and that, in some cases, tributary and mercantile institutions were closely interlinked. In the case of Louangphabang this was the basis of its economic survival.

Nan and its Mekong outpost, Chiang Khong

In about 1787, a small group of Siamese settlers took advantage of the gradual decline of Burmese power in the upper-Mekong region and re-established the northern township of Nan. In the wake of the prolonged warfare between the Siamese and the Burmese, Nan had been "completely deserted." "It had no ruler to care for it, and most of the people had evacuated the town, fleeing into the jungle and mountains" (Wyatt 1994: 89). The primary challenge for the new settlers was to bring the extensive rice plains that lay around the township back into production. Irrigation works that had fallen into disrepair were renovated and new canals were carved into the river plain. Nan's labour force was boosted as it became a

---

2 These approaches have also been influential in analyses of Thai history. For a critical discussion see Bowie (1992).

haven for Shan and Siamese refugees from the remnants of Burmese oppression further to the north (Wyatt 1994: 87–95).

By the 1830s, Nan was one of the main centres in northern Siam, its nineteenth century prosperity reinforced by a series of upper-Mekong military campaigns. With Chiang Saen left to the jungle after the defeat of the Burmese garrison in 1804, the way was clear for Siamese expansion up the Mekong. In the major campaign of 1805, most Siamese forces concentrated on the Burmese-dominated Shan states, to the west of the Mekong, but the ruler of Nan was instrumental in conquering the east-bank districts of Viangphoukha and Louangnamtha as well as much of Sipsongpanna (Flood and Flood 1978: 274, 278–281; Wenk 1968: 90; Wyatt 1994: 100). To meet Nan's labour demands many residents of the upper-Mekong towns and villages were forcibly resettled south of the Mekong to cultivate Nan's abundant rice plains and support an ambitious program of hydraulic and religious works. Further campaigns on the upper-Mekong's east bank were conducted in 1812, 1851 and 1857, each yielding more war captives and consolidating the productive base of Nan's tributary state (Archer 1896: 83; Davis 1984: 31–32; Flood and Flood 1965: 93, 109–110, 118–119; McGilvary 1912: 363; Wyatt 1994: 104–105, 118–120). The effect of Nan's growth was extensive depopulation and underdevelopment in the areas that now lie within north-western Laos. Viangphoukha, "once an important centre and apparently very densely populated" (Izikowitz 1979: 24), lay deserted for most of the century. By the time McCarthy (1900: 156) passed through in 1892, the paddy fields "had been left fallow for many years, and the whole place was now a dense jungle." The large rice plain at Louangnamtha was also deserted for over 70 years when its residents were resettled between Nan and the Mekong (Archer 1896: 84; Lefèvre-Pontalis 1902: 159; Pavie 1901: 227).

Nan's trans-Mekong territory was sparsely settled, but it had strategic importance for regional trade. One of the main caravan routes between Yunnan and northern Thailand passed through Louangnamtha and Viangphoukha to cross the Mekong at Chiang Khong (Map 2.2).[3] When the British explorer McLeod (1867: 29, 40–42) arrived in Chiang Mai in the early 1830s, he found that this caravan trail was the "road travelled by the Chinese caravans," even though the Chinese merchants complained about the abandoned towns and sparse settlement along the road. The more lucrative route to the west of the Mekong – through Kengtung – was "closed ... from the excessive jealousy of the Siamese towards the Burmans" (McLeod 1867: 29). In the 1890s, the caravan trail through Louangnamtha was still regionally important, and early French adminis-trators noted the busy dry season passage of mule caravans along the route:

---

3 For a detailed discussion of the Yunnanese caravan trade, see Hill (1982: chapter 5) and Forbes (1987).

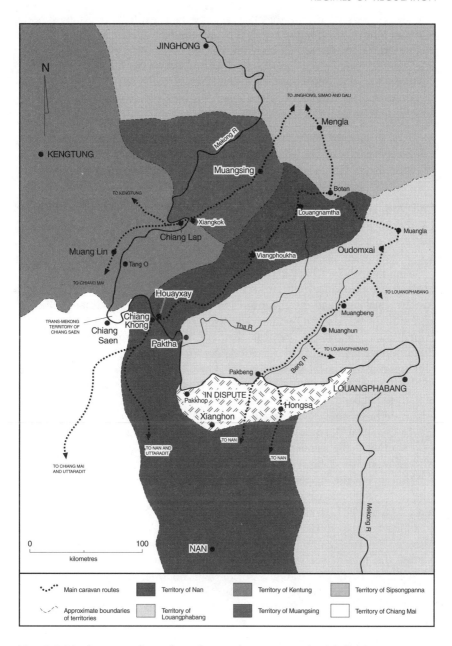

Map 2.2 North-western Laos: late nineteenth century territorial divisions

"this was the thang-luong, that is to say the main route from Xiang Khong [Chiang Khong] to China, across Sipsong-panna" (Lefèvre-Pontalis 1902: 154).[4] On the southward journey the Yunnanese muleteers carried silk, tea, salt, opium, furs, metal goods, hats and Chinese baubles to sell in the northern-Siamese markets and in villages along the route. The major cargo acquired on the return trip through Laos was raw cotton cultivated by Khmu, Lamet and Yao in scattered hill plots:

> It is almost exclusively this product [cotton] that makes up the return cargo of the mule and horse caravans which come, each year, from Yunnan-Fou [Kunming], Tali [Dali], S'sémao [Simao] ... (Reinach 1911: 299)[5]

The Yunnanese would also pay "fabulous prices" for deer antlers (Bock 1884: 230), a product readily available in northern Laos, as were the gall bladders of bears, which were eagerly sought by Chinese pharmacists to the north (Izikowitz 1979: 315).

The township of Nan itself was not well placed to regulate this caravan trade. From the Mekong there were several caravan trails to Nan but it was equally easy to head to the more lucrative markets in Chiang Mai or Uttaradit (Map 1.1).[6] On the Nan River there were serious rapids which impeded access to the central Siamese markets, reducing the town's desirability as a trading destination. Nan's main strength in relation to regional trade lay at its Mekong outpost of Chiang Khong, the "second city of Nan" (Garnier 1885: 9). The rulers of Chiang Khong had close relations with Nan, dating, in recent history, from 1792 when the "governor of Chiang Khong moved his family and all his manpower" to Nan, seeking refuge from the Burmese forces just up river at Chiang Saen (Wyatt 1994: 94–95). Following the destruction of Chiang Saen in 1804, Chiang Khong was re-established and soon emerged as the most important riverside settlement on the upper-Mekong, for a time unchallenged on the long stretch of river between Jinghong and Louangphabang (Anon 1990; Anon n.d.; Carné 1872: 245). Chiang Khong was Nan's most important administrative outpost and, to this day, the two towns are said to be *phiinɔɔŋ kan* (older and younger siblings) and many residents of Chiang Khong still maintain contact with relatives in Nan.

Chiang Khong's strategic position in regional trading systems had several components. In relation to the caravan trade, it was an ideal place to levy ferry tolls, to collect taxes on traded goods, to extort protection

---

4 *Thaaŋ luaŋ* is Thai for highway. For the importance of this route, see also Lefèvre-Pontalis (1902: 100, 113, 289) and Pavie (1906: 276, 279, 360).

5 See Map 1.1 for the locations of these Yunnanese towns.

6 See Garnier (1885: 12–13); Hallet (1890: 104, 209–210); Smyth (1898a: 114–115, 121–133); Pavie (1906: 262–265); and Le May (1926: 178–195).

money and to impose frontier duties (Hallet 1890: 163; Hong 1984: 88–89). By controlling one of the few suitable river-crossing points, Nan was able to gain a share in the regional caravan trade despite the notable lethargy of its own commercial life (Smyth 1898a: 116). Chiang Khong was also an important trade and tribute centre for the scattered mountain villages on the opposite bank (Pavie 1906: 348). Taxes, such as bees wax and cardamom, were paid to the Siamese overlords in Chiang Khong and, in the local markets, the hill-dwellers exchanged their surplus rice, forest products, baskets and silverware for Siamese iron goods, clothing and pottery and for European goods bought overland by buffalo and elephant from Chiang Mai.[7] This exchange across the Mekong was sufficiently vigorous to alarm the early French administrators in the region (Lefèvre-Pontalis 1902: 115). Trading monopolies on goods from the hinterland were a feature of chiefly power throughout the region and Chiang Khong was an ideal place where such power could be exercised (Condominas 1990: 84; Pasuk and Baker 1995: 7). The upland Khmu and Lamet in Chiang Khong's trans-Mekong domain were also required to undertake regular upkeep of the caravan trail, building bamboo bridges across streams and setting up rest houses at the stopping points along the route (Izikowitz 1979: 23; Lefèvre-Pontalis 1902: 114, 146–150). Finally, Chiang Khong was also well placed to control the passing river traffic: boats entering Chiang Khong's territory were required to stop at a riverside frontier village to pay a toll, and taxes were collected from traders engaged in commerce along the Mekong and its tributaries (Lefèvre-Pontalis 1902: 100, 127). It also served as one of the upper-Mekong ports in the trade between Chiang Mai, Nan and Louangphabang (McGilvary 1912: 154; Orléans 1894: 607–609).

Chiang Khong's profitable position in upper-Mekong trading systems is said to be reflected in the name of the town itself. Literally, its name can be translated as the "town (*chian*) of things (*khɔɔŋ*)," but locals suggest that "Chiang," in fact, derives from *siaŋ*, meaning to risk, lose, waste or squander. In times past, they suggest, Chiang Khong was a popular "gambling" centre where traders and travellers from Laos, China, Burma and Siam came and, inevitably, lost their goods to the sharp-dealing locals. Chiang Khong is, then, the "town where you lose your things," a town where the passages through the borderlands could be profitably intercepted.

In brief, Nan's position as a tributary state was primarily based on its uncontested control of the surrounding rice plain which was populated, in part, by refugees and war captives from areas further to the north. However, this classic form of tribute extraction was supplemented by

---

7 See, for example, Smyth (1898a: 174–175); Lefèvre-Pontalis (1902: 114–117, 147); Ellis (1960: 125); and Izikowitz (1979: 310–311).

Chiang Khong's regulation of trade on the upper-Mekong. Through its conquest of north-western Laos, Nan had, for a time, secured unchallenged control of these market networks but the large swathe of trans-Mekong territory was vulnerable to incursions. In the latter half of the nineteenth century Chiang Khong's strategic position came under serious challenge as the area became an arena for territorial competition and alternative centres of power started to intervene in local and regional trade. The territorial ambiguity, that Thongchai (1994) rightly identifies as being characteristic of the region in the decades prior to colonial rule, arose not out of nonchalance and neglect but out of spatial competition.

After recovering from the Siamese aggression of the 1850s, the main Shan state of Kengtung consolidated its hold around the Mekong and extended its influence into a substantial part of what is now north-western Laos (Map 2.2).[8] The area was gained through gradual settlement, both by upland Lahu settlers, who moved into areas depopulated during Burmese rule (Lefèvre-Pontalis 1902: 138), and by lowland Shan who established villages along both banks of the Mekong, including strategic settlements at the mouths of small east-bank tributaries. The most audacious incursion was by Shan sapphire miners who were well entrenched at Houayxay, directly opposite Chiang Khong, by the 1880s (Smyth 1898a: 153–156).[9] On the upper-Mekong, the Shan settlers had a reputation for piracy, harassing passing caravans and boats and, on one occasion, launching an attack on Chiang Khong itself (Izikowitz 1979: 25; Lefèvre-Pontalis 1902: 132–133; McCarthy 1900: 136). Kengtung taxes were levied throughout the area, even in some villages on the "Siamese" bank close to Chiang Khong (Lefèvre-Pontalis 1902: 138).

Kengtung's key upper-Mekong outpost was Muang Lin, about 90 kilometres upstream from Chiang Khong (Map 2.2). Though it had fallen under Siamese sway in the first half of the century (Wyatt 1994: 121), and was ravaged in the campaigns of the 1850s (Scott 1901 Vol. 2: 387), it was soon resettled by Kengtung and emerged as a "common market centre of a large number of hill tribes that inhabit the mountain ridges in all directions round about" (McGilvary 1912: 327). As early as 1867, the *French Mekong River Expedition* found it to be an important regional market centre and were disappointed to find that British cloth was already being sold there (Carné 1872: 255; Garnier 1885: 25). The chief of Muang Lin was said to be heavily involved in opium trade (McGilvary 1912: 368) and was renowned for his harassment of traders on the upper Mekong's west-bank

---

8 Shan "incursion" into Siamese territory on both the west and east banks of the Mekong has been well documented. See Archer (1889: 9); Hallet (1890: 196–198); McCarthy (1900: 146); Lefèvre-Pontalis (1902: 121, 126–127, 132, 298); Mitton (1936: 212–213); and Mangrai (1965: 253–254).

9 Some of the descendants of the sapphire miners still live in Houayxay. Said to number only about twenty families, they are sometimes referred to as the "real" Houayxay people.

caravan routes (Lefèvre-Pontalis 1902: 301). Muang Lin was also well placed to profit from river traffic, lying just a short distance from the rapids at Tang O (Map 2.2), the terminus for traders from Louangphabang who poled dugout canoes up river to exchange salt for opium (Garnier 1885: 19; Scott 1901 Vol 2: 387). At Tang O, river cargoes had to be carried overland by bullocks provided by the local "mandarins, who raise or lower the cost of transport according to their interests or their whims" (Carné 1872: 254). Upstream from Muang Lin, Kengtung also claimed the riverside trading town of Chiang Lap (Map 2.2) where an important cross-river ferry operated on the main route between Kengtung and northern Laos (Pavie 1901: 207–208; Scott 1901 Vol. 1: 364; Smyth 1898a: 144–145). The town was an important depot for distribution of salt from the wells at Boten, north of Louangnamtha, and Lao and Lü traders travelled there to exchange salt for betel nut and opium (Scott 1901 Vol 1: 364).

In the 1880s, growing Shan influence on the upper-Mekong prompted the Siamese resettlement of Chiang Saen, abandoned to the jungle since the defeat of the Burmese garrison in 1804. This was an initiative of Bangkok and Chiang Mai, with Nan refusing to participate, reluctant, it seems, to support an upper-Mekong rival to Chiang Khong (Hallet 1890: 203; Le May 1926: 214). Chiang Saen soon developed as a river port and as a marketing and taxing centre for a strip of villages along the opposite bank (Map 2.2). "The Musur [Lahu]," writes McCarthy (1900: 149), "came down from the surrounding hills, bringing chiefly cotton and wax, which they bartered for areca nuts and betel leaves." The diversion of tribute and trade generated a series of boundary disputes with Chiang Khong which required adjudication by a representative of Bangkok (Lefèvre-Pontalis 1902: 130–131, 137–138). Chiang Khong's concerns were well placed. Chiang Saen had superior transport connections with northern Siam and, despite some early difficulties (Le May 1926: 214), would become a second major trading centre on the upper-Mekong, a position it held until the late 1960s.

In the far north of Nan's domain, there were more disturbing developments. In the early 1880s, a dispute over Mekong ferry tolls prompted a small upper-Mekong state to break away from its overlord, Kengtung. It established a new settlement on the large rice plain at Muangsing, only 60 kilometres north-west from Louangnamtha (Mangrai 1965: 239–240; McCarthy 1900: 151). Muangsing was well placed in relation to both the Yunnanese caravan trade and the salt trade and soon emerged as an important upper-Mekong entrepôt (Map 2.2). Visiting in the early 1890s, Lamington (1891: 708) described it as "by far the best market I had seen" and a "trading station of some importance." McCarthy (1900: 160) observed settlers from Kengtung and Sipsongpanna on the surrounding rice-plain and "many camps of Chinese traders ... [who] went no further than Sing, and when they had got together a sufficient quantity of raw cotton, they returned to Yunan." Upland villagers from the surrounding hills came to the town's market to trade (McCarthy 1900: 160; McGilvary 1912: 363). The rough trail that ran from Muangsing to the Mekong at Chiang Lap become the most important caravan route in northern Laos (Lefèvre-Pontalis 1902: 289; Pavie 1901: 207–208) and was the subject of a vigorous dispute. Forces from Muangsing took control of the trail but were "not strong enough to cross the river, and the Keng Lap [Chiang Lap] district ... remained tributary to Kengtung" (Scott 1901 Vol 1: 364).

But it was Nan that had most to lose, with the new caravan trail drawing traffic away from the old route through Chiang Khong and towards the Shan communities of Chiang Lap and Muang Lin. Nan had resisted the establishment of a settlement at Muangsing – "the usual practice having been to 'dacoit' the settlers" (McCarthy 1900: 151) – and quickly moved to extract tribute and establish village outposts in Louangnamtha and Viangphoukha as alternative trading centres (Lefèvre-Pontalis 1902: 153, 259; McCarthy 1900: 161; McGilvary 1912: 331–332). The early French administrators fully appreciated the importance of Muangsing as a threat to Siamese power in the region and delighted in comparing the vibrant commercial activity at Muangsing with "the wretchedness" of the markets in Chiang Khong and Chiang Saen (Lefèvre-Pontalis 1902: 261).

The Lü of Sipsongpanna were also active in north-western Laos as they recovered from Siamese incursions in the first half of the century. By the last decades of the century, the Lü state of Mengla had taken control of the regionally important salt wells at Boten (Map 2.2), though they lay in the upper-reaches of the Tha River, an area claimed by Nan (McCarthy 1900: 161). The wells at Boten supported a widespread trade as the salt – packaged in small and readily portable parcels – was distributed throughout the region by Yunnanese, Lao, Lü, Shan, Khmu and Lamet traders.[10] Not only could the Mengla Lü "live to a great extent on the results of the sale of salt" (Izikowitz 1979: 314) – exchanging it for cotton, opium, forest products and rice – but they could also tax the passing caravan traffic that the salt wells attracted. When Louangnamtha was resettled by Nan, the new settlers were involved in border skirmishes with the Lü, but the result was that the territory of Mengla was extended even further and a border post inscribed in both Lü and Chinese was erected a short distance outside the newly settled Siamese outpost (Lefèvre-Pontalis 1902: 160, 163–164). Lü settlements also extended down the caravan trail towards Chiang Khong, where they were active participants in regional and local trade (Izikowitz 1979: 25–27; Lefèvre-Pontalis 1902: 98, 153).

---

10 For information on the vitally important salt trade, see Lamington (1891: 711); McCarthy (1900: 162, 166); Scott (1901 Vol 1: 364); McGilvary (1912: 396); Izikowitz (1979: 314); Hill (1982: 107–108); Chiranan (1989: 66–68); and Damrong (1994: 104–107).

Louangphabang and the Mekong tributaries

> It differs from the other Lao[11] cities in having no great rural population and extensive rice-plains near it (McGilvary 1912: 156).

Louangphabang's regulatory challenges were fundamentally different to those of the small hydraulic state of Nan. Located on a narrow spur of riverside land, it had a very limited area suitable for rice cultivation and was forced to rely heavily on trade with rice-producing villages along the Mekong and its tributaries (Smyth 1898a: 178, 201).[12] The valley of the Tha River (Map 2.2) was a crucial resource and it was described by Lefèvre-Pontalis (1902: 140) as "the granary of Luang-Prabang." Travelling upstream from Paktha in 1894, he was surprised at the number of rice-growing villages along the banks and in the surrounding hills (Lefèvre-Pontalis 1902: 140). Much of the rice was produced, not in irrigated paddy by the lowland Lao, but in dry-rice fields cultivated by the Khmu and Lamet. "Without the agriculture of the Khas [hill-dwellers]," Lefèvre-Pontalis observed, "the Lao would not have a grain of rice to put between their teeth" (Lefèvre-Pontalis 1902: 140). The overall level of trade in Louangphabang may have been disappointing to colonial adventurers (Evans 1990: 31) but this commercial relationship with the hill-dwellers was a central feature of the pre-colonial economy.

Some of the upland rice, together with forest products and cotton, was transported to Louangphabang by the Khmu and Lamet themselves. They constructed simple rafts by lashing bundles of bamboo together and covering them with a flimsy decking. Laden with rice, these were floated down the Tha River and the other navigable tributaries, then along the Mekong itself to the busy markets at Louangphabang. When they reached their destination, the rafts were dismantled, the bamboo sold and the highland traders returned to their villages on foot (Halpern 1959; Lefèvre-Pontalis 1902: 141; McCarthy 1900: 155; Roberts et al. 1967: 249). However, the trip down the Mekong on tiny rafts was long and hazardous and, more often, the hill-dwellers sold their rice to traders who established rice barns and temporary market-places at the mouths of the tributaries and at other places where tracks from the highlands met the Mekong (Izikowitz 1979: 310–311; Lefèvre-Pontalis 1902: 89; Orléans 1894: 397; Pavie 1901: 208). When sufficient quantities were accumulated, the rice was transported downstream, sometimes in large canoes – the biggest were

---

11 In writings of this era "Lao" refers to both present day Laos and northern Thailand.

12 Bowie (1992: 805) has argued that "most northern Thai villagers were not self-sufficient in rice production." In the much less ecologically favourable northern Laos the problems of self-sufficiency must have been significantly more marked (Halpern 1964a: 87–88).

30 metres long and could carry six tonnes[13] – but usually on cargo-carrying rafts made by lashing two large canoes together with bamboo. The rafts travelled in large numbers to Louangphabang where they lined the riverbank, forming what amounted to a floating market. Smyth (1898a: 178) provides a vivid description of this riverine trade between Paktha and Louangphabang:

> They are like floating villages, with enormous round-roofed sheds covering them almost completely. They are over a hundred feet long and twenty or thirty feet wide, and have their ends turned up. There are three or four oars a side, and about ten at each end working transversely to keep the structure straight when in the rapids. They carry between thirty and forty people according to size, and travel practically with the stream alone ... When they reach Luang Prabang the rice and cotton is unloaded and the raft broken up. Some of the Lao crews are' away months on these journeys seeking cargo. Part go up to bargain with the ... [hill dwellers], while others build a temporary village by the main river, and proceed to make the raft.[14]

It is likely that some of this trade took the form of tribute payments from upland communities to lowland village chiefs and the paramount chief in the royal capital. Louangphabang had a network of lowland administrative centres along both the Tha and Beng Rivers (Map 2.2) from which tributary relations with uplanders could be managed. Tributary relationships with the hill-dwellers were also elaborately enacted and legitimised in Louangphabang's state rituals (Stuart-Fox 1993: 114). However, managing such a spatially dispersed network of tributary relationships was problematic and there were limits to the effectiveness of politico-religious power. Lefèvre-Pontalis (1902: 139, 142) noted that some of the lowland

---

13 For details on canoe transport, see Smyth (1895: 47–49); Picanon (1901: 309); Reinach (1911: 361); Franck (1926: 287–288, 297); Coolidge (1933: 149, 163–164, 177); Legendre (1936: 142–143); and Credner (1966: 310).

14 Other descriptions of large-scale raft transport on the Mekong are provided by Carné (1872: 212); Orléans (1894: 375); Smyth (1895: 47–49); Pavie (1901: 208; 1906: 65); Reinach (1911: 361); Franck (1926: 324); and Coolidge (1933: 151, 198–199). During the 1940s and 1950s, large cargo boats powered by truck engines took the place of rafts, though the practise of lashing boats together to form larger vessels persisted until at least the 1960s (see, for example, Ellis 1960: 123, 139; Wollaston 1960: 169, 183). Most of the large-scale river trade travelled downstream. There was some upstream traffic in wooden canoes that were laboriously poled up the river (Coolidge and Roosevelt 1933: 206; Picanon 1901: 340–341; Rowley 1960: 170). This upstream traffic proceeded as far as the impassable rapids at Tang O (Map 2.2) where traders from Louangphabang travelled to exchange salt for Kengtung opium (Scott 1901: Vol 2: 387). Some traders also continued "up the Nam Tha [Tha River] in their canoes in order to sell their wares in the Lamet district," returning with loads of highland rice (Izikowitz 1979: 54). There was also some river trade on the Mekong above Tang O (Woodthorpe 1896: 585).

chiefs seemed to have tenuous relations with their upland subjects and it was not unknown for tributary communities to revolt and cross into the territory of neighbouring states (Lefèvre-Pontalis 1902: 142; Smyth 1898a: 172).

A more effective regulatory strategy, it seems, was to engage the upland communities in commercial exchange and a rudimentary system of politico-spatial specialisation occurred where lowland settlements concentrated on handicrafts and trade, while the uplanders focussed on agricultural production (Halpern 1964a: 87, 92; Izikowitz 1979: 27; Lefèvre-Pontalis 1902: 140). Key lowland settlements, including Louangphabang itself, were located at strategic transport junctions where trade with the upland communities could be regulated. Barter was the most common basis for exchange, with hill-dwellers trading primary produce for iron goods, fabric, ornaments and pottery produced in lowland Lao communities. The region around Louangphabang is noted for its village handicrafts and it is possible that this developed not only to support the royal court but also to encourage trade with uplanders (cf. Berdan 1989: 88). Salt from the salt-wells in the northern reaches of Louangphabang's domain was also highly sought after by the hill-dwellers (Izikowitz 1979: 27, 310). Lowland traders and village shop-keepers also introduced European manufactured goods – cloth, thread, needles, dyes, condensed milk, matches, sugar, kerosene and mirrors – that were imported from trading centres in northern Siam (Orléans 1894: 480, 488, 607–609). Cash transactions also occurred: Siamese *ticals*, Indian *ruphees* and locally smelted silver circulated widely in the region (Reinach 1911: 327–328).

Trading relations between upland and lowland communities were often managed by the institution of *lam* (literally, interpreter). According to Halpern (1959: 121) the *lam* was a lowland intermediary who was approached by uplanders "whenever they had some forest products to sell or wanted to buy salt or clothing." The *lam* would arrange a transaction with a merchant or even engage in direct trade himself, in which case he may have "enjoyed a complete monopoly with all their trade funnelled through him" (Halpern 1959: 121). Though Halpern's observations were made in the latter stages of the colonial period, when the institution was in decline, his work suggests that earlier *lam* may have combined the positions of tribute collecting chief *and* commercial agent. He writes that *lam* were often village or district headmen who paid taxes for the uplanders and managed their relations with central authorities in return for agricultural labour and an assured supply of forest products and game (Halpern 1959: 121).

From the relatively scanty evidence it also seems likely that more "independent" forms of trade were also emerging. Some of the most active traders were Chinese merchants based in the lowland settlements. In 1892, Archer (in Forbes 1987: 43) reported that Louangphabang's external trade with Siam was "carried on chiefly by Chinese traders" and a few years earlier, Orléans (1894: 375) had found that many of the rafts moored at Louangphabang's riverside market were owned by Chinese. Even in the remote upper-reaches of the Tha River, Lefèvre-Pontalis (1902: 144) found that Chinese merchants were settled in a village that lay on one of the "principal cross-roads in the region" The nature of the relationship between Chinese merchants and tributary overlords is difficult to judge but, following Berdan (1989), it is possible that they established their role as suppliers of luxury goods to the chiefly elite, gradually expanding their role into more generalised commodity trade. They may also have played a role as commercial agents in dealings with external states and as local tax and revenue collectors (Hong 1984). Chinese merchants would later become very influential in Laos and the origins of their influence in the pre-colonial polities requires further investigation.

Like Nan, Louangphabang also controlled some important caravan routes in the north-west. Oudomxai - an important trading centre for minerals, cotton, salt and cattle - was a meeting point for several caravan trails heading into Laos from Sipsongpanna.[15] Over the years, the town had been contested with the Lü of Sipsongpanna (Jumsai 1971: 142–145) but, in the last decades of the century, Louangphabang had secured full control. Visiting in 1895, Pavie's men found Louangphabang's interests in Oudomxai represented by a commissioner accompanied by 50 troops "whose presence had brought peace to the country" (Pavie 1906: 374). From Oudomxai, the Yunnanese caravans took several routes southward: some followed the Beng valley – where there were at least two lowland administrative centres (Pavie 1906: 373–374) – while others took more direct, but rugged, routes south-east towards Louangphabang. During the caravan season, the authorities from Louangphabang installed cross-river ferries at Pakbeng and collected tolls on the passing traffic (Lefèvre-Pontalis 1902: 89). Opposite Pakbeng, there were numerous caravan trails that linked riverside market villages and provided direct routes into northern Siam for Yunnanese traders keen to avoid the tax agents in Louangphabang (Lefèvre-Pontalis 1902: 90–91; Orléans 1894: 489, 609; Pavie 1901: 227). There was keen competition with Nan for control of these strategically important routes.[16]

---

15 For details of the caravan routes between Sipsongpanna, Oudomxai and Louangphabang, see Neis (1885: 388); Orléans (1894: 419–420); McCarthy (1900: 161–164); Pavie (1901: 258–259, 305); Picanon (1901: 342); Lefèvre-Pontalis (1902: 89, 176–178); Reinach (1911: 369); and McGilvary (1912: 390–91, 402–403). For details of trade at Oudomxai see Lamington (1891: 712); McCarthy (1900: 166); Picanon (1901: 323); and Pavie (1906: 374).

16 When Louangphabang was attacked by a force from northern Vietnam in 1887, Nan occupied some of the strategic riverside villages (Pavie 1901: 227). Soon after, when officials in Louangphabang were preoccupied with the French, Nan begun to levy tolls at Pakbeng itself (Lefèvre-Pontalis 1902: 89).

To summarise: during the nineteenth century, both Nan and Louangphabang had important interests in the areas that would become north-western Laos. These pre-colonial states were supported by the direct extraction of tribute from peasant producers, by tolls and taxes on trading activities and by the commercial exchange of manufactured and imported goods for agricultural produce. In Nan, the tribute generated by the nearby rice plains was probably the primary focus, though the Mekong outpost of Chiang Khong was an important base for the collection of taxes and tolls and for exchange with the hill-dwelling communities on the opposite bank. However, being a relatively small township with a sparsely settled hinterland, Chiang Khong lacked the power to maintain this strategic position in the face of incursions from Kengtung, Chiang Saen, Muangsing and Sipsongpanna. By the end of the nineteenth century, Nan's upper-Mekong influence was greatly reduced, despite belated attempts to resettle both Louangnamtha and Viangphoukha. By contrast, Louangphabang's north-western territories remained largely intact for most of the nineteenth century. Heavily dependant on trade, it was essential that it retained control of the valuable rice growing areas in the Tha and Beng valleys and it maintained a string of small administrative and trading centres along both rivers and at important land-transport junctions such as Oudomxai. With this superior administrative network Louangphabang was well placed to defend its domain and, despite some border tension with Nan along the Tha River and to the south of the Mekong, its core north-western territories remained intact.

The French Colonial Failure: 1893–1953

In 1893, following an exercise in gun-boat diplomacy on the river below Bangkok, France gained control of all Lao territory to the east of the Mekong. After negotiating the Franco-Siamese treaty, Auguste Pavie, the French colonial hero in Laos, travelled north to Nan "to receive, from the hands of the authorities, the administration of the territories located on the left bank of the Mé-Khong" (Pavie 1906: 261). He continued along the rough caravan trails to Chiang Saen and drifted downstream to Chiang Khong, informing the upper-Mekong Siamese chiefs about the treaty and introducing himself to the minor chiefs in the newly acquired east-bank territories. Pavie (1906: 267) was pleased to find things in good order on the east bank and writes that he was received "with eager joyfulness." He insisted that the authorities in Chiang Khong return 1894 tribute that had been collected on the east bank and, in an expansive mood, he dismissed as false a rumour that the French would put a stop to sapphire mining by the Shan settlers at Houayxay (Pavie 1906: 268–269). He then set off down-river towards Louangphabang in good spirits leaving, he wrote, "everywhere, our new subjects content and full of hope" (Pavie 1906: 268).

41

Despite the optimism, Pavie and the early French administrators in northern Laos faced a major, and ultimately insurmountable, regulatory challenge. The tributary and trading economy that the French inherited on the upper-Mekong was complexly and multiply connected with the political and economic systems of surrounding Siamese, Burmese and Chinese townships. By contrast, linkages across the eastern highlands to the commercial centres of colonial Vietnam were tenuous and poorly developed (Lamington 1891: 714–715; Orléans 1894: 329). Moreover – as much as trade proceeded the flag elsewhere in Asia – the pre-colonial penetration of French trading or industrial capital into northern Laos was minuscule. If Laos was to pay its way as a source of raw materials for French manufacturers and as a market for French merchandise the entire "natural and historical orientation" of the region had to change (Gunn 1990: 40; see also Stuart-Fox 1995a). Existing patterns of interconnection had to be disrupted and a new regime of regulation put in place. The French challenge was clearly expressed in an ambitious map prepared by Orléans (1894: facing 650) where the upper-Mekong lay at the centre of a large "zone of expansion open to French trade through Tonkin [northern Vietnam]."

There were several possible routes from northern Vietnam into Laos.[17] Some French observers advocated using the Black River and the Ou River (Map 1.1) as a link between northern Laos and Hanoi. In the early 1890s, French merchants had used this route to supply a new trading store in Louangphabang (Smyth 1898a: 207). But there were dangerous rapids on both rivers and, for some colonial observers, overland tracks running north-east from Louangphabang offered more promise (Pavie 1903: 35; Picanon 1901: 343–348). Visiting Chiang Khong in 1896, a British official was told that there was already a good road from Louangphabang to northern Vietnam – wishful thinking no doubt, but an indication of French spatial aspirations (Archer 1896: 81; see also Lefèvre-Pontalis 1902: 114). The Vietnamese colonial outpost of Dien Bien Phu (Map 1.1), located on a tributary of the Ou River and only "four or five days' march" along a well maintained road from the Black River (Lamington 1891: 715) was proposed as a possible trading entrepôt for Lao, Chinese, Vietnamese and French traders (Lefèvre-Pontalis 1902: 322–323). From Dien Bien Phu there were rough tracks and river routes, not only to Louangphabang, but also to the north-western market towns of Oudomxai and Muangsing.[18]

---

17 For a discussion of overall French transport plans in Laos, see Stuart-Fox (1995a: 123–128).
18 However, some French writers were pessimistic about the routes between northern Laos and northern Vietnam. They advocated a rail link from central Vietnam to the Mekong in southern Laos, with the north supplied by a river steamboat service upstream to Louangphabang (Orléans 1894: 487–488, 535–536). One writer advocated a compromise. French goods, he argued, should be imported via northern Vietnam with northern Lao exports taken down the Mekong to the proposed southern railway for transhipment to Vietnamese ports (quoted in Picanon 1901: 339).

The French advocates of the routes between northern Laos and Vietnam hoped that they would bring about fundamental changes in the established patterns of local and regional trade, "completely alter[ing] the economic future of Upper Laos" (quoted in Stuart-Fox 1995a: 126). French goods, they anticipated, would flow into Louangphabang and the north-western trading centres for distribution by agents of French commercial houses. French goods would be exchanged for local produce and forest products – at newly established periodic markets – ensuring regular supplies for the export houses of Vietnam rather than Chinese traders in Siam. Competition from French merchandise would spell an end to the down-river trade in foreign goods carried from the trading centres in northern Siam, and it may even be possible, some writers hoped, to divert Yunnanese caravan traders away from Laos and Siam towards the commercial opportunities of northern Vietnam (Lefèvre-Pontalis 1902: 311–326; Orléans 1894: 488–491; Reinach 1911: 350–352, 366; Smyth 1898a: 208; Stuart-Fox 1995a). In order to achieve this realignment, the French had to secure control over the key marketing locations in northern Laos.

Making new boundaries: Muangsing, Boten and west-bank Louangphabang

Much has been made of the creation of colonial boundaries in the borderlands, of the supposed historical rupture that occurred when "sharp and clear-cut" colonial demarcation, backed by the modern technology of mapping, displaced the supposedly fluid, ambiguous and non-bounding spatial practices of the past (Thongchai 1994: 111; see also Anderson 1991: 170–178; Keyes 1993: 11; Leach 1960; Reynolds 1991: 21–22; Steinberg 1971: 7; Stuart-Fox 1997: 21). But perhaps there was more regulatory continuity than this widely-held view allows. The chief of Muangsing, for example, had fought with Kengtung for control of Chiang Lap, reluctantly accepting the Mekong as a pre-colonial demarcation (Scott 1901 Vol 1: 364). To the north, a "low mud wall with a bamboo palisade on the top" (Lamington 1891: 709) separated Muangsing's territory from the southern states of Sipsongpanna. One of these states – Mengla – had extended its boundary southward to take in the salt wells in the headwaters of the Tha River, erecting a boundary marker as a reminder to the Siamese settlers at Louangnamtha. In the lower reaches of the Tha River, Nan and Louangphabang were involved in a longstanding boundary dispute (McCarthy 1900: 154–155, 162). There were detailed documents setting out the trees, rest-houses and other markers that defined the boundary, but the documents held in either capital did not agree (Lefèvre-Pontalis 1902: 141–142). And, further up the Mekong, there were arguments between Chiang Khong and Chiang Saen about whose territory included a number of east-bank tributaries (Lefèvre-Pontalis 1902:130–131, 137–138). When the French negotiated the colonial boundaries on the upper-Mekong, their motives were similar to the territorial demarcators who preceded them: they wanted to secure access to strategically important territory that would facilitate their control of trade and natural resources. This regulatory goal was evident in all of the major boundary negotiations the French undertook.

The northern boundary with China was settled without major difficulty, given China's preoccupation with Japanese aggression in the first Sino-Japanese war. Visiting the areas north of Louangnamtha in 1894, Lefèvre-Pontalis had asserted French rights to the salt wells at Boten in the headwaters of the Tha River. Watersheds of tributaries such as the Tha River were, he argued, "boundaries traced by nature" (Lefèvre-Pontalis 1902: 164) and he had the boundary post erected by the Mengla Lü taken down. French control at Boten was crucial, not for the small territorial gain, but to secure the invaluable supply of salt, to control the lucrative trade that the salt wells generated and to provide a link into the commercially important areas to the north: "localities of Sipsong-panna, provided with markets, visited by numerous Chinese caravans and linked to the major Yunnanese centres by numerous routes and paths" (Lefèvre-Pontalis 1902: 314). In subsequent negotiations, concluded in June 1895, the Chinese gave up Mengla's claim to the salt wells and handed Boten to the French (Prescott 1975: 450).[19] In the same agreement the French won preferential terms for French goods entering Yunnan and rights to navigation along the Mekong into China (Anon 1896: 299; Chandran 1971: 12).

The famous boundary dispute with the British over Muangsing was harder to resolve.[20] British claims, backed by a military force that crossed the Mekong in 1895, were based on Muangsing's previous payment of tribute to Burmese rulers and its history of association with the Shan state of Kengtung (which came under British control in 1890). The French disputed this, claiming that Muangsing had fallen within Nan's domain and had been validly ceded to them in the Siamese treaty of 1893. From a French point of view, Muangsing was a key element in enforcing a new regime of trade regulation. It was one of the most important trading centres in the upper-reaches of the Mekong and, outside Louangphabang, probably the busiest market town in northern Laos. It commanded what had become the most important caravan route in Laos and was only a short

19 It was only this small piece of territory, not the entire province of Louangnamtha, as suggested by Stuart-Fox (1997: 25), which the French gained on this section of the border.
20 For detailed accounts of this dispute, see Hirshfield (1968) and Chandran (1977). For accounts of some of the main local participants, see Pavie (1901; 1906); Lefèvre-Pontalis (1902) and Mitton (1936). For some of the ongoing implications for Franco-Siamese relations, see Goldman (1972).

distance from the important salt wells at Boten. The French feared that British control in Muangsing could be a base for extending British commercial influence throughout the north-west. Already, British wares – "Manchester goods" and "Bryant and May's wax matches" – were sold in the market there, imported by traders from Burma (Lamington 1891: 708; see also Lefèvre 1898). French concerns were heightened by rumours that the British were improving the route between Kengtung and Muangsing by constructing a bridge across the Mekong at Chiang Lap, and that they were planning to install Burmese boats on the upper-reaches of the river (Woodthorpe 1896: 584–585). The Mekong rapids had dampened French hopes of a river route into China, but the prospects of a British barrier at Muangsing that could "throttle French commerce up that channel" (quoted in Hirshfield 1968: 43) was still intolerable, especially since the Yunnanese town of Simao had been opened to French commerce (Chandran 1971: 12). The Mekong, the French argued, was the obvious boundary between the colonial possessions.

Fortunately for the French, British views were more ambivalent (Smyth 1898a: 145–151). No doubt, they were keen to limit French expansion in the upper-Mekong region and were particularly concerned about French commercial inroads into Yunnan. Some British business interests were lobbying for a railway linking Siam and Yunnan via the upper-Mekong and one proposed route crossed the Mekong at Chiang Lap, and ran through Muangsing to Sipsongpanna (Lamington 1891: 720). But the railway lobbyists had little support in the Foreign Office (Chandran 1971: 11) and it was ultimately recognised that Muangsing – "distant," "unhealthy" and "roadless" (quoted in Chandran 1977: 341) – was a low priority for the British in comparison with their extensive commercial interests in northern Siam. In an agreement signed in 1896, the French rights over Muangsing were recognised and the upper-Mekong itself became the boundary between French and British colonial possessions. In return, the British achieved a guarantee of the neutrality of most of Siam, thwarting French influence beyond the Mekong watershed.[21]

The dispute over west-bank Louangphabang, though less contentious, was the most prolonged. In the case of Muangsing, France argued that the Mekong itself represented the most suitable border but, to the south, they were active in pursuing Louangphabang's "traditional" claims on the opposite bank. Soon after the 1893 treaty with Siam, French trans-Mekong ambitions became clear when a senior official from the Louangphabang court was sent across the river to collect tribute and

---

21 In 1914, the French had to fight for control of Muangsing again when the local chief fled into Sipsongpanna and led a Lü revolt against French outposts in the north-west. Three expensive military expeditions were required to restore order (Boulanger 1931: 356–357; Gunn 1990: 142–144).

administer the west-bank territories (Jumsai 1971: 222–226; Smyth 1898b: 244–245). A high priority for the French was to gain control of the extensive teak reserves that lay across the river, but they were also keen to secure control over the caravan routes that linked Nan and Uttaradit with the Mekong, routes that were in direct competition with the planned routes that would direct northern Lao trade to Vietnam. The market villages along the Siamese bank of the Mekong could provide the French with good bases for regulating and taxing trade and extending their commercial influence southward towards Nan. However, the most pressing consideration was, once again, salt. In 1897, a force from Louangphabang occupied Hongsa and nearby salt wells in response to military action in the area by Nan (Jumsai 1971: 222, 225). Salt was in short supply in French territory and settlers from the east bank soon arrived to establish an export trade with Louangphabang. Despite vigorous Siamese protests to Paris, Louangphabang retained control of the area and later extended its claim to the limit of the Mekong watershed. The area had been excluded from the Anglo-French declaration of Siamese neutrality and, in 1904, it was ceded to the French in return for a relaxation of a number of the terms of the 1893 Franco-Siamese treaty (Boulanger 1931: 347–349; Prescott 1975: 433). The French gained all of the territory that had traditionally been claimed by Louangphabang, extending upstream as far as Paktha (Prescott 1975: 434, 441). Though they lay within the Mekong watershed, Chiang Khong and Chiang Saen remained in Siamese hands – Louangphabang had no recent claims to them – but the French had already moved to break Siamese power in these upper-Mekong trading outposts.

French action on trade

It is eighteen years since Laos has become a French possession, but the internal conditions of commerce and exchange have not varied. (Reinarch 1911: 353)

The task of establishing a French administrative presence in north-western Laos fell to Lefèvre-Pontalis, a close colleague of Pavie. Travelling up river from Louangphabang in July 1894, he noted the strategic importance of towns like Pakbeng and Paktha where, he hoped, trade could be profitably developed under French control (Lefèvre-Pontalis 1902: 91–93). But his goal lay further upstream, at Siamese Chiang Khong. Here, it was his task to set up a "commercial agency" and, after much cajoling of the local chief, Siamese labourers were put to work constructing the agency on a riverside site that, Lefèvre-Pontalis was pleased to find, had previously been occupied by the chiefs of Chiang Khong "at the most flourishing period" of the town (Lefèvre-Pontalis 1902: 106). Soon after, he continued upstream to establish a second agency at Chiang Saen (Lefèvre-Pontalis 1902: 120–138). The spatial anomaly of French agencies on Siamese soil had been provided for in the treaty of 1893 and was reinforced by the exclusion of Siamese officials and tax collectors from a 25 kilometre strip of territory running along the Siamese side of the Mekong.

The French moved quickly to supplant Siamese power in these upper-Mekong trading towns (Lefèvre-Pontalis 1902: 95–139). Soon after his arrival, Lefèvre-Pontalis intervened in communications between the chief in Chiang Khong and local chiefs on the east bank, introduced new arrangements for the collection of east-bank taxes and even attempted to persuade Lü settlers around Chiang Khong to cross the river and return to their former homes, now under French control. The operators of the cross-river boat service were instructed to berth just below the French agency, where passports would be issued for all travellers. This, the French concluded, would be the best way to supervise relations between the east and west banks, to compile statistics on the Yunnanese caravan trade passing through Chiang Khong and, above all, to monitor the movement of east-bank Khmu who were travelling in large numbers to work for British firms in the teak forests around Chiang Mai. Economic independence on the east bank was to be achieved by establishing a market in the Shan settlement of Houayxay and by the construction of village rice stores that would encourage the Khmu and Lamet to store surplus rice, rather than selling it and putting themselves "at the mercy of the Thaïs" when supplies ran out (Lefèvre-Pontalis 1902: 115). In Chiang Saen similar initiatives were put in place to break the links between the east and west banks (Archer 1896: 77–80). Visiting the two upper-Mekong towns in 1896, the British Consul in Chiang Mai found that Siamese power was practically extinguished and that "the Mekong has now become to all intents and purposes a French river" (Archer 1896: 82).

The results for French commerce were, however, disappointing. The agencies at Chiang Khong and Chiang Saen were bases for the *Syndicat Français du Laos*, a group of Parisian merchants who hoped to open the upper-Mekong to French trade (Gunn 1990: 20–21; Reinach 1911: 247). The *Syndicat* did succeed in establishing a "well stocked" store in Louangphabang but "the goods did not … seem to find their way out again" (Smyth 1898a: 207) and there is no evidence that French merchandise was sold through the upper-Mekong agencies or that they had any success in capturing local or regional trade (Smyth 1895: 57–58). By 1895, the *Syndicat* had collapsed (McCoy 1970: 77; Stuart-Fox 1995a: 134). Archer, the British Consul, was disturbed by French political influence, but in relation to French commerce he saw no cause for alarm:

> I need hardly say that as there is no French trade on the Upper
> Mekong, the term "Commercial Agent" is a misnomer, and that

47

the Agents at Chiang Khong and Chiangsën are ... "Consular Agents," or more correctly speaking "Political Agents." (Archer 1896: 8)

The commercial failure of the agencies was soon recognised by the French themselves and their political functions were incorporated into the French administration of "Haut Mekong" (Reinach 1911: 248). The riverside agencies at Chiang Saen and Chiang Khong were abandoned and the small Shan settlement of Houayxay became the centre for French administration on the upper-Mekong.

With the demise of the commercial agencies, French intervention in cross-border trade was limited and relatively ineffective. Export taxes were placed on rice, cardamom, wax, ivory, boats, livestock and a range of other locally produced or collected goods (Picanon 1901: 255–258). Though the taxes made an important contribution to Lao colonial revenue, they had little effect on the continued flow of exports across the Mekong. Most northern Lao exports continued to pass along Chinese trading networks into Siam where transport infrastructure was more developed, prices were better and a wider range of manufactured goods was available for exchange (Picanon 1901: 280, 329–330, 340–341, 345; Reinach 1911: 287, 354–356; Smyth 1898a: 208–209, 212–213; Stuart-Fox 1995a: 122, 135). By 1914, the Siamese rail-head at Uttaradit had become the main centre for northern Lao export trade (Brenier 1914: 224–226). Despite the ambitious colonial plans for new trade routes, the only French competition to Siamese infrastructure was a road built from central Vietnam to Louangphabang, completed in the mid-1930s. However, the flow of cheap Vietnamese rice along this road may, in fact, have loosened the longstanding trade links between Louangphabang and the rice-producing villages of the north-west, encouraging their closer relations with Siamese traders in Chiang Khong and Chiang Saen (Izikowitz 1979: 311). French head taxes may also have encouraged cross-border sales to generate cash income in the cross-border markets of northern Siam (Anan 1983: 21; Reinach 1911: 241). The colonial dream of northern Lao produce supplying French or Indochinese merchants and manufacturers remained unfulfilled.

Action on imports was similarly ineffective. Under the terms of the 1892 *Colonial Tariff Law* "products of the mother country could enter the colony duty free while those of other countries were subject to the same tariffs as in France" (Robequain 1944: 129; see also Murray 1980: 196–198). This, however, provided little joy for Indochinese traders, as France did not produce the manufactured goods sought after in Laos and they had to rely on English, German and Japanese goods that were subject to heavy duty when they entered via Indochinese ports. By contrast, the same goods were subject to light taxes when they entered Siam or Burma and usually entered Laos duty-free along the sparsely supervised Mekong border (Bassenne 1995: 62–63; Gunn 1990: 22; Smyth 1898a; Stuart-Fox 1995a). One French writer lamented that the colonial tariff regime benefited the traders in Siam, Burma and China at the expense of traders in Indochina itself (Reinach 1911: 353–354). A visitor to Louangphabang in the 1920s confirms this conclusion and provides a vivid picture of the French failure to regulate upper-Mekong trade:

> The French had placed such a high duty on all goods entering Indo-China that smuggling has become one of the most essential and profitable if not the most honourable of the native trades. Goods are brought in from Siam at one-third the cost, and then sold in competition with the French products that must bear not only the initial entrance duty at Saigon, but also the heavy freight cost of the three week journey ... Nevertheless, these [Chinese] smugglers ... are not content with the already enormous profits to be made in the most honest transaction of their profession, but have commenced the importation from China of cheap copies of English, French and American goods ... I know this is true in my case, for after buying in a Chinese store what I believed to be a Waterman fountain pen and a pair of "Keds" tennis shoes, I found that they were the rankest imitations. (Legendre 1936: 163)[22]

More concerted regulatory efforts were made in relation to the trade in opium. In late 1895, the French declared a colonial monopoly and an official opium enterprise for northern Laos was established in Louangphabang. Independent trading in opium, including transit trade, was prohibited and smugglers faced heavy fines, prison sentences and the confiscation of property (Picanon 1901: 259–262). In the north-west, opium was grown in only a relatively small number of Hmong and Yao villages and most of it was locally consumed rather than sold to the French. Most of the opium processed at the boiler in Louangphabang was purchased from Shan traders from Kengtung, making a major contribution to French revenue in northern Laos but maintaining the old trade routes across the Mekong. The Yunnanese caravan traders were more reluctant to enter into commercial arrangements with the French and they conducted an extensive illegal trade, motivated by the high prices created by the opium monopolies in both Siam and Indochina (McCoy 1970: 86; 1972: 68, 252; Picanon 1901: 262, 285). Lü settlers along the main caravan route between Louangnamtha and Houayxay, were also active in the illegal trade

---

22 The French did not move to establish an effective customs barrier along the Mekong until the late 1930s (Levy, Lacam, and Roth 1941: 81–82; Thompson 1941: xxiii) and there is some evidence that this did disrupt cross-border trade (Charivat 1985: 98), worsening tensions with Thailand (Thompson 1941: xxiii) and, possibly, adding some strength to the Lao independence movement (Sasorith 1953: 86–91).

(Izikowitz 1985: 107). The French made vigorous attempts to suppress smuggling along the Vietnam-Yunnan border but made little effort to extend border controls into the northern regions of Laos (Brenier 1914: 87; McCoy 1972: 65–66). "Through this oversight," McCoy (1970: 87) writes, "the French made Laos into a smuggler's haven and started the contraband opium trade."

Although French regulatory action on trade was relatively ineffective, there were significant developments in the sociology of the region's trade during the colonial period. The relative peace and stability of the colonial period in Laos – coupled with the development of trading, transport and administrative structures in northern Siam – encouraged the migration of Chinese traders from the commercialised districts around Bangkok into the upper-Mekong region (Anan 1983: 34–35; Moerman 1975: 153). Some of the Chinese shopkeeping families in Chiang Khong arrived in the early decades of the century to pursue opportunities in the cross-border timber and cattle trade and to establish retail and wholesale shops. Chinese shopkeepers in the Mekong hinterland provided local traders and peddlers with manufactured goods imported, with minimal tariffs, through Bangkok. They were also active in buying natural products from Laos and dispatching them to their trading partners at the Bangkok ports (Anan 1983: 36; Reinach 1911: 350, 354–355).[23] In northern Laos there was a Chinese mercantile presence prior to the 1890s, but these developments undoubtedly strengthened their commercial position, probably under-mining the longstanding links between mercantile activity and the traditional tribute/trading elite.[24] The northern Lao institution of *lam* appears to have declined at the same time as the Chinese increasingly came to dominate long-distance wholesale trade (Halpern 1964a: 91) and, in most cases, it was Chinese merchants, rather than members of the Lao elite, who made the first tentative moves into industrial production: rice milling, sawmilling, brick kilns, dye shops, ice factories and bottling works (Halpern 1964a: 90; 1964b: 127). By the end of the colonial period the Chinese had emerged as the predominant commercial class in northern Laos.

---

23 Shan, Burmese and Indian traders were also active in the region, benefiting from the protection of British citizenship and from the favourable credit arrangements they had with British trading firms in northern Siam and Burma (Anan 1983: 22, 26; Dooley 1959: 111; Le May 1926: 197; Smyth 1898a: 116).

24 In Chiang Khong this changing balance of commercial power took on a spatial form. The first Chinese merchants were forced to set up their shops on the town's outskirts, due to the control of the central "port" areas by the descendants of Chiang Khong's traditional chiefs. However, by the 1950s and 1960s the local landowners has started to sell, and the Chinese succeeded in establishing the busy commercial strip that still surrounds the town's main temple.

Two Zones: 1962–1975

The trading and transport systems of the borderlands entered a period of rapid change during the Second World War and its post-colonial aftermath. With France powerless to defend Indochina, no less than five foreign armies occupied and attempted to exert control over different parts of north-western Laos.[25] In 1941, Thailand seized the west-bank territories opposite Louangphabang that had been ceded to France in 1907. In 1945, the Japanese army occupied northern Laos and the French forces retreated into southern China after trying to hold onto the airfields at Louangnamtha and Muangsing. Just a few months later, under the terms of the *Potsdam Agreement*, northern Laos was occupied by the Chinese Kuomintang whose economic plunder of the countryside far exceeded that of the Japanese they had been sent to disarm. For a period, there were plans to establish Muangsing as the capital of a Chinese province in northern Laos. A year later, the north-west was the last area of Laos to be recaptured by French forces following the withdrawal of the Kuomintang and the defeat of the newly emerged Free Lao anti-French forces. And, in 1953 and 1954, Vietnamese communist forces thrust into northern and north-western Laos in the build-up to the decisive battle at Dien Bien Phu. In an ultimate colonial irony, the French were defeated at Dien Bien Phu trying to block what they had been unable to achieve – the integration of northern Laos into the orbit of northern Vietnam.

After the battle of Dien Bien Phu and the granting of full Lao independence in 1953, anti-government Pathet Lao forces, supported by the North Vietnamese Army (NVA), consolidated their position within the north-west. Initially their stronghold was around Muangbeng, to the south of Oudomxai but, by the early 1960s, they had established effective control over most of Beng valley – Oudomxai itself fell in 1961 – much of the territory between Oudomxai and Louangnamtha and a large swath of territory around Viangphoukha (Deuve 1984: 96, 146, 166, 206; Devillers and Lacouture 1969: i; Thee 1973: 109; Toye 1968: 167). They had also

---

25 There are numerous fragmentary references to north-western Laos in a range of historical accounts of this tumultuous period. For details of the Franco-Thai conflict, see Sivaram (1941); Crosby (1945: chapter 19); Gaudel (1947: chapter 3); Decoux (1950: chapter 6); Direk (1966); Flood (1969); Hesse d'Alzon (1982: 93–96; 1985: chapter 7); and Charivat (1985: chapter 6). For the Japanese occupation of northern Laos and French resistance, see Sabattier (1952: 212–213, 232–233); Hammer (1966: 40); Crèvecoeur (1985: chapter 1); Hesse d'Alzon (1985: 240–247); and Deuve (1992: 3–126). For the Kuomintang occupation, see Embree (1949: 154); Hammer (1966: 135–138); Crèvecoeur (1985: 43–52); and Deuve (1992: 106–202). For the reconquest of the north by the French and the early activities of the Free Lao, see Crèvecoeur (1985); Gunn (1988); and Deuve (1992). For the battle of Dien Bien Phu and the associated incursions into north-western Laos, see Newman (1953: 140–144); Meeker (1959: 62); Fall (1961: chapter 5; 1967); Lancaster (1961: 259–263); Dommen (1964: 40–43); Hammer (1966: 293); Toye (1968: 82–101); Devillers (1969: 33, 44–45, 51–52, 61–63); and Héduy (1981: 128–131).

secured control of numerous villages along the Mekong between Paktha and Pakbeng and, by 1961, their activities against boats on the Mekong had created a partial blockade of Louangphabang (Dommen 1964: 207). In 1962, in the decisive military action of the north-west, Pathet Lao and Vietnamese troops surrounded Royal Lao Government (RLG) forces that had massed at Louangnamtha. The military outpost at Muangsing was captured and, after shelling of positions around the airport at Louangnamtha, the large RLG force fled, making its way down the caravan trail to Houayxay (Dommen 1964: 213–219; Thee 1973: 235–253; Toye 1968: 182–184; Warner 1964: 265–267).

Following the fall of Louangnamtha, the north-west was divided into two zones (Fall 1961: 337; Langer and Zasloff 1970: 74–75). The northern communist zone included Oudomxai, Louangnamtha, Muangsing, Viangphoukha and much of the Beng and Tha River valleys. Pathet Lao control over the Mekong was increased when the river port of Pakbeng fell in the late 1960s. RLG control was limited to areas adjacent to the Thai border (Map 2.3). It controlled Houayxay, a narrow strip of territory up and down the Mekong, and the districts around Hongsa and Xianghon.

The two rival states that contested Laos in this period were both heavily dependant on external assistance. Not only was the military effort itself costly, but local production and distribution systems were disrupted by warfare, large-scale refugee movement and severe limits on internal travel. In the communist north – heroic efforts in underground factories notwithstanding – China became the primary source of military supplies, manufactured good and processed foods. The most potent symbol of this alignment was the Chinese construction of an extensive road system in northern Laos. In the south, economic relations with Thailand were intensified and aid poured across the Mekong to help support the large dependent refugee population. Industrial activities in the southern zone also linked the region into international marketing networks. The external links that were strengthened in this period were to prove crucial in the era of the Economic Quadrangle.

The northern zone

By the 1950s, the Yunnanese caravan trade in north-western Laos was in steady decline. A small part of the decline may be attributed to French restrictions on the opium trade, but it was mainly due to increased availability in southern China of imported manufactured goods (especially textiles) and competition from Chinese and Shan traders based in Thailand and Burma (Anan 1983: 22–23; Forbes 1987: 24–25, 40–44). After the 1949 communist victory in China, the caravan trade diminished further as the remote regions of Yunnan were incorporated within the modern Chinese state, restrictions were placed on private trade, and supervision of

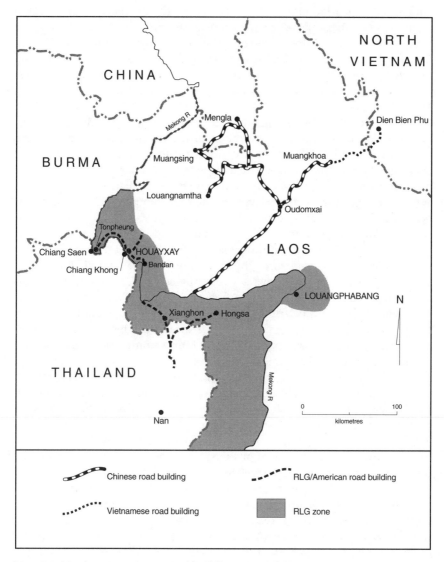

Map 2.3 North-western Laos: road building 1963–1975

the border was stepped up. In Dooley's (1959; 1963) accounts of both Muangsing and Louangnamtha, cross-border contact with China appears as an occasional trickle of refugees from Sipsongpanna, though local residents recall that the salt wells at Boten continued to attract some small-scale trade with some caravans continuing on as far as Houayxay and

Chiang Khong. Manufactured goods sold in the northern markets came mainly from Thailand. They were poled up the Tha River in wooden canoes by merchants from Louangphabang, Chiang Khong and Chiang Saen or loaded onto packhorses at small river ports along the Mekong (Rowley 1960: 149–150, 190). Some shops were also supplied by planes flown by wholesalers based in Louangphabang and Vientiane (Damrong 1994: 108–114; McCoy 1972: 254).

After the fall of Muangsing and Louangnamtha to communist forces, however, Thai commercial penetration of the north came to an end and cross-border trade with China was dramatically revived.[26] The fledgling communist state that was formed in northern Laos faced a crisis of production with almost no industrial activity in the Pathet Lao zone and agricultural production severely disrupted by bombing and widespread depopulation. Inevitably, the Pathet Lao provinces turned to China for support. An account of this trade has been provided by Langer and Zasloff (1970: 121–122) based on information from Vietnamese informants. Orders for supplies from throughout the region were compiled at Pathet Lao headquarters in northern Laos, then passed to Hanoi and, finally, to the Chinese central government. After some time, NVA and Pathet Lao representatives would be summoned to Kunming – the capital of Yunnan Province (Map 1.1) – to arrange transport of the goods to the Lao border near Muangsing. The supplies included arms, ammunition, salt, canned meat, fish sauce, sugar, milk, cigarettes, toiletries, rainproof clothing, kitchenware, sandals, shoes, blankets, mosquito nets, agricultural tools and cloth. Army supplies were distributed to local units from warehouses in Louangnamtha, while other goods were sold in the region's markets by Pathet Lao authorities to raise revenue for the local administration. Though the local population was depleted by large-scale refugee movement to Houayxay and Louangphabang (the northern towns were heavily bombed in the 1960s), the level of trade was boosted by the influx of Vietnamese and Chinese troops and thousands of Chinese road workers.

Chinese road construction in the 1960s and the early 1970s was a dramatic and long-lasting regulatory intervention in the transport and trading systems of north-western Laos (Map 2.3). The first project undertaken by the road builders strengthened the old cross-border trading link between Mengla and Muangsing. The link was completed in 1965 and later extended down the rough track to Louangnamtha (Godley and St Goar 1991: 292). Muangsing's strategic trading position was reinforced: "[t]he place looked prosperous, with a large population, animated market activities, a clear communications line to China, an adequate supply of food and commodities, and rather low market prices" (quoted in Langer

---

26 Notwithstanding claims that the China-Lao border was "virtually closed" for three decades after 1949 (Chapman, Hinton, and Tan 1992: 15).

and Zasloff 1970: 142–143; see also Khamphaeng 1996: 11). But the prosperity was short-lived. By the late 1960s, the Chinese had completed a direct link between Mengla and Louangnamtha, via the border village of Boten, bypassing Muangsing and ending its position as a regional trading centre (Godley and St Goar 1991: 294). Later road-building efforts would be concentrated on areas to the east.

Information on trading conditions around Oudomxai is scanty. During the 1950s, the town was subjected to devastating attacks by NVA forces (Meeker 1959: 61–63) and later was heavily bombed by RLG and American aircraft. Locals recall abandoning the town, living in caves and tunnels in the surrounding hills and cultivating fields at night. By one account (Langer and Zasloff 1970: 121), Oudomxai fell within the region of northern Laos that was supplied from Vietnam, and NVA units were busy building a road from Dien Bien Phu to the Ou River at Muangkhoa (Godley and St Goar 1991: 295). In the late 1960s, however, Oudomxai became a focus for Chinese activity in the north-west. In a new phase of road construction, thousands of Chinese labourers and engineers built roads from Boten to Oudomxai and onward to Muangkhoa to the north-east and Pakbeng to the south (Godley and St Goar 1991: 294–297, 302–309). Chinese and Vietnamese road-building met at the Ou River, creating a new east-west trading and transport link – the dream of French colonial administrators – that would support much of the north-west during the war years and well beyond (Taillard 1989: 84–85).[27] The road to Pakbeng also opened up an important supply route to the Mekong, consolidating communist control of the Beng valley, and threatening the RLG strongholds on the opposite side of the river. It has become the most important transport route in north-western Laos. With the establishment of a Chinese consulate, Oudomxai became the centre for Chinese influence in Laos.

The southern zone

In 1962, RLG forces abandoned Houayxay, hastily crossing the river to Chiang Khong, fearing that communist forces were pouring down the trail following the fall of Louangnamtha. But the communist forces paused well to the north – probably reluctant to provoke Thailand and America with a drive to the Mekong – and Houayxay was soon reoccupied, becoming the RLG's main north-western outpost. The government moved to consolidate its hold on territory up and down the Mekong. A road was constructed along the bank of the river from the village of Bandan upstream to Tonpheung, directly opposite Chiang Saen (Map 2.3). Refugee settlements

---

27 The Vietnamese later strengthened this east-west trading link by funding the upgrading of the route from Oudomxai to Xamnua and onward across the border (Taillard 1989: 85).

were established along the road and, for a period, consideration was given to building up Tonpheung as a trading, military and administrative centre, probably due to its superior supply lines through Thailand and its better defensive position. Later, the road north towards Louangnamtha was improved as far as the border of the Pathet Lao zone and villages along it were "pacified" with schools, wells and irrigation projects. Most infrastructure in RLG areas of Laos was funded by the Americans, and a busy USAID office was established in Houayxay (IBRD 1975; Rantala 1994: 126).[28]

A combination of factors created the environment for an unprecedented expansion in industrial production in the RLG zone. The riverside road from Bandan to Tonpheung opened up large areas of forest and several sawmills were soon established along the river. The timber industry was encouraged by the Americans who were undertaking major construction projects as part of their military build-up in Thailand. Locals recall that RLG army officers, keen to secure their economic influence, were heavily involved. At the industry peak, there were more than ten sawmills operating along a 90 kilometre stretch of river (see page 183). The second export industry, for which the region became notorious, was the manufacture of heroin (McCoy 1972: 242–354). During the 1960s, a string of heroin refineries commenced operations along the Mekong. They were supplied by opium caravans from the Shan states and there was vigorous competition between Shan traders, the Lao military and Kuomintang forces (remnants that had fled China after the communist victory) for control of the cross-border trade. This conflict culminated in the 1967 mini "Opium War" fought out in the muddy grounds of a sawmill (and heroin refinery) near Tonpheung. The Burmese opium was refined into heroin in factories upstream and downstream from Houayxay and then exported to Vietnam (to supply addicted GIs), to America and to Western Europe. The price of the high quality heroin produced around Houayxay was high enough to place it beyond the reach of most Asian addicts.

For many people living along the border, this period is remembered as the golden era of trans-Mekong commerce and sociality. A large dependant refugee population, generous foreign aid, revenue from timber and heroin

---

28 Attempts were also made to consolidate RLG control of the areas opposite Pakbeng. An important base for RLG, American and Thai (mercenary) troops was established in the "forward area" of Xianghon, with a smaller base at Hongsa (Anon 1966: 68, 80; Cross 1992: 109; Roberts et al. 1967: 266). The old caravan trails running between Nan and the Mekong were upgraded to carry Thai trucks which supplied anti-communist forces and carried food and consumer goods to the Mekong where they were used to lure villagers across from the Pathet Lao-held areas around Pakbeng. Thai truck drivers and mechanics, recruited from Chiang Khong, were paid 800 *baht* a month, with 200,000 baht promised to their families in the event of their death. Regular air services were also established between Houayxay's upgraded airport and Xianghon.

and a substantial military presence all encouraged intensive cross-border trade. Early each morning, for example, large numbers of petty traders would cross from Chiang Khong to Houayxay to sell rice, vegetables, fish and groceries in the busy morning market where heavy demand ensured good prices. Foreign beer, spirits and cigarettes were shipped or airlifted into Houayxay and distributed by Thai and Lao traders as far afield as Chiang Mai and towns in north-eastern Burma. Cross-river boat operators in Chiang Khong made a good living supporting the busy traffic to and from Houayxay and carting timber, spare parts and fuel for the sawmills on the opposite bank. There were few restrictions on cross-border travel, with cargo and passenger boat services free to call at both Thai and Lao villages. Residents of Chiang Khong received medical attention in Houayxay's hospital (built by the French and supported by American aid), went to Houayxay's cinema at night and courted trans-border lovers with romantic picnics on the Mekong islands. "It was like one village," a resident of Houayxay told me, referring to his regular trips across to Chiang Khong. "I could even travel to Chiang Rai without a pass."

The level of cross-border commercial activity increased when a good road finally reached Chiang Khong in about 1968.[29] Until then, Chiang Khong's only connection to the provincial capital of Chiang Rai was a rough, and often impassable, cart track along the valley of the Ing River (Map 1.2). Almost all non-locally produced supplies came down the river from Chiang Saen – a hazardous journey on one of the least navigable sections of the upper-Mekong. With the new road link, supplies could be bought direct from Chiang Rai to Chiang Khong, bypassing the commercial rivals up river at Chiang Saen. Many of the wholesale shops that line Chiang Khong's main street were first established in the late 1960s and, up until the Pathet Lao victory in 1975, they enjoyed a boom atmosphere, with ready supply, high demand, low transport costs and easily evaded customs duties.

Restricted Access: 1976–1988

In late December 1974, the sleep of one of the cross-river traders in Chiang Khong was rudely interrupted when a small artillery shell smashed through the wall below his bed. Rushing outside, he looked across the darkened

---

29 The construction of this road was motivated, in part, by national security concerns. In one of the ironies of the borderlands, the mountain districts around Chiang Khong had become a base area for Thai communist rebels, while the area around Houayxay was an anti-communist stronghold. At one stage Kuomintang forces were recruited by the Thai government to fight a series of battles against communist rebels around Chiang Khong (Bo 1987: 135–139). However, they were not completely successful and the road between Chiang Khong and Chiang Rai was vulnerable to attack until the *Communist Party of Thailand's* "surrender" in the early 1980s.

Mekong and saw that Houayxay was burning. Occasional stray shells whistled overhead. For the second time in three months, sections of the RLG forces stationed there had rebelled, tired of the corruption of their officers in the bloated trading economy and keen to get in on the act by cultivating opium themselves (Brown and Zasloff 1986: 318). Pathet Lao forces took advantage of the fighting to occupy the riverside villages around Houayxay. A peace deal was brokered with the rebellious RLG soldiers, but the end was in sight. Three months later, USAID abandoned Houayxay in the face of increasing harassment and disruption of activities at the all-important airport (Rantala 1994: 161). In August 1975, the Pathet Lao announced that Houayxay had been liberated (Brown and Zasloff 1986: 324). In December, the Pathet Lao took control of government in Vientiane itself. A new era in the regulation of borderlands trade and transport was about to begin.

Closed borders

The "liberation" of Houayxay by Pathet Lao forces did not bring an immediate stop to cross-border trade despite a general escalation in border tension between Thailand and Laos. Though the level of trade was diminished by the withdrawal of USAID, local traders in Chiang Khong report that they quickly established trading relations with the new authorities, their trading status enhanced by the flight to Thailand of most of the Chinese merchants in Houayxay. After the Thai economic blockade of Laos, which began in November 1975, cross-border contact at Chiang Khong continued, but within a year, the border closure was enforced on the upper-Mekong following the seizure of power by a staunchly anti-communist group in the Thai military coup of October 1976. Some Chiang Khong traders resorted to smuggling – paddling loads of Aspirin, fish sauce and sugar across the Mekong at night to be enthusiastically and profitably received by Lao traders and officials in Houayxay – but their taste for adventure was soured when several were shot dead by Thai border police who patrolled the high river-banks. Restrictions were occasionally relaxed when provincial authorities in Houayxay had a load of logs they wanted to exchange for Thai consumer goods and construction materials (IMC 1987: 76; Stuart-Fox 1986: 79–80) but, for the vast majority of traders, the upper-Mekong was a closed border until 1988.[30]

This dramatic regulatory intervention had profound effects on the patterns of upper-Mekong production, transport and trade. Starved of

---

30 For details on the fluctuating state of Thai-Lao border relations during this period, see van der Kroef (1982), Anon (1985); Stuart-Fox (1986: 190–195); Tanyathip et al. (1992); Mayoury (1994: 69–80); and Maana (1994).

markets, capital, spare-parts and fuel, the timber industry that had flourished around Houayxay collapsed, a set-back from which most of the sawmills never recovered. Thai boat operators, who had come to dominate the upper-Mekong trade, were forced to sell their boats at bargain prices to Lao operators or let them rot on the muddy banks at the unused ports at Chiang Khong and Chiang Saen. A fledgling Lao river boat industry emerged to take their place. The shopkeepers in Chiang Khong remember this as a terrible period. With the cross-river wholesale trade eliminated, they were forced to rely on local retail sales, some resorting to peddling their wares in the rural villages surrounding Chiang Khong. The establishment of a Lao refugee camp to the south of Chiang Khong provided some business but many shopkeepers were forced to close their shops, leave town and establish businesses in more prosperous areas of the north. By 1977, the boom of the war years had come to an end.[31]

The isolation of north-western Laos was compounded by the closure of the Chinese border several years later. Following the Pathet Lao victory in 1975, the Chinese kept up a strong influence in the north, maintaining an active consulate at Oudomxai and proceeding with the construction of a road towards Louangphabang (Godley and St Goar 1991: 309). They also entered into an agreement with the new government to construct a riverside road linking Louangphabang and Pakbeng (it was never built) and provided support for the establishment of a weaving factory and brickworks in Oudomxai (FEER 1976: 206; FEER 1979: 231). However, relations started to sour as Laos sided with Vietnam in the conflict with the Beijing-backed Pol Pot regime in Cambodia (Stuart-Fox 1980). As regional tension escalated, the Lao government sought the closure of the Oudomxai consulate and, after China's punitive invasion of Vietnam in 1979, asked the Chinese government to withdraw the 5,000 road workers still in northern Laos (Chiou 1982: 300–301; Godley and St Goar 1991: 309). Precisely when the border was closed is not clear, but by 1979, cross-border relations had deteriorated dramatically, with reports of Chinese troops massed near the Lao border, shelling by Chinese border guards and incursions into Lao territory (Chiou 1982: 301). There was a brief clash at Boten. Border tension mounted further with allegations that the Chinese were supporting anti-Pathet Lao insurgents operating in the north-west, charges that gained weight with the resettlement of Lao (Hmong) refugees in southern Sipsongpanna (Anon 1985: 22; FEER 1981: 182, 184). This, a local official told me, was a time of "misunderstandings," and the flow of Chinese goods into the moribund markets of Louangnamtha and Oudomxai was reduced to a trickle.

---

31 For the similar experiences of other border towns in Thailand, see Bunyaraks (1977: 14–17).

Trade regulation in a communist state

Within Laos, the move to establish a Soviet-style "command economy" also had profound effects on trade (Evans 1991a: 84–85). In the early years of socialist enthusiasm and economic nationalism, restrictions were placed on commercial exchanges between rural areas and the major towns, strict limits were placed on inter-provincial trade and travel, price controls were put in place and the trading stock of some of the larger traders was seized. Gradually, a system of state stores – with heavily subsidised stock – was established in an attempt to supplant the independent trading system, already weakened by the flight of many merchants and shopkeepers across the Mekong to Thailand. As part of the drive towards self-sufficiency, and to quarantine Laos from foreign commercial pressures and exploitation, a state monopoly on foreign trade was established (Evans 1988: 6–10, 55–58; 1991a: 97, 108; FEER 1976: 201; 1977: 217–218; 1978: 234; Stuart-Fox 1986: 36–37; Vokes and Fabella 1995: 108).

The fundamental problem faced by the new state was, however, the low level of economic surplus that could be mobilised to promote economic growth (Evans 1991a). Most mercantile, industrial and manufacturing capital had been spirited across the Mekong in the waves of refugee exodus that followed the Pathet Lao victory. In the dominant agricultural sector incentives to produce surpluses were diminished by the absence of tradeable consumer goods, suppressed agricultural prices and restrictions on inter-provincial movement of produce. Agricultural taxes were also relatively ineffective in mobilising peasant surplus, and there were reports that some producers restricted their output, or even destroyed crops, to minimise payments to the state (Evans 1991a: 95; Thalemann 1997: 90). As early as 1978, this crisis of accumulation had prompted some questioning of the wisdom of the heavy restrictions on trade. As in the tribute-trading economy of the pre-colonial era, exchange of consumer goods for forest and agricultural products was crucial in maintaining the flow of rural surplus to the lowland centres of power. The poorly developed and sparsely supplied state distribution system of the late 1970s could not manage the task on its own:

> [V]illagers in each village must be allowed to set up their own trading unit to perform the dual duty of purchasing agricultural products from their village to sell to state shops ... and of purchasing essential goods needed by the villagers to sell to them. At the same time, we must encourage certain private traders who own transport to buy goods from state shops to sell to ethnic groups in the mountainous areas and to buy products from them. (GLPDR quoted in FEER 1979: 230)

In 1980, the Lao President went further, declaring that "it is inappropriate, indeed stupid, for any party to implement a policy of forbidding the people to exchange goods or to carry out trading" (quoted in FEER 1981: 182). A number of the early restrictions were relaxed and some private involvement in trade was permitted, though officially private involvement in cross-border trade was limited to trading companies holding government licences (Evans 1988: 58; Vokes and Fabella 1995: 108). The change in policy direction produced the desired results:

> Increased consumer goods were imported ... for sale to farmers in return for state procurement at negotiated prices. One immediate result of these increased incentives was a 16.5 per cent increase in rice production. Government purchases of rice rose six times, and tax income tripled ... (Evans 1991a: 101–102)

The continuing importance of external trade in maintaining the domestic economic system was reflected in the presence of considerable unofficial cross-border trade which, in many areas, was actively encouraged by provincial authorities. In the north-west, a border market operated between 1978 and 1986 on the Lao-Burmese border, just north of the Golden Triangle. Bypassing the closed Thai-Lao border, Thai shopkeepers from nearby Chiang Saen and Mae Sai, travelled through Burma and across the Mekong to the small Lao village of Muangmom (Map 1.2) where a twice-monthly border market was held. The market was patronised by state trading companies and independent traders from towns all over northern Laos. Provincial authorities facilitated access to the market by extending the riverside road north from Tonpheung. Though the level of trade was relatively low, demand was high and profits were good, and the market provided the basis for the establishment and gradual consolidation of a new class of Lao transport operators and traders (see chapters 5 and 6). It also encouraged the redevelopment of trading networks that had been disrupted by the military partition of the previous era. Gradually, the networks of distribution from Muangmom extended outwards – from Houayxay and Louangphabang to Viangphoukha and Hongsa and then to Louangnamtha and Oudomxai.

To the north, the trading system was somewhat different – dominated by state trading and transport companies in Oudomxai and, to a lesser extent, Louangnamtha. With the Thai and Chinese borders closed, trade turned towards Vietnam and the Soviet aid imported through Vietnamese ports.[32] State-owned trucks maintained a northern trading life-line with Vietnam, along the roads that had been constructed during the war years. A fleet of Oudomxai-based tankers operated by the *Lao State Fuel Company* also plied these routes, supplying the north-west with Vietnamese fuel. The importance of the trading links with Vietnam was symbolised in the pairing

---

32 Taillard (1989: 85) suggests that Oudomxai's trade was oriented towards Houayxay-Chiang Khong, underestimating the impact of the restrictions on the Thai-Lao border.

of these northern Lao provinces with provinces in northern Vietnam (Taillard 1989: 85). Thai goods from Muangmom arrived in the northern markets, but they were small and desultory affairs. Some trader's recollections indicate that restrictions on private trade persisted longer in the Vietnamese-dominated northern towns than they did in Houayxay or Louangphabang.[33] "You had to buy everything from the state stores," one recalled, "you couldn't even sell things along the street."

Conclusion: Rediscovering the "Periphery"

The relatively restricted trading conditions of the late 1970s and early 1980s were something of an anomaly in Lao history. However, for many observers of contemporary developments, this restrictive decade has become a powerful and timeless motif of longstanding Lao isolation. The historically brief experience of closed (but *not* completely closed) borders has, it seems, written Lao peripherality deep into contemporary consciousness.

By contrast, my aim in this chapter has been to rediscover a history of the north-western Lao borderlands, to show that upper-Mekong communities have had longstanding experience of managing uneven and unequal connections with other places. My analysis of nineteenth century trade adds to the work of a number of writers who have challenged the popular "myth of the subsistence economy" (Bowie 1992) and pointed to the role of local and regional trade in consolidating lowland power, generating intra-state and inter-state conflict and maintaining international alliances (Cushman 1975; Evers, Korff and Suparb 1987; Junko 1992; Mayoury and Pheuiphanh 1989; 1994; Pasuk and Baker 1995; Sarasin 1977; Wilson 1990). My work also challenges the conventional wisdom, put eloquently by Thongchai (1994), that the nineteenth century borderlands were characterised by a territorial nonchalance, most clearly expressed in the absence of clearly defined boundaries. The upper-Mekong trade routes, and the resources and market towns that lay along them, were highly valued assets and there is ample evidence that disputes about boundary delineation and enforcement preceded the colonial map-making of the 1890s.[34] Indeed, as Evers et al. (1987: 756–757) have argued, the common view that control over manpower in the nineteenth century was more important than control over territory may obscure the extent to which manpower (in the form of armies) was required to maintain control

---

33 In the late 1970s, there were large numbers of Vietnamese troops in the northern areas of Laos near the Chinese border (Evans and Rowley 1990: 64).

34 See, for example, Lamington (1891: 709); Lefèvre-Pontalis (1902: 89–90, 130–131, 141– 142, 160, 163); McCarthy (1900: 154); Scott (1901 Vol. 1: 364); Wijeyewardene (1991); Mayoury (1994: 56); and Vickery (n.d.). For a similar argument in relation to African boundaries, see Thompson (1995).

of trade routes (see also Pasuk and Baker 1995: 9, 44). Any ambiguity or fluidity in the borderlands arose out of dispute and conquest, not out of nonchalance.

There is also a need to reassess the twentieth century history of the borderlands. Analysing the boundary making of the 1890s, Thongchai (1994: 129) concludes that the new colonial geography displaced "indigenous knowledge of political space," substituting rigid demarcation for the supposed fluidity and ambiguity of the past. "[M]odern geography" he writes *"eliminated the possibility, let alone opportunity, of those tiny chiefdoms being allowed to exist as they had done for centuries"* (Thongchai 1994: 129, my emphasis). But, in fact, the trading relations of the small states in the upper-Mekong were only slightly affected by French colonial rule. Boundaries were redrawn, but the French were unable to translate the discursive power of colonial maps into a new regulatory regime that incorporated north-western Laos into the trading and transport systems of Vietnam. As transport and trading networks in northern Thailand developed, northern Laos was increasingly drawn into commercial connections with Bangkok, Chiang Mai and Chiang Rai. Cross-border interactions flourished during the post-colonial 1960s and 1970s. Even during the brief period of closed borders between 1976 and 1988, alternative and informal trade routes were actively pursued and formal trade links were strengthened between northern Laos and Vietnam. In brief, an *over*-emphasis on the rigid demarcations of the twentieth century – like the *under*-emphasis on the demarcations of the nineteenth century – obscures the subtle and complex realities of borderlands history.

This is much more than arcane historical argument. As I will repeatedly argue in the chapters that follow, contemporary developments in north-western Laos need to be understood in terms of the regulated interconnections of the past. Journalistic and academic images of Lao isolation and vulnerability do not do sufficient justice to the historical depth of its experience in managing external connections. This historical experience is shaping the contemporary development of the Economic Quadrangle. As Appadurai and Breckenridge (1995: 16) have written, "localities are 'sites' of complex and specific negotiations between history and globality."

CHAPTER THREE

North-Western Laos and the Economic Quadrangle

Introduction: Rhetoric and Reality

In the latter half of the 1980s and the first half of the 1990s, there were a series of important developments in the trading and transport systems of north-western Laos. Many of the connections that were severed or hindered after the Pathet Lao victory in 1975 were re-established, and ambitious plans were developed for their intensification and restructuring. The "vision splendid" (Chapman and Hinton 1994: 1) of an upper-Mekong Economic Quadrangle encapsulated these changes and promoted ambitious hopes for the future. A deceptively simple notion, it suggested that economic cooperation between the connected borderlands of Laos, Burma, China and Thailand was a recipe for regional prosperity. For Laos, in particular, the Quadrangle was said to represent an opportunity to move towards subregional integration; to turn its back on its past of isolation and peripherality; and profit from its strategic position on one of the emerging crossroads of South-East Asia.

This chapter seeks to go beyond the rhetoric and provide an assessment – focusing on trading and transport systems – of the Quadrangle's uneven and partial development in north-western Laos. To place Lao developments in context, the first section briefly examines some of the regional components of the Quadrangle. The chapter then focuses on trading systems within Laos and argues that contemporary changes have been relatively modest and represent a resumption of longstanding trading connections. In addition, these connections are now more firmly under the control of Lao traders and transport operators than they have ever been. However, plans for developing transit routes across northern Laos appear to foreshadow more radical change. The second half of the chapter outlines the three most popular transit options before dissecting some of the provincial, political and commercial rivalries that lie behind them. While these attempts to reorient borderlands trade are broad in scope, they are also deeply enmeshed in local interests: "global schemes are revealed in their provinciality" (Fardon 1995: 4). Ongoing state regulation is one component of this provinciality and, in the conclusion, I argue that the region's states have maintained an important role in the Quadrangle's development, despite predictions that trans-border economic relations will render the state irrelevant. In brief, the chapter argues that while the rhetoric of the Economic Quadrangle has emphasised transformation, cooperation and free trade, the current reality has as much to do with continuity, competition and regulation.

Components of the Quadrangle

The concept of an Economic Quadrangle in the northern borderlands of South-East Asia first emerged in the early 1990s. As with "growth triangles" and "growth areas" elsewhere in Asia,[1] the main idea underlying the Quadrangle was that opportunities for economic growth and development will arise if the border regions of adjoining countries are permitted and encouraged to cooperatively exploit their complementarities. "Located within the same economic space it would make good economic sense if areas in these sub-regions could harness their economic potential for the mutual benefit of the region" (Hasnah 1996: 1). These trans-border zones are, according to Ohmae (1995: 5), the new "regional economies ... where the real work gets done and real markets flourish." In the case of the upper-Mekong these arguments are seductive: they represent a formula for trans-border prosperity based largely on the indisputable reality of geographic proximity. As a prominent Thai banker argued at a conference in Beijing, "the resources from Burma and Laos [can] be given added value with the help of technology, funds and other necessary infrastructure from Thailand and China" (BP/RT 6 July 1993; see also GOT 1994).

Given the poor state of communications in the upper-Mekong region, infrastructural development has always been the highest priority in Economic Quadrangle discussions (ADB 1996c). In the creation of what has been called a "Mekong corridor" (Chapman, Hinton, and Tan 1992), most interest has been expressed in road links between Thailand and China. The main proposal was that a circular road be developed, linking Chiang Rai and the Yunnanese capital, Kunming, via both Laos and Burma (Map 1.1). As early as 1993, work had started on the link through Burma – via Kengtung – but the road had been abandoned by 1995, a legacy of lingering

---

1 For example, the Indonesia-Malaysia-Singapore growth triangle; the Indonesia-Malaysia-Thailand growth triangle; the Brunei-Indonesia-Malaysia-Philippines growth area; the Hong Kong-Shenzhen-Pearl River growth triangle; and the Tumen River (China-Russia-North Korea) growth area (Hasnah 1996; Ohmae 1995: 84; Parsonage 1997; Yuan 1996).

military insecurity and corporate bankruptcy. Most attention then shifted to the road links through Laos which are discussed in detail in the second half of this chapter. There has also been considerable interest in reviving French colonial dreams of a "river road to China" (Osborne 1975) and – following several survey missions along the river – a series of plans have been developed for improving upper-Mekong navigation. This is also discussed in more detail below. Even the ambitious nineteenth century plans for rail-links between Thailand and Yunnan were reborn, despite the massive cost of the projects and uncertainty about the future level of traffic (BP 7 September 1994; BP 13 December 1994). Finally, some improvements have been made to regional airports and air services, with the lavish airport at Chiang Rai a potent symbol of that town's desire to become the Quadrangle's air-transport hub (BP 4 August 1994).

The main aim of these transport projects is to promote the flow of goods, capital and labour between the Quadrangle countries. To this end, there have also been sustained calls for institutional reform to take place alongside infrastructural development. As Ohmae (1995: 4), one of the most active proponents of the new "regional economies" has argued, state regulation and mediation is an impediment to the development of new trans-border markets which, if given the opportunity, will "work just fine on their own." Economic growth, he writes, will be much more rapid if traditional nation states – "unnatural, even impossible, business units in a global economy" – greatly limit their intervention in the new trans-border economies (Ohmae 1995: 5; see also Hasnah 1996: i). An ADB-sponsored survey of firms with interests in the Mekong region found that "bureau-cracy and nontransparent regulations" were the most serious impediments to trade (Brimble 1994: 7). Commercial and political interests in Thailand, in particular, have lobbied hard for the reduction and "harmonisation" of financial and non-financial trade barriers and the development of regionally standardised trade and investment laws (BP 16 September 1994; BP 31 August 1996; BP 8 July 1997). Officials in Laos have also lobbied for the reduction of Thai tariffs on agricultural products in an attempt to address the substantial trade imbalance between the two countries (BP 21 July 1994; BP 3 January 1995). There have even been ambitious, though poorly developed, plans for the Quadrangle to become a "quasi free trade zone" (BP January 7 1994).

In the climate of the late 1970s and early 1980s, this level of regional cooperation seemed unlikely, but in the following decade a series of international and domestic developments appeared to lay the ground-work for an upper-Mekong Quadrangle. First, there was a general decline in regional tension coinciding with the end of the Cold War. In Thailand, this geo-political shift was symbolised by Prime Minister Chatichai's 1988 call to turn the region's "battlefields into marketplaces" and given practical effect with political and commercial diplomacy in Laos, Burma and China

(Mayoury and Pheuiphanh 1994: 34, 77–78; Pasuk and Baker 1995: 351). There were still some points of tension – such as a bitter border dispute between Thailand and Laos (Mayoury and Pheuiphanh 1994: 56–80) – but these were increasingly subordinated to the broader goal of economic cooperation. Relations between China and Laos were also placed on a more stable footing in the early 1990s and, together with Burma, they signed an agreement that their upper-Mekong borders would be a frontier of "peace, friendship and cooperation" (BP 19 April 1994).

Factors within the four Quadrangle economies were also important in restructuring the region's interconnections. In Thailand, highly politicised environmental constraints were encouraging a search for non-domestic sources of timber, minerals and energy (Hirsch 1995). After the national Thai logging ban in 1988, Thai loggers and sawmillers began beating a path to Vientiane and Rangoon to negotiate access to cross-border resources (Sesser 1993: 111). In north-western Laos, they became active in reviving the sawmilling industry (see page 166). Thailand's domestic power needs were also a pressing concern and Thai consortia became involved in lignite mining at Viangphoukha and Hongsa – where a coal fired power station is also planned[2] – and in reviving old plans for hydro-electric projects on the Mekong and its tributaries.[3] Some Thai businesses also saw an increasingly open southern China as a lucrative market for their manufactured goods and, with wage growth in Thailand, as an alternative production site that could make use of cheap Chinese labour (Chapman and Hinton 1993: 14; Chapman and Hinton 1994; Vatikiotis 1996b: 187). Upper-Mekong tourism opportunities were also attractive to some Thai businessmen (though less attractive than the breathless accounts in the Thai media would suggest). In some sections of the Thai business

---

2 The mine at Viangphoukha is being developed by a consortium of Thai companies involved in mining, construction and manufacturing. The Lao government has a one quarter interest. The operators of the mine plan to extract up to one million tonnes of lignite per year for at least ten years. The lignite will be trucked to Thailand where it will supply cement production plants in areas close to Bangkok. A major lignite depot, with cross-river vehicular ferries, has been constructed a few kilometres to the south of Chiang Khong. The lignite mine at Hongsa is being developed by a Thai industrial group with a history of involvement in tin mining, electronics and rubber-related industries (BP 13 December 1993). The one quarter share held by the Lao government is controlled by a state enterprise – *Agriculture and Forestry Development Company* – with close links to the Lao military (see page 179). It is planned that the mine will supply an adjacent 600 megawatt power station to be constructed by a number of major Thai investors. The Lao government is expected to get almost 30 billion *baht* in corporate taxes from the operation of the project (BP 13 December 1993). If the power station goes ahead it will be a massive investment of over 25 billion *baht* (TN July 16 1994) and the station will be larger than all but one of the domestic power stations in Thailand (BP 28 March 1994). There are mounting concerns in Thailand about the environmental impacts of lignite-burning power stations and the Hongsa development provides a welcome opportunity to shift the focus of such concerns across the border.

3 In the north-west there are plans for dams on the Tha River and on the Mekong itself, just above Pakbeng (ADB 1996c: project profile A2; Compagnie Nationale du Rhône 1994). For a general discussion of hydropower development in the Mekong basin, see Choung (1996).

community, the old concept of *sawanaphuum* (the "heavenly land") was revived – "[t]hey imagined a prospering mainland South-East Asia dominated by Thai capital emerging as a major force in the economy and politics of Asia" (Pasuk and Baker 1995: 351). In northern Thailand, widespread property development and land speculation occurred in border districts as small and large investors alike sought to secure a strategic position in the hoped-for "golden" Quadrangle.

In China, the southern province of Yunnan was also experiencing sustained economic growth (Chapman, Hinton, and Tan 1992: 16; Feng 1993). Revitalised state and private enterprises in Yunnan were said to be keen to secure southern outlets for their growing industrial output, with millions of tonnes of goods stockpiled there due to bottlenecks at Chinese east-coast ports (TN 15 December 1993). A major Mekong river port near Simao (Map 1.1) was constructed to facilitate the down-river trade, and border trading-posts were carved out of the jungle at a number of locations further south. In the southern districts of Yunnan, there was rapid economic growth and social transformation as immigrants from other regions arrived to exploit commercial opportunities along the border (Chapman, Hinton, and Tan 1992; Evans 1996). A new class of southern Chinese entrepreneurs also looked across the border to investment opportunities in both Burma and Laos. Like Thailand, China is also interested in the hydro-electric potential of the Mekong and, by the early 1990s, had commenced construction of a major Mekong dam, with long-terms plans for a cascade of dams along their section of the river.

In north-eastern Burma, the domestic environment for investment, infrastructure development and trade was made more attractive by the 1989 collapse of the *Communist Party of Burma* and the signing of a raft of cease-fire agreements between Rangoon and rebellious ethnic groups (Porter 1995: 15–20). There has been significant growth in trade and investment in Burmese districts bordering China, though the more westerly routes towards Mandalay and Rangoon (Map 1.1) are developing much more rapidly than the "Quadrangle routes" towards Thailand (Porter 1995: 48–67). Though there is a busy commercial life on the Thai-Burmese border at Mae Sai-Tachilek (Map 1.2), development in the eastern districts was compromised by the ongoing activity of Shan rebel groups (BP 23 March 1995).[4] Possibly concerned about their degree of control in the Mekong hinterland, the Burmese government has been the least active party in Quadrangle discussions.

Laos, the fourth country in the Quadrangle, has also experienced important domestic developments. These are discussed in detail in the following section.

---

4 The important border-crossing between Mae Sai and Tachilek was closed for almost a year after an attack by Shan rebels in March 1995.

Re-establishing Trading Connections

The incorporation of Laos into the Economic Quadrangle has been facilitated by a series of policy initiatives that have encouraged a more open and market-oriented economy. The package of polices, usually referred to as the "New Economic Mechanism" (NEM), has been described in detail elsewhere (Bourdet 1996; Ljunggren 1992; Pham 1994a; Than and Tan 1997; Vokes and Fabella 1995) and need only be summarised here, highlighting some of the important implications for the north-west. There is no doubt that the effect of the policies has been to liberalise trade and passage in the borderlands but they have also provided incentives and opportunities for new forms of collaborative and competitive regulation. As I wrote in the Introduction, and as I will repeatedly demonstrate in this and the following chapters, *liberalisation does not necessarily amount to de-regulation.*

When the NEM was introduced in 1986, one of its main aims was to stimulate trade and to encourage the distribution of commodities throughout the country. Some loosening of the controls on private sector involvement in trade had occurred in the early 1980s, but there was still considerable uncertainty and much of the trade, while officially tolerated or ignored, was often, in fact, illegal (Vokes and Fabella 1995: 108). In early 1987, private traders were officially permitted to compete with state enterprises on internal trade and, soon after, they were also permitted to participate in many areas of import and export trade, though some "strategic goods" were excluded (GLPDR 1988b; GLPDR 1988d; Vokes and Fabella 1995: 109). In the following year, the remaining restrictions on inter-provincial trade and travel were abolished, the government declaring that "[l]egal commodities can be sold over the country without any form of restriction" and ordering the eradication of "all commodities checking points along various communication lines within the country" (GLPDR 1988a: Articles 6 and 8). All of these initiatives regularised patterns of internal and external trade that were already (re-)emerging. Other reforms encouraging private involvement in trade included relaxation of controls on currency exchange, elimination of subsidies to state and cooperative stores with the adoption of market pricing arrangements and expansion of the banking sector (GLPDR 1988c). Between 1988 and 1990, the number of privately operated shops increased by almost 55 per cent, while the state and collective sector declined by almost 70 per cent (GLPDR 1991b: 5):

> There are many stores and some department stores established in urban areas, which gradually improved the quality of services to customers. In rural areas they have reorganized the old market centers and constructed new market centers to answer the requirement of local people. (GLPDR 1991b: 8)

69

Not only did the private sector share of retail activity increase – from 46 per cent in 1986 to 76 per cent in 1990 – but the overall level of retail activity increased more than 300 per cent (GLPDR 1991b: 10; Vokes and Fabella 1995: 115).

In north-western Laos, the expansion in private trade was facilitated by improved border trading conditions with both Thailand and China. By 1987, the border between Houayxay and Chiang Khong was being opened on a temporary basis to enable the operation of occasional border markets on the Lao side of the river. By 1988, substantial import and export trade had recommenced, though there were still numerous restrictions on free passage (Thai traders, for example, had to stay within 50 metres of Houayxay's immigration office). After vigorous lobbying by provincial chambers of commerce, the Thai government resolved to address problems of border trade with Laos (Anek 1992: 95–96) and, in early 1989, border crossings at both Chiang Khong-Houayxay and Chiang Saen-Tonpheung (Map 1.2) were officially re-established (Anon n.d.: 16; Tanyathip, Watcharin, and Maana 1992: 236). In late 1993, the crossing at Houayxay was upgraded to an international border crossing, having little effect on Thai-Lao trading conditions but serving as an important symbol of upper-Mekong cooperation and enabling international tourist entry and exit. In 1994, provincial authorities on both sides of the border entered into an agreement that allowed for longer hours of border passage – though this was still not implemented in late 1996 – minimisation of provincial taxes and charges and, most importantly, for the sale of electricity from Chiang Khong to Houayxay (RT/SWB 19 October 1994). A part-time border crossing was also established at the Lao village of Bandan – some 20 kilometres downstream from Houayxay – to enable the operation of a weekly border trading market. A border crossing was also established with considerable fanfare to the south of Hongsa, mainly to service the large lignite mining development taking place there, but also opening up an alternative trading route between northern Thailand and northern Laos and reviving some of Nan's nineteenth century links with the region.

Since the recommencement of cross-border interaction, there have been significant increases in both import and export trade passing through Chiang Khong-Houayxay. Pent-up demand for Thai manufactured goods resulted in a mini-boom in imports from Chiang Khong between 1988 and 1990, followed by something of a slump in the following two years, and a return to rapid growth since 1993 (Table 3.1). Lao exports had a more modest start, largely a reflection of the parlous state of north-western Lao sawmilling, but experienced sustained growth in the following years. In 1992 and 1993, the balance of trade at Chiang Khong-Houayxay was about equal but, by 1995, the value of imports to Laos from Thailand was outstripping Lao exports by about 80 per cent, a pattern common

Table 3.1 Import and export trade, Chiang Khong-Houayxay 1988–1995

Year	Imports to Laos (baht)	Exports from Laos (baht)
1988	30,610,000	6,640,000
1989	50,086,000	16,254,000
1990	83,113,000	28,590,000
1991	44,319,000	24,689,000
1992	36,851,000	37,564,000
1993	63,003,000	63,499,000
1994	110,430,000	86,176,000
1995	154,790,000	86,340,000

Source: Fieldwork 1994-1995, 1996; GOT (1989; 1992; 1993b; 1995a; 1995b; 1995c); and GLPDR (1994e).
Note: These figures should be taken as indicative only, and are likely to understate trading volumes given frequent evasion of customs taxes and other charges (GLPDR 1994e 70–71).

throughout Laos (Vokes and Fabella 1995: Table A12). There has also been growth in trade at Chiang Saen-Tonpheung, but this border crossing is much less strategically placed and has experienced only a fraction of Chiang Khong-Houayxay's trading volumes (GLPDR 1994e: 58). Informal reports from customs staff at the new border crossing south of Hongsa also suggest that current trading volumes are low but there are indications that this could increase substantially.

The trade that now passes through Chiang Khong and Houayxay is managed in several different ways.[5] Fuel, the major export commodity, is sold by production companies in Thailand to the *Lao State Fuel Company*, with a local trading company in Chiang Khong preparing the customs paperwork and arranging for the trucks to cross the Mekong on the vehicular ferry. During 1994, fuel pumped into river tankers at Houayxay supplied all of the towns in north-western Laos and, when the road north from Vientiane was impassable, Louangphabang as well. Several other trading companies in Chiang Khong are involved in the sale of construction materials (for infrastructure projects in Laos) and occasional large consignments of manufactured goods. Despite the reforms of the NEM, Lao regulations usually require these Thai companies to work in conjunction with Lao companies in Houayxay. These enforced partnerships are not without their problems, with regular disputes over the allocation of tasks and profits. "The Lao company . . . invests nothing. All it does is sign the papers," one Thai trader complained (quoted in Supalak 1993).

---

5 For a detailed discussion, see GLPDR (1994e).

Most of the trade in Thai manufactured goods, construction materials and processed food is conducted by independent Lao traders from towns throughout the north and north-west. These traders make regular trips to Chiang Khong where they are supplied by a revived and active wholesale shopping sector and a large "dry goods" market that is held in Chiang Khong each Friday. Almost all the traders head downstream to Pakbeng – where trucks are dispatched to Oudomxai and Louangnamtha – or to Louangphabang, two days journey along the river. The town of Oudomxai is the most important north-western entrepôt for these traders. Their activities are discussed in detail in chapter 6. It is important to note that the long-distance trading networks that distribute Chiang Khong's merchandise throughout northern Laos are exclusively Lao. Chiang Khong's residents are heavily involved in small-scale cross-border trade with Houayxay, but Lao passport and visa regulations prevent them from travelling further afield.

Lao exports at Houayxay are comprised mainly of timber, non-timber forest products and agricultural products. Seed, fruit, bark, grass and resin accounted for over 40 per cent of exports during 1994, a percentage substantially higher than in other parts of Laos. These are collected and cultivated by villagers throughout northern Laos and pass along an extensive chain of small-scale traders and larger trading companies to ports at Pakbeng, Louangphabang and Houayxay before being shipped to Thai buyers. Many boat loads of forest products are said to pass upstream, beyond Chiang Khong-Houayxay, to Burmese river ports, where the cargo is unloaded and then smuggled into Thailand near Mae Sai (Map 1.2) (GLPDR 1994e: 56, 63). The timber trade is much more concentrated, with the 12,000 cubic metres of sawn timber passing through Houayxay during 1994 deriving almost entirely from three north-western Lao sawmills, all operated by Thai entrepreneurs. During 1995, additional Thai investment saw three new sawmills commence operation in north-western Laos, increasing the flow of timber across the Mekong to Chiang Khong's busy timber yards. The timber trade is discussed in detail in chapter 7.

Cross-border relationships have also improved with China. In 1992, provincial authorities in Houayxay entered into an agreement with Simao district in Yunnan (Map 1.1) to provide facilities for trade and tourism along the Mekong river (RT/SWB 7 October 1992). With its new river port, Simao was keen to secure downstream facilities. Other provincial agreements have provided for Chinese involvement in infrastructure projects in the north-west – roads and a small hydro-electricity dam to supply Oudomxai – and for cooperation in relation to "mineral survey, agriculture, trade, tourism and health" (BP 5 July 1994). These agreements have been accompanied by a revival in border trade. By the late 1980s, the border crossing at Boten was open for local trade between

Mengla district and Louangnamtha and, in late 1993, it was upgraded to an international border crossing, serving as the main land trading point between China and Laos (VT 23 December 1994). A second north-western border crossing has also been established near Muangsing. Though this is officially only a local border crossing, it services some long-distance trade that heads down the old caravan route to Xiangkok and onward to Burma and Thailand.[6] The old Lü settlement of Mengla is still the predominant Chinese-Lao trading town, though it has been radically transformed by central Chinese investment and immigration. A border trading village, with neatly laid out rows of concrete shop-houses, has also been established at Mohan, just a few kilometres north of Boten.

It is difficult to assess the level of trade with China in the absence of reliable customs figures. One report, quoting official Yunnanese sources, suggests that Lao-Chinese border trade was in excess of seven million American dollars – approximately 180 million *baht* – in 1993 (RT 13 February 1994). This is about 50 per cent higher than the level of trade at Chiang Khong-Houayxay during the same year, but this Lao-Thai trade has increased substantially since, while local reports are that Lao-Chinese trade has plateaued or even decreased as a result of unfavourable currency movements. A large proportion of Lao-Chinese border trade is conducted via the border crossing at Boten but, unlike Chiang Khong-Houayxay, only a relatively small percentage is trade with north-western Lao provinces. Most of the border trade at Boten is directed to provinces in central and southern Laos who have no common border with China. This very long-distance trade is conducted mainly by Lao trading companies who deal in Lao coffee and scrap metal and buy Chinese machinery and electronic goods. There is also some export of Lao timber and forest products, but at a relatively low level. North-western Lao trade with China is mostly undertaken by independent traders, many of whom are also involved in trade with Thailand (see page 148).

What, then, has been the effect on trade of the regulatory changes that have occurred since the late 1980s? Essentially, their impact has been to *re*-establish and strengthen the longstanding connections between north-western Laos, northern Thailand and southern China. As in the late nineteenth century, and for most of this century, manufactured goods sold in the markets and shops of north-western Laos are imported predominantly from Thailand, and Chiang Khong has resumed its role as an important upper-Mekong trading centre. The main change has been that most imported goods are now manufactured in Thailand itself, rather than in Japan or Europe. Chinese goods are also flowing again across the northern borders, especially into the nearby markets in Louangnamtha and

---

6 *World Bank* funds have been allocated to upgrade the rough track between Muangsing and Xiangkok.

Oudomxai. As in the past, Mengla is the primary border trading town with the salt-producing village of Boten the main border-crossing point. This reconnection with Thailand and China has been accompanied by a reduction in trade with Vietnam. With the opening up of the traditional Thai-Lao-Chinese supply routes, and the collapse of Soviet aid, the short-lived interest in the east-west trading corridor to Vietnam has diminished (Ljunggren 1992: 130; Vokes and Fabella 1995: Tables A12 and A13).

However, there has been one important change in north-western Lao trading and transport systems, an ironic change given the Quadrangle's emphasis on regional integration. Now, most cross-border trading systems are dominated by *Lao* traders and transport operators rather than the ethnic Chinese and Thai entrepreneurs of the past. The origins of this change lie in the post-1975 period when many of the established merchants and transport operators left Laos or, in the case of Thai boat operators, were excluded from it. This allowed small-scale Lao operators to gain a foothold in the restricted – but lucrative – trading economy that was in place up until the mid-1980s. In the more vigorous trading environment of the late 1980s and 1990s, these Lao traders and boat operators have prospered, as have Lao truckers following the privatisation of state-owned trucking fleets in 1990. While the reforms of the NEM have opened Lao borders to trade, there are still sufficient restrictions (in most areas) to hold Thai and Chinese traders and transport operators at bay. Thai trading companies have made some inroads, but they too are caught up in a bewildering array of deals, disputes and compromises with commercial counterparts in Laos. Even in the timber industry, where Thai capital has made significant inroads, there are indications that Lao interests are being vigorously reasserted, with the recent allocation of national logging rights to three state-owned military enterprises. Lao liberalisation appears to be managed in a way that gives domestic traders, transport operators, entrepreneurs and officials an important stake in external trading connections. These issues are explored in detail in chapters 5, 6 and 7.

Of course, the main hope of the Quadrangle promoters was that transit trade between Thailand and China would increase dramatically. In 1992 and 1993, things looked hopeful, with the value of transit trade booming as hundreds of imported cars were dispatched by trading companies in Chiang Khong to eager buyers and agents in Mengla. Customs records in Chiang Khong indicate that over one billion *baht* worth of cars were exported via Laos in 1993. Some good profits were made, and the trade became an influential motif in Quadrangle promotions but, when the Chinese government enforced heavy duties and import restrictions on their remote southern border, almost 900 luxury cars were left to gather dust and mud in fields throughout north-western Laos (GLPDR 1994e: 67). By early 1995, two of the companies that had been most involved in the trade with China had closed their offices in Chiang Khong and there were many reports of large financial losses and unpaid debts. Losses incurred by Lao banks – that provided credit to car traders – also prompted the Lao government to place restrictions on vehicle imports (Sundberg 1994: 88). In 1994, there was very little transit trade heading north to China, though a number of Chinese vessels came to Houayxay to pick up Thai cargoes, including 2,000 tonnes of dried longan from Chiang Mai and 200 tonnes of rubber from southern Thailand. Some Lao traders also sold consignments of Thai manufactured goods and rice when they travelled to Mengla.

Thai imports from China are also at a low level. During 1994, some machinery, technical equipment, construction materials and agricultural products came down the Mekong in Chinese boats and some Chinese imports were also trucked to Pakbeng and then bought up river in Lao boats. In late 1996, I also witnessed several boatloads of Chinese apples being unloaded at Chiang Saen and was told that there had been some increase in Chinese river traffic since 1994. However, an elaborate showroom established in Chiang Khong to sell high quality imported Chinese merchandise is now closed due to lack of business – it has become a Toyota car yard. In the first six months of 1995, the value of Thai-China trade passing through Chiang Khong-Houayxay was reported to be only 13 million *baht* (BP/RT September 12 1995) and in September 1996 the Thai consul in Yunnan expressed concern about the sluggish activity on this new trading corridor (Business Day 13 September 1996). Indications are, however, that senior Lao trade officials are less concerned, conceding that they place greater priority on developing bilateral trading ties (TN 15 December 1993).

During the period of my research, it appeared that "fraudulent" transit trade through north-western Laos was somewhat busier. During 1994 and 1995, some of the most active trading companies in both Chiang Khong and Houayxay were involved in dispatching regular cargoes of cigarettes, cloth, and electrical goods up river to the small village of Muangmom where they were transferred across the river to Burma (Map 1.2). The goods travelling along this route were goods originating outside Thailand (mainly from Singapore) and it appears that they were imported duty-free at Bangkok as transit cargoes, exported to Laos – where no duty was paid because they were in transit to Burma – and once they were in Burma spirited back into Thailand at the busy border crossing at Mae Sai where they were sold for a handsome profit. Tourists buying cheap cigarettes from touts in the busy Mae Sai market were undoubtedly unaware of the level of cross-border economic integration that had contributed to their good fortune. Sometimes the journey through Burma was dispensed with altogether: if the traders received word that there would be no customs patrols, the goods were shipped just a short distance upstream from

Houayxay and unloaded into trucks waiting in the small Thai villages dotted along the river-bank. In 1996 I also heard rumours that a prominent Thai businessman and politician was active in the export of water up river from Chiang Saen to China. Of course he claimed that the water was fuel, but it is likely that the fuel – imported into Thailand tax-free as a transit cargo – was profitably sold on the domestic market through his national network of service stations. All in all, it seems that some of the most profitable Quadrangle trade has been based on the manipulation of tariff regimes, rather than on their eradication.

Transit Routes Through North-Western Laos

The main transport route in north-western Laos runs down the Mekong from Houayxay to Pakbeng, then north along the road to Oudomxai, and further north again to Mengla in China. The route is a product of longstanding navigation along the Mekong and Chinese road-building efforts during the 1960s and 1970s. Map 3.1 sets out estimated freight flows along the various segments of this route during 1994. On the river stretch between Houayxay and Pakbeng, downstream traffic consisted mainly of Thai manufactured goods purchased by Lao traders in Chiang Khong while upstream traffic consisted of timber and forest products. There was also some domestic freight – rice and beer in particular – and substantial passenger traffic along the river.[7] On the road section from Pakbeng, northbound traffic consisted of Thai manufactured goods destined for Oudomxai, Louangnamtha, Muangsing, Phongsali, Xamnua and Phonsavan (Map 1.3). Southbound traffic consisted of timber and forest products and Chinese imports purchased in Mengla. Most Chinese imports arriving at Pakbeng were shipped downstream for domestic sale in Louangphabang and Vientiane, though some were sent upstream for export to Thailand. There was also considerable small freight and passenger traffic on the road.

The promoters of the Economic Quadrangle foreshadow dramatic interventions in the transport systems of north-western Laos. Whereas the current system mainly services bilateral trade between Laos and its neighbours, and links the main trading towns of Houayxay and

---

7 The river section between Houayxay, Pakbeng and Louangphabang is navigable year-round by boats of up to about 120 tonnes but it is a hazardous exercise requiring exceptional skill and concentration and a number of boats are lost each year. There are no navigation aids on this stretch of the river, save for a few concrete channel markers erected by the French. Information on navigability is based on field observations and discussions with boat operators. A detailed description of river conditions is provided by BCEOM (1994: 85–87) but they are wrong to suggest that the section from Houayxay to Pakbeng is only navigable by 15–tonne boats in the dry season. Taillard (1989: 67) is also wrong to suggest that there is only light traffic above Louangphabang. The section between Louangphabang and Houayxay is, in fact, much busier than the section between Louangphabang and Vientiane.

Map 3.1 North-western Laos: patterns of regional trade in 1994

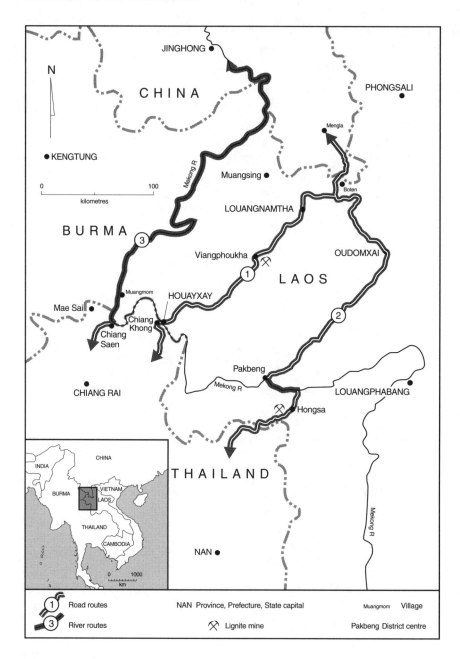

Map 3.2 North-western Laos: transit routes between Thailand and China

Oudomxai, the Economic Quadrangle transport network would concentrate on transit links between northern Thailand and southern China. Two road routes through north-western Laos (Map 3.2, Routes 1 and 2) have been the subject of increasing interest as progress on the route through Kengtung in Burma has ground to a halt. A third route, involving navigation along the Mekong itself, also has some strong backers. While support for the creation of these various transit routes is often couched in regionally integrating terms, the nature of the support is often, in fact, deeply provincial and competitive. Moreover, while cross-border linkages are often seen as a challenge to state authority, they provide states – at national, provincial and local levels – with renewed opportunities for intervention in sub-regional trade and transport. These large-scale infrastructure projects are the latest attempts to regulate the passages through the upper-Mekong borderlands.

Route 1: Chiang Khong-Houayxay-Louangnamtha-Mengla

The route that has received the most attention is the one that is now least used. Following the path of the nineteenth century caravans, it runs from Houayxay to Louangnamtha and then across the border to Mengla (Map 3.2, Route 1). Despite some improvement in the 1960s and 1970s, the road is in very poor condition. In 1990, the *Lao National Transport Study* described it as a "seasonal track" only passable, with difficulty, in the dry season (SWECO 1990: 12.2). Truck drivers and traders in Houayxay told me that, until recently, the 194 kilometre trip to Louangnamtha involved up to two nights on the road. Improvements undertaken by the lignite miners at Viangphoukha have reduced the arduous trip to 14 hours, though delays caused by breakdowns and bogging are still common and in the wet season – and for two or three months afterwards – the trip is still impossible. During the period of my research the road carried only a trickle of supplies from Chiang Khong-Houayxay to the markets in Louangnamtha and Muangsing and a similarly small amount of transit trade between Thailand and China. Figures provided by the *Department of Transport* in Houayxay for the 1994/1995 dry season indicate that less than one truck per day made the trip to Louangnamtha, with as few as five trips in November. Even during the dry season, many traders chose to travel to Louangnamtha via the longer but more reliable route through Pakbeng and Oudomxai and the heavily laden timber trucks from the mill at Louangnamtha travelled to the port at Pakbeng throughout the year.[8]

---

8 There is considerably more traffic on the branches of the road north of Louangnamtha, which were upgraded by the Chinese in the 1960s. Cross-border trade with Mengla generates traffic between Louangnamtha and Boten and there is also considerable traffic between Louangnamtha and Oudomxai. There is local traffic between Louangnamtha and Muangsing and some cross-border traffic heading north on a good road from Muangsing.

Since early 1993, this muddy and little-used track has been on the agenda of ADB-sponsored discussions on regional development and, in September 1994, its upgrading was endorsed as one of the highest priority transport projects in the greater Mekong subregion (BP 15 September 1994). The proposal put by consultants to the ADB was that the road be developed as the Lao link in a circular road running from Chiang Rai to Kunming via both Laos and Burma (PADECO 1994: 25–27). Soon after, an ambitious plan for the Lao section was released by *The Economic Quadrangle Joint Development Corporation* (EQJDC), a joint venture of the Lao government and a northern Thai property development and construction firm. The EQJDC's plan was for the road to operate as a toll-way, with revenue generated mainly by transit traffic. They estimated that up to 20,000 vehicles would use the road each year (BP/RT 4 September 1995). The EQJDC intended to develop a series of commercial, service and industrial zones in nine villages along the route. There were also plans for "four cargo stations, up to 20 service stations, tourist rest areas, two shopping centres, border duty-free shops, and up to 10 hotels and resorts" and the EQJDC was granted extensive rights to timber and minerals in a substantial strip of territory along either side of the road (BP/RT 4 September 1995; PADECO 1994: A114). Some work has been undertaken on the road but in late 1996 a spokesman told me that they are now concentrating only on building a number of bridges along the route and that the completion date for the road has slipped to 1999 or beyond. Press reports have indicated that that the EQJDC is having substantial difficulties raising sufficient capital from cautious Thai investors, a situation that is unlikely to improve following the economic turmoil in Thailand that broke out in late 1997 (BP/RT 30 January 1996; Business Day, September 13 1996; RT 23 July 1997).

Route 2: Nan-Hongsa-Pakbeng-Oudomxai-Mengla

The second proposed transit route between northern Thailand and Yunnan (Map 3.2, Route 2) incorporates the road from Pakbeng to Oudomxai and Mengla which, as noted above, is now the most heavily used section of road in the north-west. From Pakbeng north, the road is paved – with the original bitumen laid by Chinese army engineers – though it is heavily potholed and travel times are slow. The 144 kilometre trip from Pakbeng to Oudomxai takes up to eight hours in the old Soviet-built trucks that service northern Lao trade (see page 114). Despite its central role in sub-regional and local trade, there has been little interest expressed in this road in ADB-sponsored discussions of transport in the Economic Quadrangle. In the early 1990s, the Chinese government did express interest in rehabilitation of the road but later directed most of their energies towards proposals for navigation along the Mekong (BCEOM 1994: 105).

During 1994, consultants to the *Mekong Secretariat*[9] proposed that this route be extended south into Nan province in northern Thailand, eliminating the need for river transport between Chiang Khong-Houayxay and Pakbeng (BCEOM 1994: Annex 12). The terrain opposite Pakbeng is very rugged, so it is proposed that a vehicular ferry run 26 kilometres downstream to meet a track south to Hongsa. The developers of the lignite mine at Hongsa have already constructed a good road from the mine to the Thai border. Despite the need for a ferry trip along a rocky section of the Mekong, proponents of this route argued that it would be "outstandingly advantageous" over the alternative route through Louangnamtha (Route 1), capturing the bulk of transit trade passing through Laos as well as opening up an important new bilateral trade route between northern Laos and northern Thailand (BCEOM 1994: Annex 12). They rejected the EQJDC's ambitious vision for the road to Louangnamtha, arguing that "[e]ven after rehabilitation the road will remain much winding [*sic*] with steep slopes and hazardous passages on top of cliff edges" (BCEOM 1994: Annex 12). In more recent discussions references to the ferry service have been dropped, with some proponents now arguing for a Mekong River bridge in the vicinity of Pakbeng (RT 23 July 1997).

Route 3: The Mekong

The Mekong River itself is probably the most potent element in the Economic Quadrangle's promotional myth-making. But it is also highly problematic. As noted above, most river traffic on the upper-Mekong passes downstream from Houayxay to Pakbeng and, further on, to Louangphabang. Traffic upstream from Chiang Khong – where there are many rapids, rock outcrops, narrow channels and sandy shoals – is very light. Lao river boats regularly venture only as far as the village of Muangmom where goods are unloaded for export to Burma, though some do travel as far as the Chinese border to collect cattle (Chapman 1995: 12, 15–16).[10] Chinese boats can only come down river during the wet season and, in 1994, less than 20 came to Houayxay to collect Thai cargo, most arriving empty despite the much-reported desire of southern Chinese enterprises to export via Thailand. There are only a handful of Thai cargo boats operating on the upper-Mekong, though a number of

---

9 The *Mekong Secretariat* has its origins in the *Mekong Committee* which was formed in the 1950s to encourage cooperation in river management between Thailand, Laos, Cambodia and Vietnam. In 1975, Cambodia withdrew from the *Mekong Committee* and, in 1978, the *Interim Mekong Committee*, supported by a *Mekong Secretariat*, was formed. In 1995, a new structure – the *Mekong River Commission* – which included Cambodia, but not the upper-Mekong nations of China and Burma, was established.

10 Most of the Lao river boats small enough to travel on the upper-reaches of the river lack the engine power to make their way safely through the rapids at Tang O and further up river.

unsuccessful attempts have been made to establish river-cruise services upstream into China.

In October 1994, officials from China, Laos, Thailand and Burma agreed on the draft of an *Upper Mekong Navigation Agreement* aimed at developing upper-Mekong river trade beyond the current low levels. Under the agreement, upper-Mekong ports would be formally opened to international river traffic, with Chinese and Thai vessels permitted to travel as far downstream as Louangphabang – an increasingly popular tourist destination (BP 11 October 1994). Cargo traffic would be concentrated on the stretch between the Chinese border and the Thai town of Chiang Saen (Map 3.2, Route 3) where the river route would meet the Thai road network and a possible future extension of the northern Thai rail-line. One report has estimated that cargo along this stretch could reach one million tonnes per year, mostly lignite mined in Yunnan and exported to power stations in northern Thailand (BCEOM 1994: 79). This would, however, require substantial channel blasting, and both Burma and Laos – who control the relevant stretch of river – have expressed serious concerns about the environmental effect this may have. The navigation agreement still awaits formal approval from the four governments but China is keen to push ahead and is pursuing bilateral negotiations with the downstream nations (SWB/RT 16 November 1994).

Routes, regulation and competition

> Routes may be seen most abstractly as a form of regulation.
> (Ispahani 1989: 2)

The regulation of transport and trade through the development of new transport routes is a very competitive process, especially in an environment where there is uncertainty about the level of traffic that may result. There are a number of elements to this regulatory competition. First, the developers of new routes and associated commercial infrastructure are keen to maximise the return on their investment by attracting as much traffic as they can. The first route to be developed will have a competitive advantage, so timing is crucial. Lobbying of government and international agencies, glossy consultants reports, public relations stunts, marketing pitches to potential creditors and statements discrediting alternative proposals all aim at achieving rapid, and solid, commitment to one project. In the north-west these promotional activities are taking on an increasingly desperate air as investor confidence has been shaken by economic turmoil in Thailand and a shift has occurred in the centre of gravity of Mekong interest southwards towards Vietnam.

Towns and provinces along the routes also have vested interests, with opportunities for infrastructural improvement, business expansion, tourist influx, local taxation and windfall profits on property speculation eagerly embraced by government officials and local entrepreneurs. As Harvey (1989: 295–296) has argued, increased mobility often generates intense, and uncertain, rivalry between competing localities. Provincial administrations in Laos, despite efforts to centralise financial control, derive a large percentage of their revenue from trading taxes and are keen to maintain control of the key trading routes. In Thailand, provincial taxation is less important but provincial officials and businessmen are keen to secure both the direct benefits of trade and the secondary investment that tends to follow. It is not surprising that some of these local actors have been active participants in the marketing campaigns supporting alternative transit routes through Laos. In the following pages, I explore some of the specific dimensions of regulatory competition surrounding the transit routes through north-western Laos. This contemporary competition echoes some of the spatial rivalries of the nineteenth century.

In the northern Thai provincial capital of Chiang Rai, government officials, an active chamber of commerce and hordes of hopeful investors have been promoting the province as the northern Thai transport, communications, financial and tourism hub for the Economic Quadrangle (TN 8 February 1994; BP 17 March 1994; Hinton 1995: 4). The town is a relative newcomer to upper-Mekong trade and transport, having exercised none of the influence of Nan or Louangphabang in the nineteenth century. However, by the 1950s and 1960s, with improved road connections to Chiang Mai and Bangkok, it became an important conduit for northern Lao trade through the river port of Chiang Saen (Donner 1978: 755–756). Chiang Rai grew steadily in the 1970s – becoming an important marketing centre for northern Thai agriculture – and in the *Sixth National Economic and Social Development Plan* (1987) it was designated as a "growth center of the northern region" with hopes that it could become the international centre for northern mainland South-East Asia (Duangjan 1992: 8–9).

In the early 1990s, Chiang Rai's development hopes were focused primarily on Burma – on the busy border trade at Mae Sai, on the cultural attractions of Kengtung and on the economic boom taking place on the Burma-China border (Arunrat and Narumon 1994; Phornphimol and Saykeew 1994; Porter 1995). However, uncertain security in the Burmese borderlands has directed increasing attention towards Laos and the trading town of Chiang Khong. In 1995, when the Thai-Burma border crossing at Mae Sai was closed due to Shan rebel activity, Chiang Khong became the province's most important international trading point. It is no surprise, then, that provincial authorities and business groups in Chiang Rai have applauded the EQJDC's plan for upgrading the road that runs from Houayxay to Louangnamtha and the Chinese border. The road would cement Chiang Khong's position as a key upper-Mekong trading town.

To add strength to the plan, Chiang Rai's provincial governor has lobbied hard for the construction of a Mekong River bridge at Chiang Khong and proposed that a Thai consulate be established across the river in Houayxay (BP/RT 19 May 1995; BP/RT 4 September 1995; BP/RT 30 January 1996). With the vice-president of the *Chiang Rai Chamber of Commerce* working as a senior adviser in the transport Ministry, he had well-placed support (BP/RT 28 July 1994). There have also been local reports of extensive illegal land dealing and property speculation around Chiang Khong and ambitious talk of the town's transformation with industrial estates, golf courses, tourist resorts, shopping malls and picture theatres. In the battle to attract investment, and to realise the profits from existing ventures, the prospect of a road north to China is a valuable asset.

At the northern end of the road, in Louangnamtha, the mood has been more sober, but there is also strong support for the EQJDC's proposal. Louangnamtha has never been an important trading town. During the nineteenth century it was abandoned for 70 years and, after its belated resettlement in the 1880s, it lived in the commercial shadow of the more prosperous Muangsing. When Chinese road-building in the 1960s by-passed Muangsing, Louangnamtha briefly occupied a more strategic position but was itself bypassed when a road was built direct from the Chinese border to Oudomxai (see page 55). The level of trade in Louangnamtha is relatively low but, echoing their colleagues in Chiang Rai, local officials and entrepreneurs are keen to promote it as the northern Lao transport hub in the Economic Quadrangle. They see the road south to Thailand and north into China as the key to the province's future prosperity. Control of the important border crossing at Boten reinforces the province's claim to a more important role in regional trade. However, despite heavy marketing of Louangnamtha's strategic position, investor confidence appears slow to develop. In early 1995, when I last visited the town, the only notable investment linked to the road was a small rustic resort being built on its southern outskirts. There are also said to be plans for a golf course. Keen to arouse more investor interest, the EQJDC is heavily promoting the cultural attractions of the area and has employed a consultant to document the "customs and lifestyles" along the route (Prachan 1994a; 1994b). A photographic smorgasbord of "hill-tribe" girls is on display in the company office in Chiang Khong, and museums are under construction in Louangnamtha and Houayxay. How successful this display of cultural sensitivity is in securing financial support for the road, and associated investment, remains to be seen.

However, there are also some regulatory tensions within Laos along this route. The operators of the lignite mine at Viangphoukha – by far the most important enterprise along the road – have already made a substantial investment in road-works north of Houayxay. When I visited the mining company in early 1995, they were adamant that the EQJDC would not be developing the road between Houayxay and Viangphoukha. This section, they said, was their responsibility alone, a view endorsed by a senior official of the *Department of Communications*. In late 1996, I was told that there were "overlapping contracts" on the road and that the details of the overlap – including the financially crucial question of whether or not the lignite trucks would be required to pay a toll – had not yet been worked out. The reluctance of the lignite miners – with their anticipated 100 trucks per day – to see a series of toll stations erected along the road is understandable, especially after the substantial investment they have already made in improving the road.

The second alternative transit route also has strong provincial support. The northern Thai city of Nan has featured very little in the Economic Quadrangle plans and there are a number of indications that, along with other northern provinces, it is reluctant to be drawn into the Chiang Rai-focused vision (TN 5 February 1994; TN 8 February 1994). During the twentieth century, Nan has become more isolated from the main currents of regional trade. Administrative reorganisation saw its trading outpost, Chiang Khong, fall under the influence of Chiang Rai, and the market villages further down the Mekong were lost to the French. Except for a brief period during the Lao civil war, when supplies were trucked north to anti-communist forces south of the Mekong, Nan's linkages with Laos have been broken. However, the establishment of a second lignite mine near the Lao town of Hongsa has revived Nan's upper-Mekong aspirations. Since an international border crossing was opened to the south of Hongsa in 1994 – a major media event allegedly attended by a crowd of more than 20,000 – authorities in Nan have been promoting their province as the alternative northern Thai route into Laos and onward to southern China and Vietnam. Traders in Nan even offered to fund the construction of a bridge across the Mekong near Pakbeng, until they realised how much it would cost (BP 1 November 1996). Provincial authorities have predicted that a tourist, commercial and industrial boom will follow the opening of the border crossing and are lobbying for an upgrading of Nan's transport links with central Thailand (BP 6 December 1994). Provincial authorities have even suggested that their road link to Laos justifies placing the northern regions' second major university in Nan, rather than Chiang Rai, the other obvious contender (BP 6 December 1994; RT/BP 13 July 1997).

Already, Nan appears to have made some inroads into Chiang Rai's dominance of northern Lao trade. By early 1995, some Lao traders were travelling to Nan rather than Chiang Khong to buy manufactured goods, foodstuffs and construction materials, though their numbers were limited by higher wholesale prices and transport costs and by the appalling state of the road between Hongsa and the Mekong. Their numbers are likely to increase because the border crossing with Nan is well placed in relation to both Louangphabang and Pakbeng. Several northern Lao sawmills are also keen to export their timber along the roads towards Nan, rather than bringing it up river to Chiang Khong. The development of trade across this border would also serve the interests of military-backed commercial and political interests in Laos who are active around Hongsa and who hope to develop the town as a northern Lao "special economic zone." Lao officials are also reported to prefer an upper-Mekong bridge near Pakbeng, because it would lie wholly within Laos and there would not be the jurisdictional problems they encountered with the trans-border bridge at Vientiane.

As far as transit trade with China is concerned, the route from Nan does appear to have some advantages over the route from Chiang Khong, although the transit distance through Laos is considerably longer. The main advantage lies in its better position in relation to Bangkok. At present, most goods shipped from Bangkok's ports to the far north of Thailand travel through Phrae (Map 1.1), which is much closer to Nan than it is to Chiang Khong. There is a strong feeling among traders, shopkeepers and customs officers that the development of the Nan route may lead to the bypassing of Chiang Rai province altogether. Nan's transit option has also attracted some support from powerful allies – provincial officials and road construction companies in southern China. For some time, the Chinese have expressed interest in upgrading the route to Pakbeng, originally built by their army engineers more than 20 years ago. Over the past two years, there have been a number of high-level discussions between officials from Yunnan and Nan on options for funding the route (BP/RT 3 October 1995; BP 1 November 1996). Chinese interest in the road to Nan may well have been heightened by their exclusion from developing the road from Louangnamtha to Houayxay, despite considerable interest having been expressed by Yunnanese officials and road construction companies. The spate of Chinese hotels being built in Oudomxai over the past few years – in contrast to the situation in Louangnamtha – seems to indicate Chinese investor confidence in it maintaining its current position as a sub-regional transport and trading hub and as a longstanding centre of Chinese influence in northern Laos. There are also rumours that Oudomxai province is attempting to secure control of the border crossing at Boten, to reinforce its position in Lao-Chinese relations.

The Chinese are also strong supporters of the third transit route – the upper-Mekong itself. They have been the most active in developing proposals for upper-Mekong navigation and improved river infrastructure. Running along remote and undeveloped sections of the Lao-Burmese border, the river route is, from the Chinese point of view, the least likely to be subject to national and provincial regulation. Already, there are strong rumours that the Chinese have undertaken illegal blasting of rapids on remote Lao and Burmese sections of the river. Though Lao reservations about the Chinese navigation proposals have been largely voiced in environmental terms, the difficulties of regulating and profiting from river trade are probably more pressing concerns. The preferred cargo route – from the Chinese border to Chiang Saen – would by-pass all substantial population centres in the north-west, giving Laos a very marginal position in transit trade. Lao support for the river route has extended only as far as minor port upgrading and the erection of navigation markers on the "existing natural channel" (VT 14–20 October 1994). Thai enthusiasm for the river route also appears to have waned. Despite a 40 million *baht* allocation for port upgrading at Chiang Saen and Chiang Khong, the Thai government has increasingly come to the view that road transport represents a more practical and efficient option despite the higher infrastructure costs. Prior to the Pathet Lao victory in Laos, Thai vessels dominated river traffic on the upper-Mekong (see page 131), but now there is limited enthusiasm for large-scale reinvestment. The ongoing failure of a nationally high-profile tour company to develop a viable river cruise service between northern Thailand and southern China, despite massive investment and promotion, has undoubtedly undermined Thai confidence in the potential of the upper-Mekong. Thai and Lao reservations have been reflected in the low priority given to river navigation in the ADB-sponsored discussions on regional transport linkages. The ambitious Chinese plans appear to be stalled, despite misleading claims that upper-Mekong navigation is "booming" (SWB/RT 13 September 1995; TN 6 December 1996).

Conclusion: The Demise of the State?

The Economic Quadrangle has not lived up to its ambitious plans in north-western Laos. Bilateral trading relationships with Thailand and China have been resumed, but the plans for extensive transit trade have not been realised. There is no doubt that there have been increases in trading volumes since the late 1980s, but whether or not current volumes exceed those of the late 1960s and early 1970s – when trade was stimulated by a dependant refugee population, extensive infrastructure development, a booming business in drugs and timber, and a strong military presence – is exceedingly difficult to judge. There are also some doubts that trading volumes will continue to increase, with reports, for example, of a significant decline in cross-border trade between Laos and China. "This is probably the peak," one shopkeeper in Chiang Khong told me.

The disappointing level of transit trade can be attributed largely to the painstakingly slow progress on transport infrastructure. To date, the main transport improvements have been relatively short lengths of road from the Thai border to the lignite mines at Viangphoukha and Hongsa, and there are even considerable doubts about the quality of these road-works. The failure to agree on a single priority transit route through north-western Laos – a product of commercial and provincial rivalries – has undoubtedly delayed investor commitment. Like the Chinese traders McLeod met in Chiang Mai in the 1830s (see page 30), investors may also be waiting to see if recent improvements in security in the Burmese borderlands enable a resumption of work on the more lucrative route through Kengtung (TN 9 November 1996). The broader regional context must also be considered. Recently, Quadrangle discussions have been increasingly incorporated within the ADB's greater Mekong subregion vision (which also includes the lower-Mekong nations of Cambodia and Vietnam). Within this vision, there is a bewildering greater Mekong wish-list of roads, railways, airports and fibre-optic cables (ADB 1996a; 1996b; 1996c). With a total cost of over 40 billion dollars – and the ADB itself foreshadowing relatively limited support – the competition for private sector Mekong investment will be intense. With such an array of investment opportunities, the benefits of large-scale investment in the relatively undeveloped and impoverished north-west may be difficult to promote, especially as the centre of gravity for interest and investment shifts south towards Vietnam. It is early to judge, but it is also possible that investor interest in large-scale infrastructure projects in northern Laos has evaporated altogether in the wake of the dramatic economic downturn in Thailand.

What, then, of the popular argument that trans-border regional economies – such as the Quadrangle – pose a threat to the authority of the state? In the ongoing debate about the role of the state in Asian economic development,[11] growth triangles, circles and quadrangles have been hailed by some as a victory for the free-marketeers. Ohmae (1995: 80) argues that transborder regions are the "natural economic zones" in a borderless world. States, by contrast, are a "fiction" and a "transitional form of organisation for managing economic affairs" that have now outlived their usefulness (Ohmae 1995: 80, 136). Referring to the Mekong's "*baht* defined zone of influence" he suggests that the "nation-state focused policy may be intentionally blind to these developments" (Ohmae 1995: 109). The Thai scholar Chai-Anan is a supporter of Ohmae, and gives these free-market arguments a gentle and nostalgic edge. He has suggested that the new economic, social and cultural opportunities in the borderlands amount to a "bypassing of the state." He argues that the resumption of "age old" transborder networks "implies a breakdown of the authority of the nation state because it opens more room for non-state actors" (Chai-Anan 1995). Vatikiotis (1996b: 180) also writes of a partial return to an idealised past, arguing that trans-border regionalism "has begun to reproduce elements of a pre-colonial Southeast Asia; when borders were vaguely defined, the relations between states depended on a web of personal ties and the actual power of the state was more symbolic than real." And, of course, all of these arguments resonate with recent discussions in social theory which

---

11 For a good overview see Rodan, Hewison and Robison (1997).

highlight the increasing irrelevance of the state in the face of globalisation. Summarising a large body of recent work, Eade (1997: 3), for example, writes that "[t]he significance of national state boundaries and institutions declines as global and local social relations interweave and worldwide social relations intensify."

The evidence from the Economic Quadrangle – albeit one of the most remote and least developed regional economies – suggests that there may be some confusion in this uneasy coalition of free-marketeer, liberal nostalgic and post-modern views. To date, the Quadrangle – like transborder zones elsewhere in Asia (Parsonage 1997) – has provided substantial opportunities for renewed and reinvigorated forms of state intervention. The basis for the confusion appears to lie in a preoccupation with states as bounding, enclosing and restricting entities (Chai-Anan 1995; Ohmae 1995: viii). This focus on exclusive sovereignty, as Foucault (1980: 121–122) argued, is an oversimplification of the complex field of power and can only deal with the state's engagement with external flows by declaring its increasing irrelevance. A more realistic approach lies in recognising the role of states in *regulating* and managing trans-border flows rather than *preventing* them. While states may seek to establish exclusive sovereignty within their territory, they are also actively involved in creating *overlapping* and potentially *ambiguous* spheres of economic, social and cultural influence. In particular, state power is crucial to the initiation, maintenance, management and protection of external trading networks. In the light of this more open and regulatory approach to the state, contemporary developments represent much less of a threat to state authority. The ongoing relevance of the state is reflected in several different aspects of the Economic Quadrangle's development.

In most general terms, the rhetorical emphasis on free markets and de-regulation sits uneasily with hopes that the Economic Quadrangle will provide opportunities to regularise, formalise and eradicate the illegal practices of the Golden Triangle (ADB 1993: vii-viii). At a Burmese trade fair I attended in Tachilek, government and corporate organisers were explicit in their hope that the fair would be a first stage in the conversion of smuggling into formal trade (Walker 1994: 8). In Thailand, customs officers spoke to me of their regular meetings with village leaders, where they tried to persuade them to use the official trading points in Chiang Khong or Chiang Saen rather than shipping timber, cattle and forest products between the small villages that are scattered along both banks of the Mekong. The establishment of upper-Mekong navy units represents a less gentle crack-down on such practices. Similarly in Laos, there are regular border-commissions with both China and Thailand, aimed at developing a coordinated approach to the "bad elements" who are said to congregate in border districts. Publicly, Lao officials also make much of their attempts to restrict borderlands trade in opium and heroin. Of course, the extent of state success in these initiatives is highly variable, however it is clear that the rhetoric and practices of liberalisation are intertwined with elements of regulation and control. The opening of border crossings and the construction of infrastructure are liberalising processes, but they often aim to regularise and channel the flows of trade.

Infrastructure development – "one traditional ... mainstay of state activity"– represents a dilemma for those who advocate or predict the demise of the state in regional economies (Mann 1996: 304). Even Ohmae (1995: 126, 136) recognises a need for states to act as "catalysts for the activities of regions" and lists infrastructure as one area where state intervention may be appropriate, even if only to maintain common standards. In the infrastructural development of the Economic Quad-rangle, state officials and agencies have been the *most* active participants in a bewildering program of meetings, inspection tours, feasibility studies and public relations stunts. State enthusiasm and endorsement is one part of the strategy of mobilising reluctant investors. State coordination and brokerage has also been necessary to prevent Quadrangle planning deteriorating into bitter rivalry between competing provincial and commercial interests.

State involvement in infrastructure has, however, gone well beyond the facilitation and coordination role reluctantly accorded it by free-market economists. State officials, commercially-minded politicians and even national governments have been direct and active participants in major infrastructure projects and their commercial spin-offs. In north-western Laos, the road from Houayxay to Louangnamtha is a collaborative project between the state and private enterprise. Thai investors in this project are said to have close connections with senior political figures in Laos and at least one provincial Deputy Governor has been recruited to an "advisory team" for the project (BP/RT 25 July 1995). Formally, the Lao government has secured a 40 per cent share in any revenue that the road will generate, if ever it gets beyond a series of concrete bridges linked by mud and dust. This is a mutually beneficial arrangement: state revenue will be enhanced and the central government will maintain some degree of control over a major development in one of its more remote regions; at the same time, Thai investors have secured wide-ranging rights to land, natural resources and commercial licences, rights that could not have been obtained without substantial state backing. The nature and extent of collaboration on this project has alarmed even the ADB (Nonis 1994), despite its enthusiasm to see private sector funds make some inroads into its Mekong wish-list. Given the level of state and military intervention around Hongsa, it would be very surprising if similar collaborative arrangements were not developed for the road north from Nan.

There is no clearer illustration of renewed state intervention in the borderlands than the fiscal transformations that are occurring in Laos. The dramatic increases in private-sector trade have provided a rich harvest for state tax collectors and revenue embezzlers. The percentage of Lao state revenue derived from import and export taxes increased from 19 to 48 per cent between 1987 and 1990 (Vokes and Fabella 1995: 32; see also Pham 1994b: 22) and there is no doubt this "broadening of the tax base" (Bourdet 1994: 38) has continued since. The NEM reforms did not affect high tariffs on many items and, though there have been some small changes in the new 1994 customs law, "they could not reasonably be described as a significant trade liberalisation" (Warr 1997: Annex D-2). No wonder, then, that Lao officials have vigorously, and successfully, resisted Chinese proposals that upper-Mekong navigation be made free of all taxes and charges (BP 18 October 1994). No wonder also that provincial regulators, who were granted substantial financial independence in the mid-1980s, have resisted Vientiane's attempts to bring their budgets under central control and have continued to levy taxes and maintain internal checking points that have been abolished by central decree (Bourdet 1994: 43; Vokes and Fabella 1995: 31–32; Warr 1997: 5–6). In this fiscal resistance, and in the active participation of provinces in pursuing cross-border economic agreements, there are, indeed, signs of challenges to state power – conceived in centralised terms – but the challenges represent tensions within a spatially dispersed state rather than a bypassing of it. As Jessop (1990: 316) has written:

> ... the state does not exist as a fully constituted, internally coherent, organisationally pure, and operationally closed system but is an emergent, contradictory, hybrid and relatively open system.

While the relationships between components of the state may be experiencing some renewed tensions in Laos, there is no indication that they are going to break.

Finally, the role of the military in the Economic Quadrangle must also be considered. In Thailand, during the 1960s and the 1970s, the army played an important role in the economic development of many provinces (Pasuk and Baker 1995). Many traders and entrepreneurs, aware of the history of military involvement in Thailand, commented to me that Laos is now entering a similar phase. Commercial companies run by the military were quarantined from the privatisation of the early 1990s, and are now expanding into many ("formal" and "informal") sectors of economic life. In October 1994, for example, the central government revoked logging concessions throughout Laos and transferred them to the three main military corporations. These corporations now sell timber quotas to the sawmills at ever increasing prices, impose heavy taxes on the export of sawn timber and manage the illegal export of unprocessed logs to Thailand. Their intervention, which is examined in detail in chapter 7, has dramatically changed the balance of power in Laos' largest export industry. Beyond forestry, the military is also involved in mining, construction, manufacturing, import-export trading and tourism, making it the most important domestic force in the Lao economy.

In his recent assessment of the NEM, Bourdet (1996: 92) has suggested that "[t]here is a clear dichotomy in Laos between the comprehensiveness of the economic reforms and the inertia of the political system." My observation of the Economic Quadrangle suggests that this dichotomy, may, in fact, be very blurred with persistent and substantial state/political penetration of the economy. In the following four chapters, I examine the interpenetration of state, society and economy in more detail, exploring the role of regulation in the activities of transport operators, traders and entrepreneurs. While some regulatory practices are vestiges of a more restrictive 1980s, many others have flourished as liberalised trading and transport regimes have emerged in the 1990s. One of the ironies of the region is that "open" borders can provide more opportunities for regulation than the "closed" borders they have replaced.

CHAPTER FOUR

Borders, Frontier Communities and the State

Cross-River Boat Operators in Chiang Khong

Introduction: The Irony of the *Khoji*

In a recent paper on borders in India, Krishna (1996: 207) writes of a *khoji* (a tracker) recruited by the *Border Security Force* to trace suspicious camel tracks that wound across the sand dunes from Pakistan. "The skill of the *khoji*," he writes, "is one that arises from a sensuous relationship with the land typical of nomadic and itinerant peoples" (Krishna 1996: 207). Krishna is captivated by the romantic, tactile and mobile life of the *khoji*, contrasting it with the bureaucratic lives of the border police, filing their "sterile" situation reports with headquarters every morning (Krishna 1996: 208). "The enlistment of the *khoji*," he writes, "to maintain and preserve the border, a notion that is supremely an artefact of immobile and settled societies, is deeply ironic" (Krishna 1996: 207).

The apparent irony of the *khoji* – of an unlikely alliance between nomad and demarcating officialdom – is given its resonance by recent discussions on the nature of national borders. In these discussions, borders are portrayed as artefacts of state power, violently and arbitrarily imposed by imperialism and modern statecraft as part of the effort to "marginalise or destroy various aspects of centrifugal otherness" (Shapiro 1996: xx).[1] The bounding, demarcating and "inner oriented" practices of the state, it is argued, cut across traditional trans-border and "outward oriented" linkages of ethnicity, religion, neighbourhood and travel, defining people according to the singular abstracting discourse of citizenship (Krishna 1996: 204). But, so the story goes, states and their borders are often not successful. People living in the borderlands – sensuous, tactile people like the *khoji* (not the report-filing bureaucrats who employed him) – resist the bounding practices of the state through their everyday recalcitrance,

---

1 This view of borders occurs frequently in a recent collection called *Challenging boundaries: global flows, territorial identities* (Shapiro and Alker 1996). See also Shapiro (1994).

subversion and evasion (Appadurai 1995: 214–215; Krishna 1996: 204; Soguk 1996: 298–300). As we have seen, these borderlands activities are celebrated as a denial of borders and the state power embedded in them, holding forth the prospect of frontier communities establishing renewed, trans-border forms of cultural and commercial interaction. But, on the darker side, trans-border recalcitrance can also prompt attempts to reassert control as states respond, with all the modern technology of surveillance and repression, to their renewed "cartographic anxiety" (Krishna 1996: 208; see also Shapiro 1996: xx; Soguk 1996: 299–301).

As I suggested in the introduction, this centre-periphery tension between "the local" and "the state" is often conveyed in discussions of borders in mainland South-East Asia. From Thongchai's (1994) work we have the idea that the hegemonic regime of colonial map-making and boundary demarcation disrupted the spatial practices of borderland communities. Writers considering more recent developments present a less clear-cut picture – pointing to the persistence of trans-border interaction – but sharing with Thongchai the notion of an underlying tension between bounding states and borderland communities. Rumley (1991: 148) for example, has suggested that Thailand's southern "border landscape" is characterised by peripherality from the "highly centralised Thai state." This economic, cultural and political distance from state authority is reflected in separatism, political opposition, occasional rebellion and rampant smuggling (Rumley 1991: 140–144; see also Cornish 1988: 93). In a similar vein, Grundy-Warr (1993: 46) has written of borderlanders in Thailand, Burma and Cambodia who "develop their own laws and ways of doing things irrespective of the wishes of central state authorities." He suggests that there are fundamental conflicts of interest between state functionaries and borderlanders, reflected in *intra*-state military conflict in the borderlands and in economic strategies in border regions that tend to be "exploitative" rather than "developmental" (Grundy-Warr 1993: 53–55; see also Rumley 1991: 146–147). Chai-Anan's (1995) vision, referred to at the end of the previous chapter, is more positive, suggesting that borderland communities can bypass state power through the re-establishment of old, trans-border, social and cultural networks.

This chapter argues that there is much more complementarity in the intertwining of "state" and "local" border practices than these various approaches imply. Through an examination of the activities of cross-river boat operators, who ply the Mekong between Chiang Khong and Houayxay, it highlights the extent to which members of frontier communities themselves are actively involved in the regulation of borders and in giving borderlines their particular local character. The trans-border commercial opportunities that have emerged in the era of the Economic Quadrangle often arise out of, rather than deny or subvert, state regulation. The restrictive borders of the 1980s may be fading, but new types of regulation and demarcation, characterised by a collaborative engagement with exchange, interaction and passage, are emerging. Borders can indeed function to prevent or restrict mobility – as those preoccupied with the textual rigidity of lines on maps are keen to demonstrate – but they are also powerful generators of mobility as people seek to exploit the regulatory nooks and crannies that borders create. The cross-river boat operators of Chiang Khong – like the *khoji* – have mobility at the heart of their identity, but they have no qualms about participating in the production and maintenance of borders. As I will argue, there is nothing ironic about this at all.

Cross-River Boat Operators in Chiang Khong

The town of Chiang Khong is made up of a group of linked villages strung out along the river-bank opposite the Lao provincial capital of Houayxay (Map 4.1). The commercial heart of the town is located in the central village of Wat Luang, where the main street is crowded with overflowing shops and small warehouses servicing the busy trade with Laos. In the middle of this commercial precinct a narrow lane runs away from the main street, past the temple (*wad*) from which the village takes its name,[2] and down a steep concrete ramp to the river below. This is Chiang Khong's border trading port.

Since 1988, the flow of traffic from Chiang Khong to Houayxay has increased dramatically (see page 71) and, with no bridge across the Mekong, a substantial percentage of the trade is carried by the 38 cross-river boat operators who are based at the port.[3] Every weekday morning their long narrow boats pull out into the Mekong's vigorous current and make their way upstream. They stay close to the Thai bank for a few hundred metres before cutting between the rocks and sandy islands to Houayxay's passenger and cargo ports on the opposite bank.[4] It is a small invasion force of straw hats, baggy trousers and shoulder bags as the Thai boat operators and traders step ashore with their eggs, sweating plastic bags of vegetables, chickens tied at the legs and twitching fish in four gallon tins. This is only the first cross-border journey. Throughout the day the boat operators return to Chiang Khong's port several times to collect more loads: huge bundles of quilts that barely fit in the narrow hulls; boxes of soap powder, toothpaste and Milo; bags of clothes from the Friday market;

---

2 The *wad luaŋ* is the major, or royal, temple in the town.

3 A cross-river vehicular ferry, based in the village of Hua Wiang (Map 4.1), carries bulk exports such as fuel and container loads of goods from Bangkok ports. The ferry is owned by a Thai sawmilling company with investments in Laos.

4 One of the boats calls at the Immigration Post at Hua Wiang where the border passes for all the boat operators and traders (collected each morning by a trader travelling in the boat) are stamped.

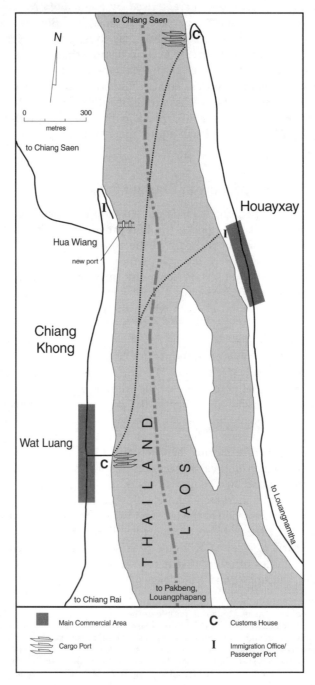

Map 4.1 Chiang Khong and Houayxay

and heavy loads of concrete, steel reinforcing and corrugated iron. Lao traders, more stylish in their baseball caps, hair pieces and vinyl handbags, sit precariously on top of their purchases, as the boats nudge their way into Houayxay's cargo port. Late in the afternoon, when all the cargo is stacked away in Lao shops, boats and trucks, some of the cross-river boat operators buy bottles of beer or rice whisky and have a leisurely drink as they drift downstream, tracing their own meandering Mekong border, before starting their engines and pulling into the muddy bank below Wat Luang.

The cargo carried by Wat Luang's cross-river boat operators can be divided into three categories. First, there are the purchases of cross-border traders operating between Chiang Khong and Houayxay itself. This trade is dominated by Thai traders who benefit from favourable short-term credit and pricing arrangements with Chiang Khong's shopkeepers and cheap freight rates offered by the cross-river boat operators. Secondly, there are goods bought in Chiang Khong by Lao traders, carried by the cross-river boats to Houayxay's cargo port, and then loaded onto Lao long-distance cargo boats for trips down the Mekong to Paktha, Pakbeng or Louangphabang. Large Lao cargo boats (between 15 and 100 tonnes) are permitted to load directly at the Chiang Khong port – avoiding the expense of the cross-river boats – but smaller Lao cargo boats (up to 15 tonnes) are confined to Houayxay where they are supplied by Chiang Khong's boat operators.[5] Finally, there are goods destined for Louang-namtha and Muangsing, which are carried to Houayxay's cargo port and loaded onto trucks for the dry-season journey north along the EQJDC's dusty track.

Moored in rows at the Wat Luang port, against a backdrop of mud and brown water, the brightly painted cross-river boats are a colourful sight. They are all made of wood and are mostly ten to twelve metres long and little more than a metre wide.[6] Their average capacity is about one and a half tonnes, with the smallest carrying somewhat less than one tonne and the largest almost two. Power is provided by four-cylinder car engines, imported second-hand from Japan and sold in motor repair shops in Chiang Khong. The engine is located towards the rear, with a long shaft

---

5 The restriction on smaller Lao boats crossing to Chiang Khong is imposed by Lao customs officers who claim that their supervision of loading the boats reduces smuggling.

6 There are two types of boat (*rya*) used for cross-river trade: *rya klab* and *rya hualɛɛm*. The *rya klab* is a simpler and older style of boat, almost entirely constructed from three pieces of wood: one along the base and one along either side. Additional small pieces are used to form the characteristic bow and stern. The *rya hualɛɛm* has a more complex construction with an internal frame and numerous narrow planks forming the hull. The *rya klab* are cheaper, use less fuel and can run in shallower water but the *rya hualɛɛm* are preferred for their greater capacity and sturdiness and are used by most of Chiang Khong's boat operators. A number of operators who now use *rya hualɛɛm* started out with the cheaper *rya klab*. By contrast, *rya klab* are by far the more popular style amongst Lao boat operators across the river.

extending through the floor to the propeller. A boxed-in section of the hull in front of the engine serves as a driver's seat and a storage box for fuel and tools. A steering wheel is connected to the rudder shaft at the rear by wire and rope lines running down the sides. Slatted wooden floors keep cargo out of the water that inevitably accumulates in the bottom of the hull and rough planks serve as removable passenger seats. It is illegal to fell timber now in Thailand – and there is nothing suitable left around Chiang Khong anyway – so most of the boats are built in the Lao saw-milling town of Bandan, about 20 kilometres down the Mekong (Map 1.2). During 1994, new boats from Bandan cost about 16,000 *baht*, with the second-hand engines costing almost as much again.[7]

All of the cross-river boats based at Wat Luang's cargo port are owned and operated by men. There is no concentration in ownership, everyone owning only one boat. Most boat operators work with their boat only one day in four – under a rostering system discussed below – and they are engaged in a number of other occupations. Many work as small-scale cross-border traders and many also have fruit orchards and rice fields in the rural areas surrounding Chiang Khong. Indeed, most earn more from their other occupations than they do from boat driving, with only the poorest relying on their boat as a main source of income. Nevertheless the boats are central to many of these men's identity. When asked their occupation they readily respond that they are boat drivers, rather than traders or farmers. They regularly socialise together, attend major ritual events as a loose group, spend an inordinate amount of time at the port when they are not working and regularly go off on weekend fishing expeditions with their rods and, occasionally, a stick of dynamite. They value the mobility that their boats give them, undoubtedly enjoying their regular trips across the border to Houayxay – where else could they see Chinese girls in mini-skirts and skin tight tops? – and occasionally to Lao villages further afield. When my neighbour's boat was sunk at the port by a runaway truck, he spoke to me with genuine distress: "Oh Andrew," he said, "I love my boat."

A lifestyle that celebrates mobility is not, however, inconsistent with one that seeks to restrict and regulate. The boat operators are all members of an association (*chomrom*) – the *Wat Luang Boat Operators' Association* – whose primary role is to maintain their monopoly on cross-river freight transport and to avoid the over-supply of boats leading to price competition between operators. The central activity of the *Association* is the coordination of a roster system whereby the fleet of 38 is divided into four groups known as *khiw* (derived from the English "queue"), one of

---

7 When I returned to Chiang Khong in late 1996 I found that new boats were now being made from metal in Chiang Khong, given the high cost of Lao timber. New metal boats were being sold for about 20,000 *baht*. There was strongly divided opinion on the merits of the metal boats.

which operates each day the port is open for trade (Monday to Friday).[8] The *khiw* system is a recognition of substantial oversupply at the port, with one quarter of the boats being quite sufficient to meet cross-river demand on all but the busiest days. It is a carefully structured system with an array of rules and regulations. *Khiw* membership is fixed and each *khiw* has its own "office bearers," record books, property (such as shade umbrellas and seats) and bank accounts. *Khiw* are referred to by their number (one to four), and the order of *khiw* operations is an idiosyncratic one-three-two-four, a result of an obscure regulatory anomaly in the late 1980s. There is joking rivalry between the *khiw* about their income-earning abilities and some boat operators even seemed to keep tabs on the number of bottles of whisky I bought for the various *khiw* in what became something of a Friday evening drinking institution.

Freight and passenger fees are set by the *Association*, and these are strictly enforced. They are strongly biased in favour of Thai traders from Chiang Khong who, for example, are charged only 80 *baht* for a full load whereas their Lao counterparts pay 170 *baht*.[9] Thai traders are also charged 20 *baht* for an unlimited number of passenger trips across the river on any one day, whereas Lao traders have to pay 30 *baht* each time they cross. Members of the *Association* who are trading on their non-*khiw* days are not charged any freight or passenger fees at all. All fees are paid to a member of the relevant *khiw* who acts as the record keeper and port coordinator. This position – known as the *kebŋen* (money collector) – is also rostered with a different *khiw* member filling it each day and not operating his boat. The *kebŋen* is the day-to-day enforcer for the *Association*, busily directing loads of cargo to boats, stepping deftly across the loaded boats to collect payments from traders and conducting vigorous negotiations when traders dispute his assessment of the amount payable. Some *Association* members are much more capable *kebŋen* than others, and they are often paid by less confident and assertive members to take their turn in the position.

At the end of the day, the members of the relevant *khiw* adjourn to one of the *Association's* sheds overlooking the port for calculation and distribution of the day's takings. This can be a prolonged and argumentative process, with the cash collected rarely matching the payments recorded in the *khiw* record book. It can be a nerve-racking time for the *kebŋen*, who may be required to make up any shortfall from his own pocket. Younger and better educated *Association* members tend to

---

8 The number of boats in each *khiw* is not equal. Given the four day rotation system, the *khiw* that operates on Monday also operates on Friday (see page 100). *Khiw* systems amongst transport operators of all types are widespread in Thailand and Laos. Their systems of operation vary enormously. During 1994 motor-bike taxi *khiw* controllers in Bangkok gained some notoriety, with frequent press reports of intimidation, extortion and violence.

9 The amounts are adjusted if particularly large or small boats are used.

dominate the discussion, thumping away at their calculators with intimidating speed. Nevertheless, there are clear rules and the formality of the *Association*'s system of regulation is, once again, highlighted. When a grand total is finally agreed, various deductions are made: fees paid to Thai and Lao immigration police; allowances for fuel; a five per cent levy to meet *Association* expenses; and numerous special payments with equally numerous special rationales. The balance is divided evenly between the *khiw* members, including the *kebŋen*, and the amount set aside for fuel is allocated according to the number of trips each member has undertaken. All payments are carefully recorded and the records are prodigiously annotated so that the fairness and propriety of the system is abundantly clear. To exclamations of *riabrɔɔy* (everything in order), the books are closed.

The daily payments made to *khiw* members vary considerably. Typically, payments are better in the dry season when the level of trade is higher. In the wet season, trade declines as roads in Laos become impassable and Lao energies are diverted to rice cultivation. Payments also vary on a weekly cycle. Fridays are usually the best days, due to the presence of a large market in Chiang Khong which attracts many Lao buyers. Monday is also often busy after the two days of minimal trade on the weekend. Given the four day rotation, the *khiw* that works Monday also works the following Friday, always considered a bonus. Individual daily payments of 400 to 500 *baht* are acceptable, disappointing on a Friday but good enough on other days. Amounts above 600 *baht* are considered good, with the 1,000 *baht* barrier only being breached a few times per year. On one occasion, when individual payments were around 900 *baht* in the normally depressed wet season, some of the *khiw* members put on a great show of excitement. One pretended to shake with nervousness as he took the money, another carefully rolled up his sleeves and brushed his hair as his name was called. The trader-wife of the *kebŋen* sat watching, drinking beer through a straw.

Maintaining Borders: Cross-River Boat Operators and the Regulation of Passage

The *Wat Luang Boat Operators' Association* places a series of restrictions on cross-river cargo transport, actively participating in the "micro-regulation" of the border. These restrictions start with its own members. Some of the boat operators are clearly more energetic than others, with a more developed "entrepreneurial" style, a better network of contacts with Lao traders and shopkeepers and, in a few cases, pick-up trucks to collect cargo from Chiang Khong's shops and markets. Given the opportunity, they could readily capture a greater individual share of cross-border freight, willingly undercutting other operators and, possibly, even acquiring more than one boat.[10] At present, the *Association* rules prevent this. Standard freight rates are set and all payments are collected by the *kebŋen*, preventing any special deals being struck between boat operators and traders. The rostering system also restricts the days of operation of each boat operator. Most importantly, however, *khiw* revenue is divided evenly between *khiw* members regardless of the number of trips they have undertaken (save for the small fuel allowance). On exceptional occasions when operators do provide freight transport on a day they are not rostered to operate, they have to pay a substantial percentage of their revenue to the relevant *khiw*.[11] There is considerable bending of the rules – a small number of operators, for example, have regular contracts with business in Houayxay and supply them every day, paying only a small "fine" to the *khiw* – but the overall system remains intact. One operator, whose extra-*khiw* activities stretched the rules to the limit, was often criticised for his avarice and I was not surprised when I saw another boat owner surreptitiously letting down the tyres on his pick-up.

In addition to limiting its more ambitious members, the *Association* also places pressure on some of its less willing workers. There is a high social expectation that all *khiw* members will be available on their rostered day, even if the level of trade is very low. *Khiw* members are also expected to return promptly to Chiang Khong for additional loads rather than spending time in Houayxay drinking, gambling and flirting. Disparaging comments about the lack of cooperative spirit are often made about those who breach these rules. One young operator, who had inherited his boat after the early death of his brother-in-law, had little interest in trading or boat driving, yet spent several thousand *baht* having his boat enlarged after fellow *khiw* members had commented that it was the smallest capacity boat in the *Association*. This expensive work was undertaken regardless of the general over-capacity at the port. Another boat operator received no sympathy or assistance from the *Association* when debts – allegedly incurred through gambling and drinking – led to a creditor seizing his boat. He was given three months to retrieve his boat, or he would lose his position within the *Association*.

One of the *Association's* main regulatory functions is to restrict entry into the cross-river freight market for other potential operators in Chiang Khong. There is a long tradition of river transport in Chiang Khong and there are many people who have the expertise to drive a boat. Financially,

---

10 Some of the most successful boat operator/traders have "assistants" who could drive additional boats for them.

11 They are exempt from this if they are using their boat for their own trading purposes, ie. carrying goods that they have bought for sale in Laos. Boat operators working as traders on their non-*khiw* days do not have to pay cargo fees so there is no loss of revenue to the *khiw*. However, I have no doubt that some use this as a cover for carrying goods for other fee-paying traders without the knowledge of the *khiw*.

purchase of a boat is no more onerous than the purchase of a motorbike, almost a standard household possession in Chiang Khong. Prior to the closure of the border in 1976, there were no restrictions on cross-border boat operations but the group of operators that became established in the few years following the reopening of the border has succeeded in creating a virtual monopoly. Most striking is the exclusion of the boat operators in the village of Hua Wiang (Map 4.1). There are about 40 under-utilised boats at the border passenger port at Hua Wiang, only one kilometre up river, but their involvement in cargo transport is limited to hand-held cargo carried by passengers crossing to Houayxay. None of them have been permitted to transfer their operations to the cargo port at Wat Luang, and there were sketchy reports of bitter and even violent confrontations when a number attempted to do so. During Thai new year, when a large carnival is held on the river-bank at Hua Wiang, the boat operators there retaliate by refusing to allow the *Association* boats from Wat Luang to pick up or drop off passengers.

New operators are only allowed to become involved in cross-border cargo transport if there is a vacancy in the *Association*, and an entry fee of at least 3,000 *baht* is required. Vacancies arise infrequently, usually when an existing member dies, becomes too old to drive a boat or takes up an alternative occupation, though in the latter case some have chosen to maintain their membership and rent their boat out. During 1994, I knew of only three new entrants into the *Association* – one a previous boat operator who had lived in Bangkok for some time, and the two others close relatives of existing members. Operators in one *khiw* prevented new entrants altogether by jointly buying the positions of departing members and "retiring" their boats. Cross-border freight transport is a tightly knit system and boat owners often commented that operations at the port were *sabaaj* (comfortable) because they were all relatives.

The *Association* is also successful in restricting operations at the cargo port by Lao cross-river boats. There are numerous small boats across the river in Houayxay and surrounding villages, many owned by friends, relatives or neighbours of Lao traders and shopkeepers who would readily use them. However, the *Association* does not permit them to call at Chiang Khong to collect cargo.[12] There are some exceptions, but the impact on the total cross-river cargo traffic is minimal and the few Lao boats that are permitted to collect cargo are usually charged a fee – often the subject of considerable argument – to compensate the *khiw* for lost revenue. The only

---

12 It is important to note that there is no reciprocal exclusion that prevents Thai boats collecting cargo on the other side of the river. There is very little cross-river cargo traffic from Houayxay to Chiang Khong because almost all Lao exports are unloaded at Chiang Khong direct from the long-distance cargo boats that ply the Mekong. On the few occasions that I saw non-timber forest products bought to Chiang Khong on cross-river boats, they were carried by *Association* boats from Wat Luang.

regular exception was provided for a Lao boat operated by a much admired woman from south Houayxay. She regularly called at the port to collect loads of vegetables and other merchandise and jokingly told me one day that she only had to pay with a smile. However, even she was confronted when she attempted to carry 12 passengers across to Houayxay, denying the *Association* over 200 *baht* in fares. After a long and vocal argument with the *kebŋen* she paid 70.

The *Association's khiw* system is a source of considerable annoyance for the Lao traders who use the port. They resentfully accept the relatively high cargo fees – though prolonged negotiations are common – but they are continually frustrated by having to wait for a vacant *khiw* boat while numerous other boats lie idle around them. On busy days, as *khiw* boats return empty from Houayxay, the traders make every attempt to call them in to berth next to their piles of cargo, or even to negotiate freight with non-*khiw* operators, much to the annoyance of the *kebŋen*. Occasionally, pressure from the traders forces the rostered *khiw* to call in other *Association* boats for assistance, though this is rare. Once, on a very busy day, the husband of one of the Lao traders, who was an experienced boat driver, was allowed to use one of the *Association's* boats to carry his wife's cargo across to Houayxay. Returning to Chiang Khong, the boat ran out of petrol, and all the boat operators watched with amused nonchalance as he drifted past a hundred or so yards out from the bank. He had challenged the system when it was under pressure, and this unplanned revenge was sweet. Traders are also inconvenienced by the long lunch breaks taken by the boat operators – sometimes stretching to almost two hours – and are not uncommonly told to take their goods back to the shops for storage if they arrive after a halt has been called to the day's work.

Chiang Khong's shopkeepers face similar frustrations. Large consignments of goods are delivered to the port in pick-ups and small trucks owned by the shops. In the dry season, when there is a wide exposed bank beside the river, their goods can be readily unloaded, but in the wet season there is limited room to stack cargo and much of it is loaded directly into the boats. As the shopkeepers wait for the *khiw* boats, the ramp leading down to the port becomes hopelessly congested, resulting in numerous minor accidents and near misses. The shopkeepers often ask why they cannot unload into the boats that lie idle. One day, tired of their complaints, the *kebŋen* exploded into rage, shouting "Andrew has only just come from Australia and he understands the *khiw* system, you shopkeepers have been here for years and still haven't got the hang of it."

The large long-distance Lao cargo boats that cross the river to load at Chiang Khong do not escape the regulation of the *Association*. One of the responsibilities of the *kebŋen* is to collect port fees to compensate the *Association* for lost cross-river revenue and to reimburse it for its maintenance of port facilities. Payments range from about 300 *baht* for a boat of 20 tonnes to over 1,000 *baht* for an 80 or 90–tonne boat. The amounts levied are much less than payments that would be made if the cargo had to be carried to Houayxay's port in the cross-river boats, but the payments are widely resented by Lao boat owners and traders and are vigorously negotiated. They are occasionally reduced if the cargo boat owners, or the traders they are carrying, are on particularly good terms with members of the *Association*. The amounts collected from the large cargo boats are added to the *khiw* total which is divided between members at the end of the day. When boats load cargo over more than one day, the amount is split between the various *khiw* according to the amount loaded each day. This allocation between *khiw* caused some of the most bitter arguments that I saw at the port and sometimes port labourers had to be called in to give their opinion on how much had been loaded over the various days. The intricacies of local regulation are not without their problems.

Boat Operators, Local Authority and the State

What, then, is the basis of the boat-operators' authority to regulate border passage at the Chiang Khong port? It certainly does not derive from any high social standing within the community. Some of the boat operators are quite affluent – with modern houses, pick-up trucks and up-to-date consumer durables – but this wealth has usually derived from strategic marriage or the sale of family land rather than boat operations or petty-trade. Boat driving itself tends to be regarded as a low status and dangerous occupation, suited to the heavy drinking, impolite and argumentative low achievers who take it on. In the eyes of some, the boat operators seem to be almost tainted by their regular contact with the disease and under-development of Laos on the opposite bank. My neighbours – a respectable family of builders, petty-landlords and unmarried daughters – were horrified when I issued a general invitation to members of the *Association* to attend a farewell "wrist tying" ceremony to mark my wife's return to Australia. "They just filled the place up," I heard one of the daughters telling her friend, referring to the five or so nominated boat operators who came to pay their respects.

Though exaggerated, my neighbour's comment highlights a crucially important issue – the power of the boat operators' spatial presence. Their authority derives largely from their literal, physical occupation of Chiang Khong's cargo port. The power of this occupation derives less from its intimidation than it does from its perceived inevitability. It is an occupation that is less authoritarian than it is domestic. And, it is an occupation that is complexly intertwined with the regulating practices of the state. When we read Appadurai (1995: 214), for example, writing of the nation state's attempt to "penetrate the nooks and crannies of everyday life," we would do well to remember that state actions can also create and reinforce "nooks and crannies" of opportunity and legitimacy. Chiang Khong's border trading port is one such place.

Local authority . . .

The port is located in Chiang Khong's central village of Wat Luang, directly below the town's most important temple. It is a place well suited for boat operations. A rocky outcrop at the southern end of the port traps sand and mud, forming a wide flat bank from which boats can be loaded until it is inundated in the wet season. This has been Chiang Khong's main cargo port for as long as anyone can remember and a busy commercial district has grown up around it. Almost all of the boat operators are residents of the village of Wat Luang. They dominate some residential clusters in the village and many have family links there that can be traced back for generations. Some of the *Association* members have been working at Wat Luang's cargo port since the 1940s and can recall carrying cargo for French administrators in Houayxay. Cross-river boat operation is part of the residential identity of the village and, within Chiang Khong, it is recognised as one of Wat Luang's occupational specialisations. Most of the Thai traders who use the port are also residents of Wat Luang, many of them the wives, relatives or neighbours of boat operators. In the local landscapes of power, Chiang Khong's cargo port is a place where the residents of Wat Luang have a natural authority.

Perched precariously on the river-bank above the port, a ramshackle collection of sheds is the focus of the boat-operators' border presence. The small front shed is the daytime centre for coordination of boat operations and in the evenings it fills with noisy *khiw* members as calculations are made and the day's takings distributed. The shed has a sense of rustic officialdom with its rough wooden table, a blackboard for occasional announcements ("warning there is an outbreak of red-eye in Laos"), a megaphone, and *khiw* record-keeping books wedged beneath the corrugated iron roof. But more impressive than this petty-port-bureaucracy is the domestication of public space achieved in the more substantial, but less accessible, shed just next to it. Here there are all the comforts of home – a television, a water cooler, sleeping mats, two broken scales used as seats, an electric fan, a small altar and rough, but substantial, cooking facilities. A poster of a naked young girl coyly clutching her groin graced the water cooler, but she was removed when they tired of her after two years. This shed is a popular rest and relaxation place for the boat operators and evening drinking sessions usually adjourn there when they become serious. Fat fish bought in Houayxay's market are chopped mercilessly into mince, while chickens, with strings around their neck, try to keep their footing on the narrow railing overlooking the Mekong and delay the inevitable hanging that awaits them. Every night a rostered group of boat operators sleep in the shed to watch over the boats, guarding against thieves and ready to bail the boats out if a sudden rain storm sweeps down the river. Prostitutes, they joke, sometimes join them. On Sunday afternoons, shouts of excitement echo from the shed as televised Thai champions land blows on their Japanese, American and Australian rivals. The shed is a boat operators' place where government officials, Lao traders and port labourers are rarely seen and where women only come to drag their reluctant husbands home after an evening of whisky and greasy food. It performs a central role in defining this little piece of border as a place belonging to Chiang Khong's cross-river boat operators.

In the midst of the boat-operators' sheds a large tree houses a female spirit of some local importance. The boat operators have a special relationship with this spirit and on particularly successful days – when total revenue approaches 10,000 *baht* – an offering of chickens, sticky rice, whisky, candles and flowers is made to her. In the rocky outcrop at the other end of the port a territorial spirit, associated with the origins of Chiang Khong itself, is also the focus for ritual activities undertaken by the boat operators.[13] Most mornings during the wet-season the spirit is asked to hold off trade-disrupting rain, with the incentive of chickens in the evening if the request is met. More substantial offerings – including a pig's head – are made on special occasions such as Thai new year and some of the boat operators also make small offerings when members of their family or neighbours fall ill. Three of the four *khiw* have *ʔaacaan* (ritual specialists) – all older men with a long history of involvement in boat operations – who perform most of the rituals. Members of the fourth *khiw* joke that they are so proficient at making money that they do not need an *ʔaacaan*, though they can "borrow" one if the need arises. This incorporation of ritual activity into the operations of the *Association*, with its focus on widely recognised territorial spirits, further reinforces the legitimacy of the boat-operators' claim to authority at the port.

Association members also regularly emphasise the importance of their contribution to the maintenance of port facilities, using this as a justification for many of the fees they extract from traders and other boat operators. Maintenance costs are funded from the five per cent levy on the daily revenue of each *khiw*, though there is always plenty left over for food and ritual expenses on special occasions. Ongoing maintenance activities include hosing down the concrete ramp every week or so with water supplied by the *Association's* pump, collecting the rubbish that accumulates at the port and occasionally slashing the weeds that

---

13 The outcrop is said to have been formed when a mythical giant dropped a basket of charcoal as he tried to cross the river. It is also said that, in times past, executions took place on the outcrop.

proliferate on the steep river-bank. More substantial projects have included a rough set of steps leading from the *Association's* sheds down to the river and a small brick wall beside the ramp, built after a truck ran out of control into a Lao cargo boat.

The large gang of port labourers is also an important part of the local landscape of power at the port. They tend to congregate in the sheds at the very top of the river-bank, somewhat removed from the boat operators, but there are strong social ties that draw them together. Many are also residents of Wat Luang and a number are the tenants or agricultural labourers of more affluent boat operators. A few boat operators work as labourers on their non-*khiw* days and a few labourers also aspire to become boat operators, occasionally driving boats as a back-up for sick or absent boat owners. The strength of the alliance is symbolised by a large sign at the port which sets out the "service" rates for both boat operators and labourers. The labourers are powerful allies for the *Association* and their substantial, muscular and masculine presence at the port is striking. To challenge the *Association* would risk jeopardising the goodwill of the labourers, who could readily delay the loading of cargo, refuse to load it altogether or demand unreasonably high payments.

... and the state

As far as boat operations are concerned, the *formal* regulatory presence of the state at the port is minimal. Inland ports in Thailand come under the jurisdiction of the *Harbours Department*, whose office serving the region is hundreds of kilometres from Chiang Khong in central Thailand. Officers of the *Department* visit Chiang Khong one day each year to collect boat registration fees, undertake desultory boat inspections and, if necessary, conduct boat driver licensing tests. The activities of the *Department* give the boat operators some formality and legitimacy, but it plays no direct role in regulating day-to-day boat operations at the port. Officials from the *Department* told me that anyone with a suitably registered boat could operate from the port, and they had no objections to Lao boats calling at the port to collect cargo. The district government office in Chiang Khong is a more immediate presence, but its role is still ambiguous. The *Association* and its *khiw* system was established at the suggestion of the district office in 1989, after the reopening of the border had led to a number of disputes between boat operators. By 1994, however, the district office's role in cross-river boat operations appeared to be limited to issuing the border passes used by the boat drivers to enter Laos. Occasionally, Lao traders and boat operators commented to me that they thought the *Association* had greatly exceeded any powers that may have been granted to it by the district office and considered writing letters of complaint to the district head, or even the provincial governor in Chiang Rai.

107

More substantial, and immediate, support for the boat operators comes from the Thai customs officers who are based at Chiang Khong's cargo port. One hot morning I stood with Lao traders while 30 tonnes of rice – which they were taking to China – was loaded laboriously into the cross-river boats to be carried to Houayxay. This was an expensive and time-consuming task – a windfall for the days' *khiw* – bought about by Thai customs' refusal to allow the rice truck to cross to Laos on the vehicular ferry based at Hua Wiang. On another occasion the uniformed officials delighted in extracting payments from a young, attractive, trader whom they caught surreptitiously loading bicycles into a Lao cross-river boat at the far end of the port. The customs officers have no direct role in the regulation of boat operations (GOT 1993a) but they can make life difficult for anyone challenging the *status quo* at the port – imposing unreasonable "service" charges, under-taking time-consuming and intrusive inspections and possibly even banning uncooperative boat operators or traders from the port altogether. The customs officers are also closely allied with the immigration police who occasionally arrest Lao traders whose border papers are not in order, imposing very heavy fines and sometimes holding offenders for several days. The customs officers are the boat operators most formidable allies.

The *Association's* cultivation of this alliance is a subtle process. Many of the customs officers also live within the village of Wat Luang, but their government accommodation is set apart from the residential heart of the village and neighbourhood socialisation with the low status boat operators is limited At the port itself, however, there are opportunities for informal – but highly visible – interaction. A "Welcome to Chiang Khong" sign above the port suggests a close relationship between the *"Boat Operators' Association"* (in large letters) and the *"Chiang Khong Customs House"* (somewhat smaller). The relative status is reversed in the subtle architectural complicity between the boat operators' sheds on one side of the ramp and the much more substantial customs office on the other. Some of the more senior boat operators occasionally sit talking with officials in the customs compound, arranging, perhaps, for the *Association* to make a financial contribution to the customs officers' "merit making" rituals. As traders, the boat operators make regular small payments to the customs officers as "administrative fees" or "service charges" for the goods they are exporting to Laos. Some of the boat operators are also involved in importing forest products, handicrafts or foodstuffs from Laos, arriving late in the afternoon with their laden boats and engaging the customs officers in quiet discussions as bribes are paid and import duties waived. The customs officers also have their own motives: there is no doubt that the limitation on the number of boats operating at the port makes their tasks of supervision and petty harassment of traders that much easier. In early 1995, they complained that the *Association* boats were not readily identifiable, and could not be easily distinguished from Lao boats that may be calling at the port. Within days, each *Association* boat had a bright new Thai flag fluttering at the rear, a powerful little symbol of the collaboration between state regulation and *Association* authority.

Equally important is the support provided by state employees on the other side of the border. It would be easy for Lao border officials to place arbitrary restrictions on the activities of Chiang Khong's cross-river boats – limiting their access to Houayxay's port, allowing only Lao boats to unload at the port, imposing expensive landing fees, or insisting that the boat operators go through immigration formalities every time they cross the river – but they have made no effort to do so. Indeed, the main border restriction imposed by Lao officials is their refusal to allow small Lao cargo boats (up to about 15 tonnes) to cross to Chiang Khong, a restriction which generates a substantial proportion of the *Association's* work. *Association* members carefully maintain their good relations with Lao officials. Each *khiw*, for example, makes a daily payment of 800 *baht* to the Lao immigration police and individual boat operators, working as traders, provide goods to Lao customs officers and immigration police on favourable terms. They also provide free transport for Lao officials when they cross for adventures in Chiang Khong. One boat operator told me that he provided pornographic videos to Lao immigration police in return for "convenience," turning a blind eye to his lack of a border pass for example. "Lao people like to watch them," he said "and some of the immigration police have new girlfriends."

In early 1995, the subtle intertwining of the boat operators' authority and state power was highlighted. Customs authorities in Houayxay put a stop to all Lao cargo boats crossing the river to load at the Chiang Khong port. It was a mock crack-down on the Lao traders who regularly loaded the large cargo boats in ways that concealed high-tax items (see page 144). All goods had to be transported to Houayxay's port in Chiang Khong's cross-river boats and loaded into the larger cargo boats under the watchful eyes of the Lao customs officers who were making a special effort to appear vigilant. Of course, *khiw* revenues jumped dramatically with combined daily takings over 10,000 *baht* a common occurrence. The *Association* members where delighted, though there was some discomfort and embarrassment that they were profiting so much at the expense of the Lao traders and incredulity that the traders were put in this position by their own government officials. There was also concern that, with significant congestion and delays at the port, there may be increased pressure from traders and shopkeepers to ease the restrictive practices of the *Association*. Soon after, they reduced their freight charges by almost 20 per cent and *Association* boats from outside the relevant *khiw* were regularly mobilised on busy days. The action of the Lao customs officers provided windfall profits for the *Association* members but it also placed their restrictive system under some pressure.

In late 1996, when I made a brief follow-up visit to Chiang Khong, some subtle adjustments seemed to be taking place in the relationship between the *Association's* authority and state authority. Most striking was the Thai navy's establishment of a river patrol unit in Chiang Khong and the construction of a small navy dock about 50 metres upstream from the boat operators' sheds. Suddenly, late night returns from fishing expeditions or assignations in Houayxay were a risky business, with stories of one "innocent" boat being shot at and sunk when it was suspected of smuggling (the border is officially closed between five in the evening and eight in the morning). Some operators lamented that when they tried to walk home along the river-bank they were abruptly turned away by armed soldiers, and many of the operators seemed less keen to sit around at the port at night and drink. A second change was the state-funded river-bank works which were gradually progressing downstream, covering the overgrown banks with concrete steps. The operators predicted that their stretch of the bank would be covered in a year or so and, while they would not be displaced, much of the natural charm of the scene would be lost. Thirdly, the state had funded a large new cargo port in the village of Hua Wiang. Although the port was still not being used, the operators were concerned that future relocation may bring them into conflict with their rivals – Hua Wiang's passenger boat operators. Others reassured themselves with the thought that the new port would serve only the anticipated river trade with China and that the relatively small-scale Thai-Lao trade would continue to pass through Wat Luang's port. Finally, there were reports that Lao immigration police in Houayxay were now less cooperative, restricting the extent to which boat operators could get involved in petty trade.

In brief, it appears that a period of readjustment is occurring, characterised by stricter, rather than more lenient, state regulation. No doubt, new forms of collaboration will emerge and there were already some compensating factors. For example, Lao officials were still placing strict limits on Lao boats crossing to Chiang Khong – meaning business was still booming – and the *Association* had even succeeded in restoring cargo fees to the 1994 levels. Others thought that the paving of the river-bank would provide opportunities for small-scale tourist enterprises, as Thais and Westerners flocked to the river to enjoy balmy evenings eating and drinking and hiring boat operators for mini-cruises up and down the river (as they do in Chiang Saen). Even the river patrol unit had its advantages, with the increased risk driving up the price of out-of-hours transport across to Houayxay. Yet there is no denying the concern and uncertainty. It may well be a coincidence, but it is significant to note that, during 1996, the small spirit shrine on the rocky outcrop at the far end of the port was relocated to a pedestal next to the boat operators' shed. *Association* members said that it had been moved to prevent it being flooded in the rainy season, but by

Plate 1 Houayxay in the 1890s (Pavie 1906: 348)

Plate 2 The French Agency at Chiang Khong (Lefèvre-Pontalis 1902: 96)

Plate 3 The cargo port at Chiang Khong

Plate 4 Cars stranded near the Chinese border

Plate 5 The road from Houayxay to Louangnamtha

Plate 6 The morning arrival at Houayxay's port

Plate 7 Port labourers launching a boat after repairs

Plate 8 *Maz* trucks waiting for customs inspection near the Chinese border

Plate 9 Cargo boats and Chinese trucks at Pakbeng port

Plate 10 Traders with their cargo on the boat trip to Pakbeng

Plate 11 Unloading cargo at the Oudomxai market

Plate 12 Pakbeng sawmill under construction

Plate 13 Timber from Louangnamtha being loaded at Pakbeng port

mid-November, when the river level had dropped significantly, no attempt had been made to return it. I also detected a much more rigid and defensive feeling in the *Association*, with significantly less tolerance than before of those who breached formal or informal rules. Finally, the threats to the boat operators' authority may also account for a number of unusually public instances of violence against trader wives. With Lao immigration police placing some limits on the trading activities of boat operators, they were suddenly more openly dependant on the commercial abilities of their wives. Some seemed to have difficulty dealing with this.

Conclusion: Collaborative Borders

The activities of Chiang Khong's cross-river boat operators provide a number of insights into the nature of national borders. First, they show that borders can be characterised by mobility, passage and exchange *in conjunction with* an array of demarcating and regulating practices. The boat operators' constant journeys between the port at Wat Luang and the cargo and passenger ports on the opposite, Lao, bank are typical of the social and commercial interactions that flourish as people seek to exploit and explore the nooks and crannies that borders create. Common images of borders as dividing barriers, walls or fences are undoubtedly appropriate in some situations but they need to be supplemented with images of borders as spatial lenses – attracting, permitting and even encouraging passage while also focusing, transforming and redirecting it. What this suggests is that the commonly noted porosity of national borders may not be a sign of their decreasing importance, but, on the contrary, of their efflorescence. As the Economic Quadrangle borders are reopened for trade and passage, customs officers, immigration police and unofficial regulators and controllers – like Chiang Khong's boat operators – spring into action. The "global flows" of the post-modern era may indeed be "challenging boundaries" as Shapiro and Alker (1996) suggest, but they also provide a myriad of new opportunities for profitable regulation in the borderlands.

Second, the regulating activities of the cross-river boat operators show that members of frontier communities can be active participants in the creation and maintenance of borders. In the "imagined communities" of maps, museums and monuments (Anderson 1991), borders can take on a stark and intrusive simplicity, but in the mud of the borderlands the local micro-geometries of regulation start to come into view. It is the active participation of frontier communities that gives borders their intricately woven and locally specific character – rich with intrigue, struggle, scandal and sex. I have no doubt that subversion and resistance is also present, but it is only one part of the story and one in which divisions and alliances *within* frontier communities are inseparable from the relationship *between*

111

frontier communities and the state. This micro-sociology of borders can be obscured by a perspective that portrays borders as externally imposed and as disruptive of local practices.

Third, the boat operators on the Mekong show that there are complex and subtle collaborations between local initiative and state power. It is easy to be dazzled by the symbols of state power at the border – immigration posts, flags, boom gates, tight trousers and guns – but these are often integrated into, and support, local landscapes of power. Moreover, state officials on the borderline – while often outsiders – are not robotic agents of a hegemonic state. They are embedded – often quite literally – in the social networks of frontier communities and are busy doing deals, making compromises and extracting favours. Their coercion and harassment can, indeed, be bitterly resented but their presence also creates opportunities for profit and legitimacy. Chiang Khong's boat operators are by no means alone in manipulating these shifting opportunities to reinforce local sources of authority.

These three observations do not fit easily within a framework that draws a strong distinction between inner-oriented, bounding and repressive states and outer-oriented, recalcitrant borderlanders. They suggest national borders which are more idiosyncratic, more locally specific and more collaborative than the violently and arbitrarily imposed border practices that pre-occupy the contemporary critics of state power. I have no argument with their attempts to challenge nationalist discourses of territory, citizenship and sovereignty or to expose the historically contingent nature of contemporary borderlines. But I do question their insistence that national borders are an initiative of hegemonic state power imposed on unwilling local communities. This is both historically dubious – an issue explored in chapter 2 – and, more importantly, it represents a refusal to engage seriously with the spatial practices of the borderlands. There is surely a danger that, in our current celebration of transgression and de-territorialisation, we blind ourselves to the lives of those who actively and willingly participate in practices of regulation and demarcation. Some may find the collaborative activities of the *khoji* disconcerting – a nomad working with border police in the sandhills of India – but to dismiss it as ironic is to assign a singularity to borders that does no justice to the varied and intriguing lives that are lived along them.

CHAPTER FIVE

Restricted Access

Carrying Cargo in the Borderlands

Introduction: Independence and Regulation

Long-distance transport operators – especially truckers – are often renowned for their vigorous independence and resistance to state authority. In a study of American trucking, Agar neatly summarises widely-held perceptions of the modern highway cowboys:

> The independent trucker ... operates without social ties, moving through challenging situations with a quiet self-reliance born of competence at what he does. He is the ultimate entrepreneur in the free market, working for whom he pleases when he pleases and making good money in the process. (Agar 1986: 11)

In Thailand, trucking independence has more negative connotations, but the emphasis on self reliance and the absence of social constraints is equally striking. "There is a general belief that truckers are constantly under the influence of amphetamines and alcohol," one report notes, "which this study finds to be the case" (Yothin and Pimonpan 1991: viii). Allegedly anti-social, reckless and mobile life-styles have positioned Thai truckers as an infamous high-risk group for both motor vehicle accidents and the transmission of the HIV virus (Yothin and Pimonpan 1991). And, in a recent study in the borderlands of Burma, Porter (1997: 228–229) has written of truckers' avoidance of the "conscription of vehicles," "unofficial taxation" and other "stabilising and bounding" practices of the state. "[H]ere is a comparatively durable 'community', largely of men," he writes "whose identity in part is predicated on distance from the range of ways – policing, customs, taxation – through which government surveillance is maintained" (Porter 1997: 229).

Yet, as Agar (1986: 11) has persuasively demonstrated, these positive and negative images of independence and evasion often conceal the complex "webs of dependency" in which long-distance transport operators

113

are situated. Transport operators rely heavily on state investment in infrastructure, on state contracts, on road-pricing subsidies and on an array of regulatory practices that restrict the level of competition. The previous chapter analysed the interplay between the very localised activities of cross-river boat operators and the bounding and regulating practices of the state. This chapter examines transport operations on a much broader scale – long-distance truck and boat operations throughout north-western Laos – but the beneficial relationship between "independent" operators and state regulation is equally apparent. The freeing up of cross-border trade in the era of the Economic Quadrangle has provided a windfall for Lao transport operators, but there are still sufficient restrictions on cross-border mobility to keep substantial competition from the large transport fleets in China and Thailand at bay. The first half of the chapter provides an overview of long-distance truck and boat operations in the north-west, highlighting the seemingly contradictory features of *low* rates of utilisation and *high* rates of return. The second half of the chapter traces the development of the regulatory regime that has facilitated these high profits. The histories of truck and boat operations are quite different, but the beneficial interplay of liberalising and regulatory practices is equally apparent. The chapter concludes with an exploration of some of the reasons why these long-distance operators seem much less actively involved in regulatory practices than the cross-river boat operators examined in chapter 4.

Long-Distance Truck and Boat Operations

Trucking

Early in 1995, I set off in an overloaded Soviet-built truck from the river port of Pakbeng, to Oudomxai, some 140 kilometres to the north-east (Map 1.2). Crammed into the decrepit cabin there were eight of us: Lao traders taking a load of Thai rice to China and friends and relatives along for the ride. One of the traders smoked continually and, in a display of masculine camaraderie, handed lit cigarettes through the tangle of bodies to the driver. We were making the journey at night and, a little after ten, we stopped in the market town of Muanghun for a long-awaited dinner – noodle soup, turkey, rice and Chinese beer. Trader's hospitality is an occupational bonus for north-western Lao truck drivers, and our *chauffeur* would enjoy it all the way to the well-stocked Lü and Chinese restaurants in Mengla. And there were other things to look forward to in Mengla. The driver showed me a small cardboard packet with an obscene picture on it. "Chinese medicine" he told me, "one of these and your erection will last for 15 minutes." After a relaxed dinner, we headed off into the black Lao night, counting off the passing kilometres and looking forward to the dubious comfort of an Oudomxai hotel. But, around two in the morning –

just after a small roadside post told us there were only 28 kilometres to go – the inevitable happened when you load 14 tonnes into a truck registered to carry only eight. Two tires blew and we ground to a halt in the northern Lao night.

We were going nowhere. A fire was started in the middle of the road and we sat around it, huddling against the cold, trying to sleep on what was left of the bitumen laid by the Chinese almost 20 years before. Someone told stories of the war – of Moroccan soldiers who liked to eat parts of their communist victims – and of the post-war "seminars" (re-education camps) in Oudomxai where huge logs were sawn by hand. Here, in the heart of the Economic Quadrangle, we were stuck with only one spare and, what's more, we were blocking the road. A truck pulled up behind us and another group of traders nonchalantly joined us around the fire. The drivers were friends and they lay together hugging on the ground, talking quietly and occasionally exploding into laughter. Our driver seemed unconcerned by the enormous tyre bill he would face in the morning. Our remoteness from any source of whisky, food or girls was a more pressing concern. To highlight our plight, international airlines slid across the sky thousands of metres above, dragging their sound behind them and contributing to the overfly payments which are an important source of foreign revenue for Laos.

Truck driving in Laos is a slow and tedious business, typified by the unglamorous, minimally decorated and lumbering Soviet-built trucks that ply the north-western roads. The pressured schedules, amphetamine abuse, spectacular accidents and drivers fleeing the scene that characterise the industry across the border in Thailand are all notably absent in Laos. At the port in Pakbeng, where drivers wait for boatloads of Thai cargo to arrive from Chiang Khong, a scene of improvised domesticity is testament to the slow pace of trade. The drivers set up camp in the cargo trays of their empty trucks, sleeping in the cabin at night and whiling away the days playing cards, eating and sleeping on dusty straw mats laid out in the shade of their vehicles. Some squat beside their trucks, hacking at worn brake pads with machetes and draining sump oil into putrid buckets. Occasionally a truck is carefully reversed down the slippery ramp, the wheels chocked with rough blocks of wood, and muddy Mekong water splashed onto the worn and dusty paintwork. One driver who regularly called at the port had adopted a baby monkey and sometimes sat there feeding it from a bottle.

The route from Pakbeng to Oudomxai and then to Mengla, across the border in China, is the major trucking route in north-western Laos (Map 3.1). From Pakbeng to Mengla and return it is not quite 600 kilometres – a day's drive for many of the world's truckers – but the *chauffeurs* in north-western Laos would be lucky if they made the trip more than three or four times a month. Each month, they typically spend about eight days on the road, averaging speeds of little more than 20 kilometres per hour. Waiting for cargoes takes up a lot of their idle time. At Pakbeng, waits of up to ten days are not uncommon. If the prospects for a load are looking particularly bad, some trucks may return to the north empty, perhaps with a few passengers to recover some of the costs. At Boten, where the trucks wait for traders heading north to Mengla, four or five days are often spent in the muddy no-man's-land just beyond the Lao border crossing. Loading cargoes adds a few days per month; customs inspections at Nateey (just south of Boten), where officials are now insisting on unloading all incoming vehicles, can add a few days more; and breakdowns can also eat up days and nights along the road.

In early 1995, there were 86 trucks registered in north-western Laos, the majority operated by independent owner-drivers. In Oudomxai – the main trading and transport centre in the north-west – there were 41, in Louangnamtha there were 28 and in Houayxay there were 17. In Oudomxai and Louangnamtha, most of the trucks are the Soviet-built *Maz*, imported via Vietnam during the 1980s to supply state-run transport companies. The *Maz* has an official capacity of about eight tonnes, though overloading is rampant and many of the drivers proudly display massively reinforced suspension which enables them to carry up to 15 tonnes. The *Maz* trucks in Oudomxai and Louangnamtha concentrate on the main long-distance freight route between Pakbeng, Oudomxai and Mengla. Typically, they carry Thai cargo from Pakbeng to the markets in Oudomxai or Louangnamtha and then head to Boten where they wait to meet up with traders travelling to Mengla to buy Chinese goods. Many of the trucks also carry timber and forest products on their southward journeys to Pakbeng. In Houayxay the smaller *Zin* – also Soviet-built – predominate. Though these can carry only five tonnes, they are much better suited to poorly formed, narrow roads, especially the road between Houayxay and Louangnamtha.[1] *Zin* trucks also service the route between Louangnamtha and Muangsing and provide local freight transport, such as the distribution of salt from the salt-works at Boten, collection of fire-wood and forest products and distribution of goods from the port at Houayxay to local businesses.[2]

Cargo trucks from other provinces are free to operate in the north-west. Trucks from Phongsali province, in particular, operate on the route between Boten and Pakbeng. Some of these come from Muangkhoa, to the north-west of Oudomxai, and others come from Phongsali itself, transporting sawn timber across Chinese territory to Boten and then to the waiting boats at Pakbeng (Map 1.2). Trucks from Phonsavan and

---

1 Some *Maz* also operate on this route, but they are limited to only seven or eight tonnes.
2 Small-scale freight transport is also provided by the ubiquitous pick-ups (typically *Toyota Hilux*) that carry passengers throughout the north-west.

Xamnua (Map 1.3) also travel to Pakbeng and Oudomxai to collect cargoes of imported goods from Chiang Khong. Finally, trucks from Louangphabang, Vientiane and provinces further south are a common sight at Boten and Mengla, involved in the cross-border trade with China. Most of these, however, return direct to the south via Louangphabang and do not operate on the north-western routes to Pakbeng or Houayxay.

Despite some competition from trucks based in other provinces – and the inconvenience and rigours of life on the road – truck driving in the north-west is widely regarded as a good way to earn a living. Truck drivers rarely express any desire to get out of the business. Truck sales are rare and only a very small proportion of sales involve drivers abandoning trucking altogether. Most drivers who sell do so to upgrade to a truck in better condition. Provincial officials indicated that most truck sales take place within a relatively narrow range of relatives, friends and commercial contacts. This tightly constrained market is reflected in the significant increase in the value of trucks, despite their substantial deterioration. In 1991, *Maz* trucks were sold for between three and five million *kip*, whereas the standard 1995 selling price for a truck in reasonable condition was around ten million *kip*, with prices further afield – in Vientiane for example – ranging between 12 and 15 million *kip*.

Examination of the finances of truck operation casts some light on drivers' reluctance to sell and on the substantial increase in the value of the trucks. Officials from the *Department of Transport* suggested that freight rates average about 50 *kip* per tonne kilometre, a figure they consider to be a very good rate of return. However, the data I collected point to much better rates, ranging from 69 *kip* per tonne kilometre on the popular Pakbeng to Oudomxai route to just above 80 *kip* on the long journeys to Xamnua and Phonsavan (where return loads are unlikely) to over 150 *kip* on the rugged and hazardous journey from Houayxay to Louangnamtha. The main costs for truck drivers are fuel, spare parts (especially tyres, given the bad road surfaces and overloading), and an array of official and unofficial fees and charges. I estimate that average costs amount to some 40 *kip* per tonne kilometre, a figure broadly consistent with other studies undertaken in Laos.[3] Table 5.1 summarises monthly revenue and costs for a "typical" truck operation between Pakbeng and Mengla.

By Lao standards, where monthly wage rates are estimated to be between 15,000 and 20,000 (Vokes and Fabella 1995: Table 7), an income exceeding 300,000 *kip* is extraordinary (though some of the successful boat operators and traders earn substantially more). Some truck drivers have been able to use this income as a pathway into wholesale trading – employing drivers to operate their trucks for them – while others have built up small fleets of trucks, though this is rare due to the extreme reluctance of most

---

3 TecnEcon Asia Pacific (1994: Part 2) and SWECO (1990: 27.7).

Table 5.1 Revenue and costs for three return truck (*Maz*) trips between Pakbeng and Mengla

Revenue (kip)		Costs (kip)	
Pakbeng-Oudomxai	300,000	Fuel and oil	450,000
Mengla-Pakbeng	750,000	Tyres	100,000
		Registration	18,000
		Fees/charges	80,000
		Maintenance	50,000
Total	1,050,000	Total	698,000
		Profit	352,000

Source: Fieldwork 1994–1995, 1996.
Notes: The table assumes three journeys per month, with cargo carried from Pakbeng to Oudomxai on the northward journey (in fact, trucks often carry loads to Louangnamtha and, occasionally, to Mengla itself) and from Mengla to Pakbeng on the southward journey. Average revenue per tonne kilometre in this case is about 61 *kip* (assuming average loads of ten tonnes) – a lower figure than indicated above given the amount of "empty running" assumed between Oudomxai and Mengla. Depreciation has not been included as a cost since trucks are, in fact, an appreciating asset. Cost per tonne kilometres is 40 *kip*. Figures are estimates only, based on a wide range of – sometimes contradictory – data collected during fieldwork.

drivers to sell. A very small number of drivers have acquired expensive Japanese trucks from Thailand. Drivers are also able to acquire expensive consumer durables – such as washing machines, stereos, televisions and satellite dishes – on their trips to Mengla and others have been able to fund home improvements and expand family land holdings. However, there are two important factors that mitigate against truck-driver affluence.

First, and most important, most drivers relied heavily on informal credit when they purchased their trucks in the early 1990s, and their trucking income now supports a network of family and friends who contributed to the purchase. Relatives are often employed by truck owners to assist with repairs, watch over the truck when the owner is absent and to help traders with loading and unloading. Second, the slow pace of trade provides numerous opportunities for idle, bored and restless truck drivers to waste money. Regular sustenance and accommodation costs are minimal – most drivers sleep in their trucks and prepare food on rough camp fires when they are not being "shouted" to meals by traders – but there are many chances to waste money playing snooker, drinking whisky, gambling and pursuing sexual adventures. The truck stops in Laos are not characterised by the blatant prostitution prevalent in Thailand (Yothin and Pimonpan 1991), but there are many small restaurants, hotels and *karaoke* bars where sexual services can be negotiated if enough time – and money – is spent. The boundaries between commercial and non-commercial sex are very blurred in Laos, and truckers also have a reputation for maintaining "minor wives" in the various towns on the trucking network. In Mengla, the commercial sex industry is much more obvious and, at the area designated for Lao truckers, the evening brings a steady flow of garishly dressed young women who, the drivers told me, charge according to their looks. The wives of truck drivers recognise the financial (and health) risks of their husbands' relaxed itineraries and a number travel with their husbands to provide companionship and supervision, arguing that this is a sound economy measure.

Cargo boats

Driving cargo boats along the Mekong is a hazardous business that requires extraordinary skill and concentration. In the wet season, the broad stretch of brown water conceals an array of rocks, rapids and sandbars which, every year, claim a vessel or two between Houayxay and Louangphabang – traders, passengers and crew drowned, trapped between the floating cargo and the roof of the boat. There are almost no navigation markers and the boat drivers rely heavily on their memory, using landmarks on the banks to guide them through the meandering channel. In the dry season the channel is much clearer, but sometimes almost impossibly narrow. As men frantically wrestle with cumbersome steering wheels, 80–tonne boats squeeze their way around the rocky outcrops with literally metres to spare. The balls of sticky-rice cast into the river, by way of offering, do little to subdue the palpable tension. "Driving a boat is hard," a young boat owner from Pakbeng told me, "because you don't have a brake."

In early 1995, there were 55 cargo boats (over seven tonnes) registered in the north-western provinces of Bokeo (36) and Oudomxai (19).[4] There were also a small number based in the Special Region. Despite having several small Mekong River ports, Louangnamtha province has no registered cargo boats, an indication of the low level of river traffic upstream from Muangmom (see page 81). Boats from Louangphabang also concentrate on the upper-Mekong route due to the lack of downstream traffic to Vientiane. Boats from Xaignabouli and Vientiane are also a common sight in the north-west, attracted by the lucrative timber trade. Almost all of the boats are privately owned by individual owner-operators, with the owners either driving the boats themselves or employing specialist drivers. Most of the owners are men, but their wives (and children) often travel on the boats with them and play an active role in managing the operations of the boat, though almost never driving. As with cargo trucks, there is almost no concentration in ownership of boats and I only encountered one example where two boats were owned by a single operator, and even he seemed keen to sell one of them.

---

4 The registration figures probably overstate the number of boats actually in use. Many boats are registered but appear to lie idle for much of the year.

The Lao cargo boats are roughly categorised according to their size: small (up to about ten tonnes), medium (ten to 30 tonnes) and large (30 to 80 tonnes). I estimate that approximately half the boats regularly involved in long-distance cargo transport on the upper-Mekong fall within the medium category, with the balance evenly divided between small and large boats. The large boats carry approximately 60 per cent of the freight traffic and the medium boats almost 40 per cent, with a minimal contribution made by the small boats.

The small and medium cargo boats – all of which are made of wood in towns and villages along the Mekong – are of a similar design. They have a cabin running the full length of the hull, with a steering wheel at the front and the engine mounted towards the rear.[5] Most of the boats have a separate driver's cabin partitioned off at the front, doubling as a sleeping area for the owner and his family. Sleeping areas for the crew and cooking facilities are located at the rear just behind the engine. At the very back there is a small toilet and washing area, extending beyond the hull and suspended over the water. Cargo is loaded into the hull through wide "doors" in the cabin. Excess cargo is loaded on top. Often the small boats double as passenger vessels, though those used regularly for passengers usually have rough wooden benches fitted and a series of windows along the sides of the cabin to provide ventilation. The small and medium sized boats are relatively cheap, with purchase prices for boats of around 20 tonnes said to be about six million *kip*. However, many of the quoted prices were some years old and there is a widespread view that government restrictions on independent timber felling and processing have reduced the level of boat construction and substantially increased the current prices of new boats.

Some of the large cargo boats also have full-length cabins, though the sides are usually opened out to allow timber and other bulky cargo to be loaded. The driver's cabin is raised well above the hull with a small set of stairs leading to it. Sleeping and living areas at the rear are much more spacious and comfortable than on the small and medium boats. However, the most common design for the large vessels is for the cabin to be located at the rear of the boat with a large open hull in front. The steering wheel, sleeping quarters for the owner and an open verandah are located in the upper section of the cabin with crew sleeping areas, kitchen and toilet located below. The engine is mounted in the hull, just in front of the two-storey cabin. About half of the large boats now have metal hulls and some also have a metal superstructure. The percentage of metal boats is set to increase now that it is no longer economically viable to build large boats from wood.[6] Up until 1995, all metal boats were built in a boat-yard on the

---

5 The steering wheel is connected to the rudder at the rear via long chains running down the sides of the boat.

6 This is a relatively recent development. In 1987 there were only seven metal boats in Laos (SWECO 1990: 16.27).

outskirts of Vientiane but, in 1996, a boat-building operation was established in Chiang Khong. The larger metal boats now cost up to 40 million *kip*.

Like the cargo trucks, upper-Mekong cargo boats have low rates of utilisation, most averaging about one return trip per month between Houayxay and Pakbeng or Louangphabang. Cruising time to Pakbeng is one full day, with the upstream journey taking about one and a half days. Travel times to and from Louangphabang are about double this. The bulk of the time, then, is not spent on the river but waiting for cargo, loading/ unloading and customs processing. Time spent waiting for cargo varies considerably, but waits of four to five days at Houayxay and Pakbeng are commonly reported. Often there is a mismatch between supply and demand at the different ports with, for example, traders unable to secure boats at Houayxay while there are many boats waiting for cargoes at Pakbeng. Most loading and unloading is done by teams of labourers who work at the various ports, carrying cargo across narrow wooden planks, clambering down muddy slopes and climbing across other boats that are moored in the way. The labourers at Chiang Khong are regarded as fast and strong but the Lao labourers at Houayxay and Pakbeng are much slower. At Chiang Khong loading usually takes about two days, though much longer loading times are experienced when there are delays in the delivery of goods from Chiang Rai and other towns in northern Thailand. Unloading at Pakbeng is prolonged by the traders who share the boat sorting their goods into the waiting trucks, carefully counting the boxes as they leave the boat. There is no warehouse at the port and, on the rare occasions that trucks are not available, the cargo has to be stored on the boat. Loading and unloading timber takes even longer, especially off-cuts and poor quality timber that is cut into small planks.

Processing of cargoes by Lao customs also causes lengthy delays. After loading at Chiang Khong, the boats cross to Houayxay where they often wait for two or three days while lengthy negotiations are held between customs officials and traders (see page 144). Boats coming up river with timber and forest products also have to berth at Houayxay for several days, waiting for export paperwork to be completed, before they can cross to Chiang Khong and unload. One boat owner told me that he had been stuck with a load of bark-fibre at Houayxay for three weeks while the trading company sorted out the export paperwork. Customs inspections are also undertaken at Paktha. These usually only take a few hours but they often prevent the boats from reaching their destination by nightfall. Boats travelling to Louangphabang also have to report to customs and police at Pakbeng.

Freight rates charged by the boat operators are based on tonnage and volume and do not usually reflect the time taken to complete the journey. The rates are negotiated between the boat owners and the traders.

Generally, rates for transport of cargo between Chiang Khong and Pakbeng are in the vicinity of 10,000 *kip* per tonne though there is substantial variation and I recorded rates ranging from 6,000 *kip* to 14,000 *kip*.[7] Factors influencing the rate include the volume of the cargo (higher tonnage rates for high volume cargoes), the size of the boat (higher tonnage rates in smaller boats) and the nature of the relationship between the boat operator and the traders (rates for neighbours, relatives or close friends may be discounted). This latter factor also affects the range of services provided by the boat owner: when there is a close relationship traders often sleep and eat on the boat and the boys who work on the boat assist with loading and unloading. Boat operators also face an array of costs, with fuel predominating. Details are set out in Table 5.2.

The profit figures in Table 5.2 confirm that long-distance transport operations in north-western Laos can be very profitable enterprises. They cast some doubt on the negative assessments in the 1990 *Lao National*

Table 5.2 Revenue and costs for one return boat trip between Houayxay and Pakbeng

	25 tonne	*60 tonne*	*80 tonne*
Revenue (*kip*)			
Houayxay-Pakbeng	250,000	500,000	700,000
Pakbeng-Houayxay	250,000	600,000	800,000
Total revenue	500,000	1,100,000	1, 500,000
Costs (*kip*)			
Fuel and oil	120,000	250,000	350,000
Wages	30,000	75,000	90,000
Registration	24,000	38,000	38,000
Fees and charges	30,000	45,000	60,000
Maintenance	40,000	60,000	80,000
Total costs	244,000	468,000	618,000
Profit	256,000	632,000	882,000

Source: Fieldwork 1994–1995, 1996.
Notes: Typically, downstream cargoes are made up of Thai merchandise purchased at Chiang Khong, while upstream cargoes are mainly forest products (especially in the smaller boats), logs and sawn timber. Revenue figures assume 10,000 *kip* per tonne with some under-loading in the larger boats. Figures are estimates only, based on a wide range of – sometimes contradictory – data collected during fieldwork.

---

7 Upstream rates for the transport of sawn timber are more standardised – usually 12,000 *kip* per cubic metre (roughly one tonne) from Pakbeng to Chiang Khong-Houayxay – though some boat owners told me that they received 13,500 *kip*. Rates for the transport of logs, at 21,000 *kip* per cubic metre, are substantially higher, probably due to the difficulty, and danger, of loading and unloading.

Transport Study which identified cargo-boat over-capacity as a major problem and urged that the fleet be reduced through natural attrition – "bankruptcies should be accepted" – and encouragement of alternative ventures (SWECO 1990: 46.4). Though rates of utilisation are low, rates of return appear to be very good. Since 1990, capacity on the upper-Mekong has, in fact, increased substantially and I met very few operators who expressed any desire to get out of the industry.[8]

The revenue from the larger (60 to 80–tonne) boats is exceptionally good, and it is the dream of many small and medium boat operators to purchase a large metal boat and achieve the comfortable lifestyles that the large boat owners are said to enjoy. Khampheng, the owner of a 30–tonne boat, regularly spoke of his desire to upgrade to an 80–tonne metal boat and concentrate on hauling timber for the new sawmill at Pakkhop (Map 1.2), where he has a relative in a management position. He was confident that the cost of a larger boat could be paid for in only two years, but lacked access to credit to finance the purchase. When I returned in late 1996, Khampheng had not achieved his dream, but some of the large boat operators had upgraded to even larger boats: one had bought a 120–tonne boat in Vientiane for almost 40 million *kip*. His wife was appalled at the cost, but even she acknowledged that they would be able to pay it off in only three years. Another large boat operator – getting around now in a smart white shirt and trousers – was purchasing two large boats from the new boat building enterprise in Chiang Khong. At the 1996 boat-racing festivities in Houayxay, his boat served as a floating viewing platform, complete with amplified music, a rustic dance floor, drinks and even monks who crouched above the carnival scene on a narrow ledge in front of the driver's cabin. Later that evening, he and a group of friends covered their table with empty bottles of beer and *Johnnie Walker* whisky – at 28,000 kip per bottle – conspicuously "sponsoring" songs played by the western-style band. One of his fellow boat owners became so involved in the occasion that he soiled his trousers.

Even the more modest income from the 25–tonne boat is an excellent income by northern Lao standards. Many boat owners of this scale are in a better position than truck drivers on comparable incomes because local construction has ensured a good supply of boats of different sizes and conditions, enabling operators to consolidate their position in the industry gradually without incurring substantial debts. In fact, a number of these operators have built their own boats – while working as government officials, school teachers or traders – gradually purchasing the timber as they could afford it. Smaller boat operators also have more flexibility than the larger operators, being able to carry cargo on the relatively unnavigable sections above Houayxay. Time spent waiting for downstream cargo at

---

8 For some comparable comments on private boat operations in China, see Taplin (1993: 77).

Houayxay can occasionally be filled by a short and lucrative run up river to Muangmom (see page 75).

Of course, there are also financial threats for boat operators. Navigation conditions on the Mekong are hazardous and a number of boats are lost each year. None of the boat operators I knew had effective insurance cover, and these accidents can drive operators out of the industry altogether. One unfortunate operator I knew also had to endure a two year prison term following legal action by sawmill owners whose equipment was lost in the Mekong rapids. Less catastrophic, but still financially significant, is the relatively rapid depreciation of the boats. Most of the wooden boats have an effective life of about ten years (though there are some notable exceptions) amounting to an annual depreciation cost of around 500,000 *kip*. The metal boats are expected to have a much longer life – perhaps up to 30 years – though their much higher purchase price suggests an annual depreciation cost of around one million *kip*. Few operators seem to make conscious provision for depreciation costs, however replacement boats are often bought with gold (or other assets) that have been acquired from the profits of cargo operations. Given the high "display value" of objects such as gold – many of the operators and their wives wear extraordinarily thick gold chains – this indirect provision for depreciation costs is transformed into a marker of an affluent and successful lifestyle.

To summarise, both truck and boat operations in north-western Laos are characterised by low rates of utilisation but high rates of return. Low utilisation arises out of the relatively low level of trade, but is compounded by the poor state of infrastructure, labour-intensive cargo handling and regular bureaucratic intervention. In the following section the context of this bureaucratic regulation is examined in more detail. While the state is an annoying constraint for transport operators, it is, at the same time, an important contributor to the regulatory environment in which they have prospered.

Long-Distance Transport and the State

Khamphouey Chantalangsi is responsible for transport regulation in Oudomxai province. One wet and sticky afternoon I went to ask him for statistics about cargo truck and boat operations. His office – tucked away in one corner of an old and unnaturally dim concrete building – contained two desks covered with cheap Chinese cloth. One desk, with a roll of barbed wire stored beneath it, seemed to be unused. On the wall behind it, a large sheet of paper displayed three hand-written English sentences: "are dreams real or only imaginary;" "there is no place like home" and "real love never runs smooth." The "o" in "love" was written in the shape of a heart. On Khampouey's desk there was a black clipboard and a pink plastic folder crammed with documents, many with multiple carbon copies. He referred to these documents often and unproductively. Occasionally, and with considerable reluctance, he also burrowed into a tall wooden cupboard filled with folders that got thicker, yellower and more confused towards the bottom. Some of the windows in the office were boarded up. Outside the door, the sound of a typewriter slowly reverberated against the concrete walls. Khampouey's secretary sat alone, surrounded by scraps of number plate metal, cobwebs and yet more abandoned files. My visit was only moderately successful.

In assessing the role of the state in north-western Lao transport operations it would be wrong to place too much emphasis on this superficial atmosphere of bureaucratic lethargy. Outside the desultory offices of transport regulation, the state is a constant and intrusive presence in the lives of the transport operators of north-western Laos. There is no clearer sign of this presence that the regular collection of numerous state-imposed access fees and service charges. To load goods at Houayxay, the local truck drivers have to pay between 600 and 900 *kip* each time they make their way down the concrete ramp to the boats waiting at the bottom. At the Pakbeng port, the drivers must pay 1,000 *kip*; at the Oudomxai market, 3,000 *kip*; on the provincial border crossing between Oudomxai and Louangnamtha, 1,500 *kip* for a rubber stamp; and to cross into China, 10,000 *kip* to the Boten police, and another thousand or so to the Chinese officials a few kilometres up the road.[9] Registration fees and road taxes are paid less regularly, the rates often settled upon by a process of negotiation between truck owners and provincial regulators like Khamphouey. Boat operators are similarly affected: port fees at Houayxay, Pakbeng and Louangphabang; payments for papers to be stamped at the major ports and at the inspection point at Paktha; payments of several hundred *baht* to Thai customs officers and immigration police in Chiang Khong; and hefty registration fees. For both truck and boat operators, many of the fees are individually trivial, but together they add up to a substantial and much-resented operating cost. Moreover, the regimes of collection, combined with the close supervision of trading operations by customs staff, result in innumerable delays. After several days of form filling and bribes in Houayxay, one boat owner could no longer contain his frustration. "Nowhere in Laos is this bad," he said, "nowhere in the world, Bokeo is the worst!"

Yet the relationship between these long-distance transport operators and the state is characterised by a fundamental "dilemma of independence," to use a term from Agar's (1986) study of American truckers. While the regulation of the state is resented, and where possible avoided, these transport operators are heavily dependant on the state to maintain

---

9 Drivers from Oudomxai province complain bitterly about the 10,000 *kip* collected at Boten. The border crossing falls within Louangnamtha province and drivers from that province are exempt from the fee.

125

the viability of their profitable enterprises. They have benefited from the NEM policies encouraging cross-border trade and private sector participation in distribution systems but, at the same time, they continue to benefit from regulatory mechanisms that shield them from external competition. The connections north-western Laos has with other places have been managed in a way that places its long-distance transport operators in a strategically advantageous position. The historical development of this intertwining of operator viability and state power is explored in the next two sections.

Trucking and the windfall of privatisation

Prior to 1991, truck operations in Laos – like many other sectors of the economy – were under the control of state-owned companies.[10] Private operations were tolerated but cheap trucks and subsidised fuel were only available to the state enterprises, and provincial authorities controlled the allocation of most cargo. In the north-west, there were three state-owned companies based in the main centres of Houayxay, Louangnamtha and Oudomxai. When these companies were formed in 1978, the truck fleets comprised mostly Soviet and Chinese vehicles left over from the war. In Houayxay, vehicles abandoned by businesses who fled to Thailand after the Pathet Lao victory in 1975 were confiscated by provincial authorities. By 1984, Oudomxai's company was the largest, owning a total of 32 trucks. In Louangnamtha there were about 20 trucks while in Houayxay, completely cut-off by road in the wet season, there were only eight. In 1984, and again in 1989, the fleets were updated with the import of new Soviet-built *Zin* and *Maz* trucks via Vietnam.[11] Many of these trucks continue to service north-western Lao trade.

With the Chinese and Thai borders closed, trucks in Oudomxai and Louangnamtha maintained the east-west trading life-line with Vietnam, using roads built by the Chinese and Vietnamese during the 1960s and 1970s (Map 2.3). When restrictions on inter-provincial trade were relaxed – and finally abolished in 1988 – trucks from Oudomxai and Louangnamtha could travel further afield, often making trips to southern provinces to collect rice and agricultural products to support the northern towns. A few years later, the Chinese border opened for trade, though Lao trucks were not permitted to enter China and had to transfer goods at the border crossing at Boten. The trucks based in Houayxay were much less mobile than those in Oudomxai and Louangnamtha. They were limited to dry season journeys to Louangnamtha and local journeys on the

10 It is estimated that about 800 state enterprises were created during the 1970s and 1980s "in all sectors of the economy" (Vokes and Fabella 1995: 64).

11 In Houayxay six of the eight trucks operated by the state company were *Zin* whereas in Oudomxai and Louangnamtha the numbers of *Maz* and *Zin* were equal.

rudimentary road system close to the Mekong. Given the bad state of the roads, the performance of the small Houayxay fleet was very poor.

In the first half of the 1980s, the truck fleets in the north-west operated as part of a national network, administered through the provincial offices of the *Department of Transport*. As with state enterprises throughout Laos, they were subject to strict central control. However around 1987, as part of the NEM, ownership of the vehicles was transferred to the provinces and the transport firms became independent provincial entities responsible for their own planning, budgeting and rate setting (SWECO 1990: 14.2). In 1990, the government decided to privatise many state enterprises in response to their ongoing poor performance and to encourage private sector participation in the economy (GLPDR 1990a).[12] Despite some initial reluctance to sell off strategically important transport enterprises, the trucks in the north-west were sold to their drivers in 1991. The larger *Maz* trucks were sold for between four and five million *kip*, though the price in Oudomxai was somewhat lower at about 3.5 million *kip*, probably due to the greater use and deterioration of the fleet there. The *Zin* were sold for two million *kip*, and a few recently purchased *Hino* trucks were sold for six million *kip* each. Given their very low salaries, few drivers could afford to buy the trucks on their own and most relied heavily on informal credit provided by friends and relatives. Most of the trucks were sold for cash, though in Louangnamtha a few drivers took over the repayments for trucks that the provincial company had bought with credit from the northern Lao branch of the state bank.[13]

The drivers who were able to enter the private trucking industry at this stage have occupied a privileged position. Not only were they able to acquire the trucks for relatively low prices – a result of the poor performance of the state trucking companies and close interpersonal relationships between provincial managers and drivers – but they also achieved a virtual monopoly on trucking operations. In developing countries, trucks are often a popular line of investment for fledgling entrepreneurs[14] – especially with increasing levels of trade – but, in Laos, domestic and international factors have placed severe restrictions on further industry expansion.

The most important restriction has been the supply of trucks themselves. With the cessation of trade and aid arrangements with the

---

12 For further information on the privatisation program in Laos, see Ljunggren (1992: 94–97); Daniel (1994); and Vokes and Fabella (1995: 64–83).

13 State operation of trucks is now limited to a small fleet of fuel tankers that carry fuel from the port at Pakbeng to Oudomxai and Louangnamtha. It is rumoured that the *Lao State Fuel Company* still holds 20 tankers in reserve in Oudomxai in case fuel supplies from Thailand (through Chiang Khong) are ever interrupted. There is also a private company – *Huakhong* – that operates three tankers as part of its fuel distribution contract.

14 See, for example, Rimmer (1974: 307); Evans (1991a: 108); Kingshill (1991: 28); Taplin (1993: 77); and Addus (1989: 427).

Soviet Union, no new trucks have been imported since the late 1980s, though engines and spare parts for the refurbishment of old vehicles can still be obtained in Vietnam. Most of the recent additions to the truck fleet in the north-west have come from Vientiane or towns in southern Laos, where prices have increased even more rapidly than in the north-west.

Purchase of trucks in Thailand is not a viable option, given the very high price of even second-hand vehicles, compounded by Lao import duties. There have also been, at various times, government restrictions placed on the import and use of right-hand-drive vehicles from Thailand – forcing expensive modifications – and also occasional bans on the import of second-hand vehicles altogether. I met only one truck operator who had bought a vehicle in Thailand, paying 40 million *kip* for a second-hand *Mitsubishi* with the profits from his trading ventures between Chiang Khong and Phonsavan (Map 1.3). Affordability aside, most drivers in the north-west regard the Japanese vehicles that are available in Thailand as unsuitable for the rugged and mountainous conditions in Laos. Compared to the Soviet trucks, their engines are less powerful, they carry less weight and their body work is not up to the rough conditions of Lao roads. Sitting among the trucks parked in the market at Mengla one evening, this point was underlined for me by a driver who knocked on the panel work of a *Hino* that had just pulled in from Louangnamtha. He compared its tinny sound unfavourably with the deep metallic thud that issued from the Soviet *Maz* parked next to it. Chinese trucks are somewhat better suited to Lao conditions, however, while not as expensive as trucks in Thailand, price is still an almost insurmountable barrier. I did not meet any cargo truck operators who had bought their vehicles in China, though a small number of pick-up operators had acquired two-tonne Chinese trucks, carrying small freight as well as passengers. As TecnEcon (1994: 1) recently concluded: "It has been observed that little or no investment has taken place in the last three or four years, in new trucks [anywhere in Laos]. The comment from the operators has been that new vehicles are too expensive."

Given the difficulties of buying a truck, entry into the trucking industry requires ingenuity and perseverance. Wiang, a trader and boat operator in Houayxay, has used local connections to obtain a decrepit old *Nissan* operated by a nearby sawmill during the 1960s and abandoned by its Thai owner in 1975. The chassis is sound and he is gradually rebuilding it using parts purchased in Chiang Khong and Mengla and scavenged from other abandoned wrecks in Houayxay. The *Nissan* engine was beyond repair and he purchased a second-hand engine in Chiang Khong which, to his disgust, he had to completely recondition. On a trading expedition to Mengla, I accompanied him to a large truck-works where we sat and negotiated the price of a Chinese truck cabin next to a cement bust of Mao dumped unceremoniously in the company office. The truck is an oily mess in his front yard but he confidently plans to drive it on trading expeditions to China once the road from Houayxay to the border is complete.

While the limit on the supply of trucks restricts domestic competition, the large fleet across the border in China is a potent threat. Since 1993, Chinese trucks have been permitted to enter Laos and travel to the Mekong river ports at Pakbeng and Houayxay.[15] During 1994, Chinese trucks were a common sight at Pakbeng unloading goods from Mengla and Jinghong onto cargo boats for journeys to Louangphabang and Chiang Khong. In fact, it is not uncommon for the Chinese trucks at Pakbeng to outnumber the Lao trucks (I never saw any Chinese trucks in Houayxay due to the appalling road conditions from Louangnamtha). Chinese trucks also support Chinese companies involved in infrastructure projects in the north-west, transporting cement and other raw materials to road and dam construction projects in Louangnamtha and Oudomxai provinces.

However, despite a series of cross-border agreements relating to transit and trade, Lao government regulation has prevented these Chinese trucks from posing a competitive threat to the Lao truck operators. Having unloaded their cargoes in Laos, they are required to return empty across the border and are not permitted to pick up cargoes for carriage within Laos (for example, from Pakbeng to Oudomxai). This is relatively easily controlled given the presence of an official of the *Department of Transport* – and the Lao truckers themselves – at the Pakbeng port and the close supervision of vehicles crossing the border at Boten. There is undoubtedly some clandestine carriage of cargo by Chinese vehicles – at Boten I saw Lao traders surreptitiously loading their goods into the cabins of Chinese cement trucks – but the overall impact on the level of demand for Lao trucks is minimal. The restrictions on Chinese trucks contrast with the relative freedom enjoyed by Lao trucks travelling to collect cargoes in Mengla, also permitted since 1993.[16]

Thai vehicles crossing on the vehicular ferry to Houayxay are subject to even more stringent controls than the Chinese trucks entering in the north. Most trucks are restricted to the immediate vicinity of the provincial capital and rarely venture beyond the port where they unload onto Lao cargo boats. I was also told that Thai trucks will not be permitted to travel to Viangphoukha to collect lignite from the mine being developed there – Lao trucks will deliver the lignite to a depot being developed to the south of Chiang Khong. The only Thai trucks that I observed travelling beyond the township of Houayxay were those operated by the Chiang Khong-based owner of the Sin Udom sawmill, some ten kilometres downstream. In the

---

15 When they enter Laos at Boten, the Chinese trucks are required to pay an entry fee of 8,500 *kip*, regardless of their destination.

16 In Mengla, the major restriction placed on the Lao trucks is that they all park together at a designated area in the town's central market. Lao trucks are also able to cross Chinese territory travelling between Phongsali and Boten. For this they pay a transit fee of 300 *yuan*.

dry season – when the road to the sawmill was passable – they made weekly trips to collect timber before returning across the river to the large timber yard on the southern outskirts of Chiang Khong. The owner of the sawmill is also the owner of the cross-river ferry and obviously has some leverage in securing access for his trucks.

The limited supply of vehicles and the constraints on the activities of Thai and Chinese operators have been the most important factors in maintaining the privileged position of north-western Lao truckers. A third, less important, factor is the presence of truck operator associations. As early as 1983, independent trucking associations were permitted, though it is unlikely that there were any in the north-west due to the predominance of the state trucking enterprises. However, following privatisation in 1991, the newly independent owner-drivers were required to form themselves into provincial associations to coordinate the collection of data, monitor vehicle operations and prevent illegal activities. The Oudomxai association also took responsibility for coordinating truck operations at Pakbeng where trucks tend to accumulate because the southward flow of timber, forest products and Chinese merchandise is usually higher than the northward flow of Thai goods. There were reports of bitter arguments and cost-cutting in the past when the cargo-laden boats arrived from Houayxay. Now, the head of the truck operators' association – who is based in a small office overlooking the port – coordinates a *khiw* to allocate cargoes to trucks.

The operation of the *khiw* is simple but effective. When the traders arrive from Chiang Khong, they are allocated the truck at the head of the *khiw*, that is, the truck that has been waiting for the longest. There may be some negotiation between the trader and the truck driver but the freight rates are set by the association and there is not a great deal of variation. There are a number of situations where the truck at the head of the *khiw* may decline the job. It may be a low-paying journey to Muanghun – about 40 kilometres to the north – and not worth the long wait at Pakbeng. Such a job will be passed down the *khiw* until someone accepts it. The drivers who decline the job do not forfeit their position on the *khiw*. More often, it is the very long-distance jobs to towns in the north-east (Phonsavan or Xamnua) that will be declined by drivers based in the north-west. Though these are well-paying jobs, they will take them a long way from home and they are unlikely to get a return load. Accordingly, these jobs are usually taken by drivers from these towns who have travelled to Pakbeng specifically to meet traders with whom they have a regular arrangement. Sometimes traders travelling to Oudomxai, Louangnamtha or Mengla may also wish to use a specific driver – a friend or close relative – who is not at the head of the *khiw*. In this case a "fee" is paid to the association to bend the rules. Usually, the other drivers do not object. The association office also informs drivers about jobs at other locations in the north-west. Most commonly these are at sawmills who contact the office when they have a load of timber to be transported to Pakbeng. In brief, the regulation of the association helps to manage tensions at the main point in the north-western trucking system where there is oversupply.[17]

Restricted access on the Mekong

The most striking feature of cargo boat operations on the upper-Mekong is the absence of Thai vessels, despite the importance of Chiang Khong to northern Lao trade. Prior to 1975, this was not the case, and Thai cargo vessels based at Chiang Khong and Chiang Saen dominated river traffic. The origin of this dominance lay in the introduction of motors on boats during the 1930s by a number of wealthy merchants. According to Izikowitz (1979: 311), this new technology led to a shift in river trade, away from the small and relatively unnavigable Mekong tributaries towards the large surplus-producing rice plains on the Siamese side of the river. Initially, motors were used on large canoes but, during the 1940s and 1950s, larger cargo boats powered by truck engines were introduced by Chinese traders in Chiang Saen, Chiang Khong and Louangphabang (Dooley 1959: 186; Halpern 1964c: 96; Lewis 1982: 289–291). Some of the wealthier traders operated small fleets of three or four boats. There are no figures from the period but the older residents recall that there were many more Thai than Lao boats and that the largest boats were based in the Thai towns. These boats plied a busy trade between Chiang Saen and Chiang Khong-Houayxay, with less frequent trips down river to Louangphabang and, occasionally, to towns in southern Laos.

During the 1960s, Thai river boat operations on the upper-Mekong prospered. For most of the decade, the river supply-line from Chiang Saen supported the vibrant war-time economy around Houayxay (see page 56). There were often several cargo and passenger services each day. In Chiang Khong, the riverside warehouses were crowded with fuel drums and sacks of rice, waiting for transport to RLG troops further downstream in Louangphabang. For the cargo boat operators in Chiang Khong, this meant running the gauntlet of Pathet Lao positions along the river – some were sunk, others were forced to the bank and relieved of their cargo – but the high profits were worth the risk. Thai cargo boats also transported timber for the busy sawmills on the opposite bank, sometimes heading off in convoy when word came that there was a load to collect. (The Lao sawmills also provided raw material for boat-builders in Chiang Saen and Chiang Khong once the suitable wood on the Thai side of the river was exhausted.) And for some operators, there were windfall profits to be made

---

17 At Boten, waiting time for cargo is usually considerably shorter and there is no formal *khiw* operating. However, drivers told me that they have an informal arrangement amongst themselves that, in effect, operates in the same way as the *khiw* at Pakbeng.

when a load of opium had to be bought downstream from Kuomintang suppliers in north-eastern Burma.

The lives of the Thai boat operators were dramatically changed with the Thai-enforced closure of the border after the communist victory in Laos. Many returned to farming, some resorted to smuggling or local trade in Thailand and a few, who had been born in Laos, moved back to their home towns. Some of the Thai boats had been destroyed in the war, some were left to rot on the muddy river-banks at the unused ports in Chiang Saen and Chiang Khong, and others were sold, at bargain prices, to purchasers from Houayxay or Louangphabang. For the first time ever, the Lao boat operators had the river to themselves.

The new Lao government made no attempt to nationalise boat operations. Whereas the trucking sector was crucial to maintaining the trading lifeline with Vietnam, the small Lao river fleet had limited strategic importance and private boat owners were permitted to continue operating provided that they were members of operator associations. Freight rates were set by the government and, according to a *World Bank* report (1987: 3), "seem[ed] to be high enough to yield adequate profits to the individual operators." Direct state involvement in river transport on the upper-Mekong was limited to three cargo boats operated by the provincial trading company based in Houayxay.

Initially, the conditions for the Lao boat operators were not ideal. With Thai-Lao trade suspended, the Lao boats were confined to distributing rice and other agricultural products and carrying Vietnamese imports that came down the road to Pakbeng. The boat operators' association regulated the allocation of cargoes to boats, ensuring that the limited demand was evenly spread. However, the situation improved somewhat with the opening of the border market at Muangmom in 1978. On market days there was sometimes even excess demand and traders in Houayxay recall being forced to carry their purchases on their backs, on horses and on bicycles because they were unable to find places on boats.

Most Lao boat operators secured their position in this trading system through operating small boats which were suited to the low level of trade. A survey undertaken in 1986 found the average capacity of cargo vessels calling at Houayxay was 14 tonnes and only four tonnes at Pakbeng (IMC 1987: 30). Many of the current boat operators talk of starting out in this period with boats of three or four tonnes, carrying passengers as well as freight between Muangmom, Houayxay, Pakbeng and Louangphabang. Most have owned several boats over the years, steadily upgrading as they acquired more capital to invest and as the level of trade increased. The owners of two of the largest boats in Houayxay, for example, have owned six and nine boats respectively.

Niang, a boat owner in Houayxay, typifies the gradual emergence of the Lao river fleet in the absence of the Thai boats. He was taught to drive boats during the 1960s by his uncle, who was forced to seek his nephew's assistance after he lost all the fingers on one hand in an accident at a sawmill. They provided passenger services between Houayxay and Chiang Saen. After 1975, he drove boats for hire between Houayxay and Pakbeng, where he met his wife. After a few years of driving he had saved enough to buy his own boat. He invested 2,600 *baht* in a decrepit three-tonne vessel that was lying idle in Chiang Khong. He replaced many of the timbers in the hull and restored the engine before putting the boat into service travelling to the border market at Muangmom. There was a shortage of boats on market days and his income was good. He was soon in a position to upgrade, spending 15,000 *baht* on a three-tonne boat (also from Chiang Khong) in much better condition. Later, he upgraded to a ten-tonne boat and moved to Vientiane in the early 1980s to join friends in a trading venture. There, he bought a 70–tonne boat with gold that he and his wife had bought with profits from their trading and transport activities in Houayxay. Niang became involved in trading in southern Laos, a venture which failed, costing him several hundred thousand *baht*. In 1988, they returned to Houayxay and the large boat was sold to generate trading capital. Over the next few years he re-established himself as a boat operator by building his own boat. However, tragically, the boat hit rocks and sank, drowning his sister and eldest daughter. After the accident he spent time driving a passenger speedboat while he built another boat, a 30–tonne vessel which he still operates on a regular, and profitable, basis between Houayxay and Pakbeng.

By the time cross-border trade recommenced in the late 1980s, there were no cargo boats left on the Thai side of the river. Lao authorities have permitted Thai cross-river boat operations between Chiang Khong and Houayxay (chapter 4) but long-distance journeys along the river to other Lao ports are not permitted.[18] Accordingly, no attempt has been made to re-establish cargo boat operations out of Chiang Khong despite the continued residence there of many former boat operators and an active cross-river boat fleet. At least one of the Thai-owned sawmills in Laos has invested in three cargo boats to carry logs, sawn timber and heavy machinery, but these are Lao registered, probably in the names of Lao managers. A Thai firm – *MP Tours and Travel* – has also attempted to establish tourist cruise services along the river from Louangphabang into China but has not succeeded in negotiating access to Lao waters.

Chinese boats are, by contrast, permitted to travel on the Mekong within Laos but they do not represent a substantial competitive threat. At present, Chinese and Lao cargo boats concentrate on different types of trade: Chinese boats service transit trade with Thailand while the Lao

---

18 During 1994–1995 there was a single exception, a three-tonne boat based at Chiang Khong that made daily journeys to Paktha.

boats carry Thai-Lao bilateral trade. They also operate on different reaches of the river: by late 1996 the Chinese boats were only coming downstream as far as Chiang Saen, operating on the stretch of river least used by Lao operators. To date, discussions on the *Upper Mekong Navigation Agreement* (see page 82) have had little effect on the monopoly held by Lao boat operators.

Conclusion: Regulatory Nonchalance?

Long-distance transport operations in north-western Laos highlight the uneven and contradictory development of the Economic Quadrangle. Cargo truck and boat operators are beneficiaries of a new trading regime in which private participation is encouraged. Many of them have prospered, earning incomes for themselves and their relatives well beyond their expectations of only ten years ago. Satellite dishes, thick gold chains, house extensions, imported whisky and Chinese aphrodisiacs are the rewards of cargo operations in an environment of increasing cross-border trade. But these cross-border connections have been carefully managed. Strict constraints on the activities of Thai and Chinese transport operators have shielded north-western operators from substantial competition. They have the Mekong largely to themselves and, on the Chinese-built north-western roads, Chinese trucks head north from Pakbeng with their cargo-trays empty. For truck operators, the high cost of imported vehicles, compounded by government import restrictions, has limited industry expansion, which may have challenged those who benefited from the windfall of privatisation. Transport operators regularly complain about state charges and inspections but they are the beneficiaries of state regulation.

However, the active participation of long-distance transport operators in these regulatory practices seems less than that of the cross-river boat operators in Chiang Khong. The association of cross-river boat operators verges on the pedantic, with its array of rules, sanctions and ritual practices. By contrast, the associations of long-distance transport operators are desultory affairs. Their only clearly defined activity is the coordination of the trucking *khiw* at Pakbeng, and even this *khiw* seems replete with flexibility and exceptions. In Houayxay, the trucker's association has no clearly defined role, and in Louangnamtha the association has ceased to exist, accounting for the fact that provincial officials could not provide me with any data on truck operations! There are also cargo boat associations but – while all operators claimed to be members – no one could tell me with any certainty what their functions were. Beyond data and fee collection, they appear to be moribund. At least as far as formal associations are concerned, long-distance transport operators' collaboration in regulatory practices seems half-hearted at best.

At one level, the reasons for this are obvious. The association at Chiang Khong benefits from the spatial immediacy of its members, with workplace, neighbourhood, ritual and recreation all closely interlinked. By contrast, the membership of long-distance transport associations is widely dispersed and, moreover, diluted with the presence of operators from other provinces. When they are at the key places of regulation – ports and border crossings – long-distance transport operators do achieve a subtle domestication of space that is similar to that achieved by the cross-river boat operators at Chiang Khong (see page 105) but their visits are often relatively short-lived and intermittent. While few Chinese truck drivers would be willing to take on the *khiw* at Pakbeng, the local, domesticated, authority of long-distance transport operators is unimpressive and not readily incorporated into local regimes of regulation.

There are, however, two other more subtle reasons for the less active collaboration of the long-distance transport operators in the north-west. The first relates to the immediacy of their relationship with state officialdom. Unlike the association in Chiang Khong, the long-distance associations have a clearly defined legal basis in government decrees and they have been closely monitored by provincial bureaucrats (see, for example, SWECO 1990: Appendix 24.6). At present, the key association office bearers are, in fact, on the payroll of the *Department of Transport* and the distinction between association and state is very blurred. The irony is that this close state supervision – rather than resulting in a proliferation of regulation – seems to have fostered organisational apathy and disinterest. Given the formal, bureaucratic structures, there seems little need to elaborate more subtle forms of collaboration. In Chiang Khong, where the relationship between association and state is more uncertain, an array of regulatory practices have been developed in an attempt, perhaps, to formalise and regularise an ambiguous position. Explicit state intervention may, in fact, discourage regulation and, conversely, a more "distant" state may result in its collaborative proliferation.

The second reason relates to the degree of threat confronting the transport operators. The cross-river operators in Chiang Khong face potential competition from other boat owners in Chiang Khong itself and across the river in Houayxay. Other small boats regularly call at the port and their activities have to be closely monitored. By contrast, the long-distance transport operators in the north-west have faced relatively few threats. Cargo boat operators have no competition and the threat from the distinctive Chinese trucks at Pakbeng is easily monitored. In the north-west there is little need for cohesive and united associations of operators to regulate external threats. Once again, regulation may be a more complex issue than is commonly thought: it appears to become more elaborate and intricate in an environment of competition; with state regulation preventing competition in the north-western transport industry, there is little need for further elaboration.

135

There are, however, a number of indications that the relatively secure position of north-western transport operators may be under some threat. There is a strong view that sees the future of the trucking industry in Laos lying with private transport companies – presumably funded with foreign capital – rather than with small-scale independent operators. In the north-west, this argument will gain strength if a good quality transit route is constructed. Pressures to lift the restrictions on the operation of foreign trucks are likely to mount and, with improved road connections, Thai and Chinese transport firms will be in a position to provide a more rapid and streamlined service than the existing independent operators with their outdated Soviet vehicles (PADECO 1994: A119–121; SWECO 1990: 40.21, 40.24). New roads, and other infrastructure projects, pose an even more immediate threat. In late 1996, I heard that a number of companies involved in these projects had begun selling very cheap used-vehicles, threatening the existing owners' monopoly on affordable vehicles in Laos. Even in 1994, I had seen ADB-funded trucks engaged in road-works in Oudomxai province unloading general cargo at the Pakbeng port, with the approval of provincial transport authorities.

Cargo boat operators also face a number of threats. Most immediate are developments in the forestry sector that have placed restrictions on independent felling and processing of timber. With the price of timber bought from sawmills rising steeply, the supply of new small and medium boats appears to be declining. As boats deteriorate beyond repair, or come to grief on the rocks, new boats are not being built to replace them, and the opportunities that have existed in the past for gradual consolidation in the industry are disappearing. It appears likely that the large metal-hulled boats will take on an even greater share of the cargo, benefiting a few of the largest operators.

Second, there are some signs of Thai interest in re-establishing limited cargo operations on the upper-Mekong, despite slow progress on the *Upper Mekong Navigation Agreement*. Two boat-building enterprises have been established in Chiang Khong and, though most boats have been built for Lao buyers, at least one is being used by a Thai operator to carry cargo between Burmese ports and Chiang Saen. There is still river navigation expertise in Chiang Khong and Chiang Saen and it is possible that the high rates of return generated by cargo boat operations will attract some Thai reinvestment, should the navigation agreement be endorsed. Links with the Thai-owned sawmills – all of whom have offices in Chiang Khong – are likely to facilitate Thai involvement in the relatively lucrative timber traffic.

Third, road building plans are also a threat to boat operators. If a good road is constructed between Houayxay and Louangnamtha, it will capture most of the river traffic that travels to and from the northern towns via the port at Pakbeng. The development of the second alternative route, through Hongsa and Pakbeng, may have less impact, unless, as its proponents envisage, Nan province replaces Chiang Khong as the main trading point between northern Thailand and Laos. The *Lao National Transport Study* predicted that as road development proceeds many boat operators will want to invest in trucks (SWECO 1990: 36.23), but the capital required to do this may be beyond them, especially if there is no market for them to sell their boats.

In chapter 8, I will provide a more general assessment of the threats facing Lao transport operators, traders and entrepreneurs. Here, however, I will confine my comments to suggesting that this more competitive environment may encourage more rigorous regulation. Already consultants to the ADB have expressed concern about the *de-regulated* state of the domestic trucking industry in Laos (TecnEcon Asia Pacific 1994: 1–9). The domination of the industry by independent operators, they argue, leads to non-economic rate setting, rampant overloading and evasion of government taxes and charges. The result is that the competitive viability of state and private companies is undermined and corporate investment is discouraged. To address this, they have proposed that the supervisory role of the truckers' associations be strengthened, that association membership be made compulsory, that increased fines be imposed for overloading and that a series of indirect taxation measures be implemented to minimise revenue evasion. These *re-regulatory* measures are, no doubt, aimed at limiting the activities of independent truckers and they point to an environment in which industry share will be more vigorously contested and defended. Independent operators may well respond with an array of practices aimed at demarcating and protecting a market niche, mobilising the close personal relations they already have with provincial officials. This is not a question of inward-looking defensiveness but of having to reassess the nonchalance with which external connections – in the context of state protection – have been managed.

137

CHAPTER SIX

Women, Space and History

Long-Distance Trade

Introduction: Mobile Women

In north-western Laos, retail outlets in the provincial capitals and district centres are supplied by long-distance traders who make regular cross-border journeys to Thailand and China to buy manufactured goods and processed foodstuffs. A majority of these long-distance entrepreneurs are women (*mɛɛ khaa*) and their distinctive appearance – make-up, nail polish, gold jewellery, hair pieces, fake leather handbags and baseball caps – gives the rustic and muddy Lao trading system an unmistakably feminine character. The main trade route followed by these women runs down the Mekong River from Chiang Khong to the river port of Pakbeng and, further on, to the northern "capital" of Louangphabang. At Pakbeng many follow the north-western route along the rough road to Oudomxai, where truck-loads of Thai thongs, washing powder and soft drinks are unloaded for local sale or distribution to surrounding provinces. Some traders continue on across the border to Mengla in southern China, where they stock up with Chinese beer, cigarettes and biscuits before heading south again to sell their latest load. From Chiang Khong to Mengla, it is a little over 400 kilometres by river and road but with the poor transport system and interminable administrative delays, a return journey along the full length of this route can easily take up to three weeks.

The literature on trade in South-East Asia suggests that women's management of such long-distance trading connections is very unusual. It is widely recognised that women dominate small-scale, local trade. "Markets," Alexander (1987: 31) writes, "are women's domains," a statement supported by studies in Indonesia (Alexander 1987; Dewey 1962a), the Philippines (Szanton 1972), Malaysia (Firth 1966: 282–286, 337–339; Strange 1981: 202–204), Vietnam (O'Harrow 1995), Thailand (Kirsch 1982; Young 1966: 102) and Laos itself (C. Ireson 1996; Lévy 1963; Mayoury 1993). But long-distance, large-scale and wholesale trade in South-East Asia seems to be usually the domain of men, typically Chinese men with interests in shopkeeping, transportation and ware-housing and an extensive network of contacts with suppliers and creditors in provincial towns and capital cities. A number of studies refer to the social and economic barriers between the two sectors, with market women rarely willing or able to make what Geertz calls the "jump from peddling to merchandising" (1963: 31; see also Alexander and Alexander 1991; Keyes 1984: 225; Preecha 1980; Szanton 1972; Young 1966: 105–108). Even when long-distance trade is undertaken on a small scale it seems to be most commonly the domain of men (see for example Bowie 1992: 808–809; Chandler 1984: 105, 121, 125; Young 1966: 105–106).

In Theravada Buddhist societies, such as Thailand and Laos, the non-participation of women in long-distance trade has been attributed to traditional religious values. In an important paper on gender in Thailand, Kirsch (1984: 229) suggests that women's economic activity has remained "petty and localised" in part due to Buddhism's valorisation of the roles of wife and mother. Keyes (1984: 229) explores the argument somewhat further suggesting that the role of *mɛɛ khaa* is underpinned by the Buddhist image of the "nurturing mother" and that petty trading is a natural extension of the domestic economy. A woman provides for her family, he writes "through her productive activities in the fields and in craftwork at home and it is but a small step to market the products of the family enterprise" (Keyes 1984: 229).

The views of Kirsch (1982, 1985) and Keyes (1984) resonate with reports of taboos and anxieties surrounding women's mobility in both Thailand and Laos, cultural forms of regulation which appear to stand in stark contrast to the celebration of the travels and adventures of men (Pasuk and Baker 1995: 69–70; Phillips 1965: 28; Singhanetra-Renard 1981: 151). In Laos, Trankell (1993: 22) reports that it was "often stated that women's life opportunities were hampered by the fact that rules of decorum restricted women's freedom of physical movement beyond what was recognised as the social space of the village." In a Lao village in north-east Thailand, Mills (1995: 257) has written vividly of potent "widow ghost" anxieties which she attributes to concerns about "the unnatural and dangerous consequences of allowing women to roam freely, their bodies and sexual powers unconstrained by the controls of society or of men." Keyes (1984: 235–236) shares some of these anxieties, writing of rural women's entry into prostitution when they are "unmoored" from Buddhist values and travel to the "hedonistic atmosphere" of Bangkok and the provincial capitals. More recently, the apparent hazards of trans-border feminine mobility have been highlighted with widespread media and academic discussion of trafficking in Burmese, Chinese and Lao girls for the purposes of prostitution in Thai brothels (Asia Watch 1993). All in all, it seems that women's mobility is a dangerous business, undermining

139

masculinity as men don nail polish and make-up to avoid the predations of the "widow ghosts" (Mills 1995: 252) and corrupting traditional femininity as women abandon Buddhism and matrilineal spirits (Muecke 1984: 466) and are drawn into the brothels of Bangkok and Chiang Mai.

This chapter provides a study of the way women manage long-distance trading connections, highlighting their success, profitability and enjoyment. There is no doubt that cultural regulation of women's mobility in Laos is significantly embedded in religion, ritual and in the widespread matrilocal focus of settlement patterns. State exhortations "[s]tressing women's traditional domestic roles as wives and mothers" also, on the face of it, do not auger well for the pursuit of independent and mobile lifestyles (Stuart-Fox 1986: 90; see also Ng 1991: 176; Savage 1996: 284–289). Nevertheless, this chapter argues that some Lao women have been able to exploit and manipulate regulatory practices and ideologies in the formation of their long-distance trading careers. The first part examines the long-distance trading activities of women who travel to Chiang Khong and Mengla to buy goods to sell mainly in Oudomxai. The second part explores the historical development of women's role in this long-distance trading system. I suggest that the disrupted wartime era of the 1960s and early 1970s loosened regulatory constraints and gave women unprecedented exposure to both mobility and trade. This experience was put to good use in the restricted – but highly profitable – trading conditions that followed the communist victory in 1975. While some writers have suggested that the strict regulation of this era threatened women's economic position, I argue that it was a crucial phase in creating their long-distance trading opportunities. In the era of the Economic Quadrangle, trading women have consolidated their position and continue to benefit from a range of regulatory practices. I conclude by suggesting that, although mobile women face cultural barriers and tensions, there are also cultural spaces that they can occupy, paralleling their strategic use of geographic space in the rugged terrain of north-western Laos. In the regulatory systems of north-western Laos, positive, profitable and rewarding travelling identities are not just the prerogative of men.

From Chiang Khong to Oudomxai and Mengla

Trade with Thailand

The Thai trading town of Chiang Khong is the most popular point of supply for long-distance traders throughout northern Laos. A large number of them come up river to Chiang Khong from Louangphabang, returning with boatloads of cement, corrugated iron, condensed milk and washing powder. Smaller-scale traders make the four hour speedboat trip from Pakbeng, returning with stock for the retail shops that sprawl along the dusty road that climbs up from the port. Others come from Oudomxai, Louangnamtha, Muangsing, Muanghun and Hongsa (Map 1.2), their vinyl handbags stuffed with thousand baht[1] notes and crumpled orders from the shopkeepers in the markets that dominate the commercial lives of the towns. Less frequently, traders from as far afield as Phongsali, Xamnua and Phonsavan (Map 1.3) make their way to Chiang Khong to buy direct, but more often they collect their orders from other traders in Pakbeng or Oudomxai. Finally, there are the long-distance traders in Houayxay itself. Using and creating far flung connections, they have established a regular trade with the other towns of northern Laos, in particular the entrepôt of Oudomxai.

There is substantial variation in trading style and scale among those who visit Chiang Khong's crowded shops. The small-scale traders are most likely to come from towns and villages relatively close to Chiang Khong, typically riverside settlements downstream as far as Pakbeng. Their trading capital is limited – usually between 10,000 and 50,000 baht – but they attempt to maximise income by concentrating on high profit items and making regular trading journeys, perhaps as many as two or three each month. Many of them are young unmarried women or older women who are divorced or separated from their husbands. Mai, for example, was one of the poorest long-distance traders I met. Unmarried, at the age of 30, she lives with her sister in Pakbeng. As a child, her family had to leave Pakbeng due to the war and they settled in Houayxay. Later, she moved to Louangphabang where she was involved in petty trade in the local market. After returning to Pakbeng about seven years ago, she worked in a small noodle shop for a few years before starting trading journeys to Chiang Khong, staying with friends dating from her childhood in Houayxay. By early 1995, she was making two or three trips per month to Chiang Khong, concentrating on selling eggs and bottled water to restaurants in Pakbeng. She makes good profits on the water, buying bottles in bulk in Chiang Khong for three baht and selling them in Pakbeng for almost six baht. Her trading investment each trip amounts to about 15,000 baht. Usually, she transports her purchases back to Pakbeng on small passenger boats, paying a surcharge for her cargo. On other occasions she minimises her transport costs by hitching a ride on a 25–tonne cargo boat owned by a relative in Houayxay or a large metal boat owned by a wealthy (married) boat operator from Louangphabang with whom she is involved in a relationship. On arrival in Pakbeng, she employs young boys – many of whom frequent the port area looking for work – to haul handcarts laden with eggs and water up the hill to her customers in the restaurants.

---

1 All transactions in Chiang Khong are conducted in Thai *baht*. Lao *kip* are never accepted by the shopkeepers. The traders exchange currency in Lao banks and there are relatively few restrictions on them doing so.

The larger-scale traders are much more likely to be married and often participate in trade with their husbands. While they may also have limited trading capital, they have much better access to credit in Chiang Khong, a factor not unrelated to their more respectable married status (see page 159). A "typical" trader in this category buys goods worth several hundred thousand *baht*, while some of the most successful are in the million *baht* range. Noot, for example, is a key member of a trading group based in south Houayxay, which includes her sister, her husband, her husband's sister and several close neighbours. She is in her early thirties and has been trading since she left school in 1980. She started out buying goods at the border market at Muangmom (see page 156), making twice-monthly journeys there by bicycle. Originally she sold her goods at Viangphoukha but later travelled further afield to Oudomxai. In these early days, her trading capital was limited to a few thousand *baht*. After the Thai border opened, she started trading between Chiang Khong and Oudomxai with other traders from Houayxay, gradually increasing the scale of her operations. Now, together with her husband, she buys goods worth about 250,000 *baht* from the wholesale shops in Chiang Khong, making monthly journeys to the large market in Oudomxai.

Most of the traders, small and large, work in informal trading groups of up to eight or ten friends, neighbours and relatives. They share cargo boats for the downstream journey and assist each other in supervising the loading and unloading of cargo. The groups are relatively informal and group membership changes, though there are usually a few core members. Group members rarely pool finances or trading stock, and often have separate regular customers. When group members come from different towns, they provide accommodation for each other and also assist in maintaining contacts with suppliers and customers. Traders often say that working in a group is much less convenient because the larger volumes prolong every stage of the trading journey and it can become difficult to keep track of their own stock (although boxes are usually marked with the trader's initials). Nevertheless, the sociality of trading groups is highly valued.

As indicated in Table 6.1, the wholesale shops in Chiang Khong – predominantly Chinese owned – sell an enormous range of manufactured goods, clothing and processed foods. There are about ten general wholesale shops – together with several specialist hardware shops – and most of them report that the vast majority of their sales are shipped across the river to Laos. Most of the larger-scale traders spread their bulk purchases between four or five wholesale shops, even though each stocks a similar range of goods. The traders say that a single shop usually has insufficient stock, especially highly sought-after items such as good quality quilts during the cold season. Price comparison between shops is also important. However, the main reason for spreading purchases is to maximise access to credit with the large-scale traders usually buying more

Table 6.1 Main products bought by Lao traders in Chiang Khong

Wholesale shops		Specialist shops	Friday market
Condensed milk	Sugar	Corrugated iron	Clothing
Orange juice	Toilet paper	Fibre-board roofing	Cosmetics
Soft drinks	Sanitary pads	Toilets	Shoes
Tonic drinks	Thongs	Charcoal stoves	Plastic toys
Ovaltine	Floor mats	Motor oil	
Instant coffee	Mattresses	Battery acid	
Tinned fish	Quilts	Cement	*Other*
Dried squid	Washing powder	Bricks	Eggs
Biscuits	Soap	Fibro sheets	Coconuts
Sweets	Toothpaste	Bicycles	Fruit
MSG	Cloth	Televisions	Bottled water
Cooking oil	Rope	Pharmaceuticals	

Source: Fieldwork 1994–1995, 1996.
Notes: There is gender variation in the purchase of some of the products. Male traders are somewhat more likely to be involved in the purchase of construction materials, but certainly not exclusively so. By contrast, purchases from the Friday market are almost exclusively the domain of women traders, especially small-scale traders.

than half of their trading stock on short-term – about a month – shopkeeper credit.[2] Some purchases, such as pharmaceuticals, electrical goods and automotive products, are made at specialist shops more oriented to the local retail trade. Even the modern supermarket makes some bulk sales to the Lao traders. Finally, the large travelling market that visits Chiang Khong each Friday is very popular among smaller-scale traders who can be seen crossing the Mekong on Friday afternoons, plastic bags laden with clothes, shoes, cosmetics and plastic toys.

After making their purchases, the traders spend hours, sometimes days, at the Chiang Khong port supervising the loading of the Lao cargo boats that head down-river to Pakbeng and Louangphabang.[3] This is a stressful and often unpleasant time. The port is hot, muddy and exposed and the women, fearful of losing their highly valued pale skin, squat in the shade of piles of boxes, fanning themselves with rough pieces of cardboard. The shopkeeper's pick-ups and trucks, which deliver the goods to the port, slip and slide on the steep concrete ramp and bog themselves in the mud

2 Some of the implications of credit relationships are discussed in more detail on page 158.
3 The smaller-scale traders use cross-river boats to carry their goods to small cargo and passenger boats moored at Houayxay's port. Small Lao cargo and passenger boats are not permitted to cross to Chiang Khong, while the large cargo boats are. For a detailed analysis of the operations of the cross-river boats at Chiang Khong see chapter 4.

143

beside the river. Accidents and near misses are common. The port labourers who load the cargo boats add to the stress, constantly increasing their charges and engaging the traders in muscular and sweaty negotiations. Inside the boats, the cargo is carefully stacked so as to minimise import duties on the other side of the river. Boxes of high-tax lemonade are loaded in inaccessible parts of the hull or concealed beneath low-tax biscuits and soap-powder.[4] Bundles of thongs, which attract a 40 per cent tax, are removed from their distinctive blue wrapping and repacked in the nondescript hessian sacks used for sweets and dried squid. No export taxes are collected by the Thai customs officers in Chiang Khong, but a range of service charges and administrative fees find their way into their tight back pockets.

Before heading down river, the traders and their laden boats must dock at the Houayxay cargo port where Lao import duty is assessed and paid. This too is a prolonged process and delays of two or three days are not uncommon. Though tedious and frustrating, this is the crucial period in the whole trading venture – Lao import taxes on many items are very high and minimisation of tax is essential for trading success. Concealment of cargo in Chiang Khong is only a small part of the strategy of tax minimisation. The Lao customs staff are fully aware of what the traders are doing on the other side of the river and, if they wished, could order thorough and enormously time-consuming inspections of the boats.[5] To avoid this, a process of regulation by negotiation is entered into. As Mali, a successful trader from Oudomxai, described it:

> Say I have 100 boxes of lemonade. I tell the customs officer that I have 50 boxes and he proposes that I pay tax on 30. I protest that this is much too expensive and that it will eat up all my profit. I say that tax on five boxes would be much better. Eventually we agree on 15 or 20.[6]

This crucially important regulatory process is collaborative and mutually beneficial. In return for accepting such blatant under-declaration, the customs officers receive substantial personal payments. While a certain amount of tax has to be collected to meet official expectations, it is in the

---

4 In early 1995, Lao customs tried to crack down on these practices by refusing to allow any Lao cargo boats to cross to Chiang Khong to load. Rather, they insisted that all cargo be brought across the river on the Thai cross-river boats and loaded, under their supervision, at the Houayxay port. They also limited the amount that could be loaded onto the boats to reduce the chances of concealment. Nevertheless, amidst the confusion of traders, cross-river boats and cargo boats at Houayxay, the practices continued.

5 In early 1995, customs officers at the inspection point just south of the Chinese border crossing at Boten started insisting that all the trucks be unloaded so that the cargo could be subjected to detailed scrutiny.

6 Of course, not all evasion is of this degree. Lemonade is a high-tax item and there is strong incentive to minimise tax. Evasion on lower tax items is often much less substantial.

interests of the local customs staff to minimise the official tax paid by the trader – the traders have limited cash at this stage of the trading cycle and the more they pay in tax the less they will be able, or inclined, to pay as personal inducements. The result is a high level of embezzlement of potential customs revenue by provincial regulators, widely recognised as an important fiscal problem in Laos. The level of tax and inducement paid by traders varies considerably according to the extent of cargo concealment, their persistence and negotiating skills and the nature of their personal relationships with the customs officers. Destination is also a factor: traders travelling to Oudomxai and Louangnamtha usually pay less than those travelling to Louangphabang, where there are many more officials who may check the customs paperwork prepared by their colleagues in Houayxay. A total payment of about five per cent of stock value is considered typical, though payments can range from one per cent – almost unbelievably good – to over ten per cent, a level at which the venture starts to become unviable. On top of customs payments, larger-scale traders also have to make payments to officials from the *Department of Trade* and local trading companies who process the official paperwork for their imports.[7]

The cargo boats used for the downstream journey are operated by boat owners from Houayxay, Pakbeng, Louangphabang and, occasionally, towns further down river (see page 119). If the boats leave Houayxay by mid-morning, they can make the trip to Pakbeng in a single day, provided there are not excessive delays at the customs and police post at Paktha, where additional inducements have to be paid as the customs paperwork does not tally with the cargo in the boat. Often, however, the final official inspections in Houayxay are delayed until later in the day, and a night must be spent moored at Paktha or one of the villages along the river. Most of the women seem to have overcome the fear that many Lao have of river travel, and the trip is often a lazy and restful time as the hours are whiled away sleeping, cooking, eating and talking. Sometimes the women may join male traders and boat operators in games of cards or even whisky drinking sessions, though the women's drinking at this stage is usually restrained because they need to keep a clear head for trading. If an unexpected stop is made for the night along the river, the traders may raid the cargo for quilts and mattresses if there are insufficient in the boat, carefully repacking them in their plastic wrapping in the morning.

At Pakbeng the cargo is loaded into waiting trucks for the road journey north to Oudomxai and Louangnamtha (see page 114). The cargo of the various traders, piled in cardboard confusion in the hulls of the boats, has to be sorted into separate trucks and this too can be a time-consuming process, made more so by the regionally renowned lethargy of the port labourers. As the unloading proceeds, the traders are regularly approached

---

7 For a fascinating study of customs evasion on the southern Thai border, see Suparb (1989).

by local shopkeepers – and sometimes traders from further afield who want to avoid travelling to Chiang Khong – who are keen to buy their goods. Many of the traders are reluctant to sell because they have commitments to regular customers in Oudomxai though, if a high enough price is offered, or if there are goods left over that will not fit into a truck, a sale may be made (cf. Mintz 1967: 108). Several of the women who regularly travel to Oudomxai have close friends and relatives in Pakbeng and they are often more willing to sell and may even have some stock specifically purchased for this purpose. Usually, a night must be spent in Pakbeng, and many of the women stay in a small ramshackle hotel located above the port, though some may sleep on the boats, sharing meals with the boat owners. Those who can, stay with friends or relatives.

When the trucks are loaded, the traders travel with them for the journey north. To Oudomxai it is a bone jarring six or eight hours, crammed into the improbably crowded and noisy cabins. There is a busy market at Muanghun, a few hours along the road, and traders who live there may stop to unload some goods before heading to the more lucrative market in Oudomxai.

The large market in Oudomxai is one of the main selling points for the long-distance traders. There are over 200 shops in four large concrete sheds, constructed by provincial authorities in 1991 to stimulate commercial activity. The market has an array of small retail shops selling tinned foods, drinks, sweets, toiletries, beer and cigarettes and many specialist shops selling clothes, footwear, stationery, tools and cassettes. The traders are rarely anxious about being able to sell their goods here, often joking that the shopkeepers fight among themselves to buy. On one of my first visits to the market, a small crowd of shopkeepers stripped bare a truck load of goods that had arrived from Pakbeng, climbing up the back and sides, burrowing under the thick canvas tarpaulin and handing the truck's contents to their companions on the ground who stood on top of the goods to establish their ownership. There were many heated arguments as shop owners fought over cartons of lemonade and biscuits, trying to steal boxes from each other's piles in the confusion. The trader – a woman from Houayxay – was powerless to control the situation and could only wander around urging the shopkeepers to share. When the booty was organised into separate piles, she went from one to the other writing down what each customer had taken from the truck. Many of them had actually placed orders on her previous trip to Oudomxai or sent messages to her with other traders or travellers. In fact, she told me, she had orders that could fill five trucks, well beyond her financial or logistical capacity.

Market-place bargaining is often written of as a central experience of women's involvement in trade, but in these transactions between long-distance wholesalers and local retailers it is relatively absent. Prices are only discussed in detail when the traders collect their payment from the shopkeepers, usually two or three days after the goods are stored away in the shops, if not already sold to the retail customers who frequent the market. The understanding is that prices will be the same as on the previous occasion and if there is any bargaining it is within a very narrow range and in a half-hearted manner.[8] The shopkeepers are advised of minor price rises when they collect the goods from the truck, not to initiate a process of bargaining, but to enable them to adjust their retail prices accordingly. If there are substantial price increases in Chiang Khong, the information may be telephoned through to large customers to give them the – rarely exercised – option of withdrawing their order. Moreover, the long-distance traders generally do not attempt to profit from excess demand by increasing their prices. Selling is easy for most of the year but there are times, especially in the wet season when roads become impassable and energies are directed to rice planting, when good and regular relationships with customers are highly valued. As Mintz (1967: 103, my emphasis) has written of personalised marketing relationships in Haiti: "the intermediary will be seen to be trading some portion of her potential profit ... in return for some measure of assurance that she will be able to both acquire stock and *then to dispose of it*." In Laos, overstocking may be an infrequent risk, but with problems of storage at Oudomxai and substantial debts that have to be promptly repaid in Chiang Khong, it could be catastrophic. Cautious pricing when demand is high is sound insurance (see also Preecha 1980: 108).

Collection of payments is another time-consuming part of the trading journey. Huge bundles of small denomination notes are meticulously counted as the long-distance traders make their way through the market, gradually filling carry-bags with *kip*. Those who are going to Mengla in China use market-place money-changers to convert *kip* into Chinese *yuan*, or even repatriated American dollars which some insist are better value across the border. Others go to the bank to buy Thai *baht*, to repay their debts and fund their next venture in Chiang Khong. Others may have heard that exchange rates in Louangphabang or Houayxay are better, and pack their *kip* away for the journey south. Traders who live in Oudomxai may settle down at home for a week or so before their next venture, sitting up at night with calculators reconciling receipts and tax-forms and hurriedly written records of sale. Traders from other towns head down the road to Pakbeng in the passenger pick-ups that frequent the route. From there it is a few hours upstream to homes in Houayxay or downstream to homes in Louangphabang. If all goes well the trip back from Oudomxai can be made in a day.[9]

---

8 Slightly lower prices may be offered to shopkeepers with whom the traders have a particularly close personal relationship.

9 By late 1996, some of the more affluent traders were taking advantage of the improved air services between Oudomxai, Houayxay and Louangphabang.

Trade with China

Trade with China is focused on the town of Mengla, an old Lü settlement that has long historical links with north-western Laos (see page 36). A spate of central Chinese investment, immigration and construction has transformed the town but the cultural links between the Lao and the Lü continue to underpin much of the cross-border trade. In the north-west, this trade is concentrated on a number of items where Chinese goods are substantially cheaper than comparable products from Thailand. Prominent among these are beer and cigarettes, completely absent from the Thai trade. Other popular items include biscuits, batteries, toys, torches, electronic goods, stationery, thermos flasks, cooking utensils, tools and toilet paper. There is also a busy trade in foodstuffs such as apples, pears, watermelons and eggs and some trade in Chinese machinery (especially small rice mills).

In the north-west, the trade is most active between Mengla and the nearby towns of Muangsing, Louangnamtha and Oudomxai, almost matching the flow of Thai goods into these towns. Chinese goods are also readily available in Pakbeng, Houayxay and even Hongsa but the number of traders involved and the regularity of their trips is substantially less than in the northern towns. Much more of the trade appears to be conducted by small-scale traders than is the case with the Thai trade. In both Oudomxai and Louangnamtha, there are many small-scale traders who make regular journeys across the border using readily available passenger transport to carry their goods on the return journey. This small-scale trade has been facilitated by the emergence of the border trading village of Mohan – only three kilometres north of Boten – with over 30 shops stocking many of the most popular items.

Alee is typical of some of the smaller-scale traders involved in trade with China. I first met her when she worked in a restaurant in Chiang Khong where she lived with her father. In mid-1994 she moved to live with her mother in Louangnamtha, joining her and an aunt on weekly trading journeys to Mengla. They take orders from the shopkeepers crowded into the Louangnamtha market, often concentrating on small, high-value items such as cassette recorders. They transport their goods from Mengla to the Lao border in small Chinese passenger mini-buses, and from Boten to Louangnamtha in passenger pick-ups. They rely heavily on avoiding import taxes, concealing their purchases in the crowded pick-ups at the customs post at Nateey. However, in March 1995, disaster struck when all their goods were seized in a customs crackdown at Nateey. When I last saw her, she was negotiating customs payments and the release of the goods with the head of customs. Although her mother and aunt were much more experienced, it was the young and attractive Alee who did all the talking.

Some traders travelling to Mengla operate on a larger-scale, though even the wealthiest north-western Lao traders buy less in China than they do in Thailand. In early 1995, I made two journeys to Mengla with Nom, a trader from Houayxay, and her husband, the owner of a Mekong River cargo boat. Nom had been trading Thai goods for some years in the north-west – she too was a veteran of the Muangmom market – selling to relatives in Pakbeng and later travelling further afield to Oudomxai and Hongsa. In 1994, she started making quick trips to Mengla to buy cheap Chinese batteries and cigarettes for shopkeepers in Houayxay (and an array of battery-operated toys for her demanding son). On one of these journeys, a friend (and customer) from Oudomxai introduced her to a trading company in Mengla that was keen to buy Thai rice.[10] Over the next few months, she and her husband took over 30 tonnes of rice from Chiang Khong to Mengla (via Pakbeng), exchanging it for several truck loads of rice mills, electrical goods, fruit and beer. These were readily sold back in Laos and she and her husband spoke optimistically of their plans to buy their own truck and take it regularly to China when the road through Louangnamtha was complete.

For larger-scale traders like Nom, the Mengla Lü are crucially important trading intermediaries.[11] Given their extreme reticence about dealing with the Chinese (see below), few north-western Lao traders would be willing to undertake trading ventures to Mengla without the linguistic and cultural similarities between themselves and the Lü. In Mengla there are a range of Lü border trading companies which prepare import and export paperwork, secure goods from suppliers in Jinghong and Kunming and conduct negotiations with Chinese officials. The assistance of these companies in negotiating Chinese customs payments is particularly highly valued and cautionary stories circulate of Lao traders who have been charged extraordinary tariffs when they had tried to act independently. Lü entrepreneurs also operate hotels – one in particular is patronised mainly by Lao traders – and run an array of restaurants and food-stalls where Lao traders can buy their sticky rice, fried fish and grilled frogs. There are also numerous Lü labourers who transport the traders' purchases around town on bicycle-hauled carts, load cargo at the central truck-stop, negotiate prices on minor purchases and help deal with the ever-vigilant Chinese traffic police, some of whom still seem unused to the presence of the Lao trucks in their midst.

However, despite the intermediary role of the Lü, north-western Lao traders remain very cautious in their Chinese trading ventures. During 1994 and 1995, I knew of several traders who gave up their trips to Mengla

---

10 There are said to be many buyers in Mengla for fragrant Thai rice – plain rice, not the glutinous rice widely grown throughout the region (Golomb 1976).
11 For some comparable observations about the role of ethnicity in cross-border trading systems, see Alvarez and Collier (1994).

149

altogether. There are several reasons for this. Many have difficulty securing credit in Mengla and are reluctant to spend large amounts of cash from their trading ventures to Oudomxai given their repayment commitments to creditors in Chiang Khong. Many traders also have strong cultural prejudices against the Chinese and regularly tell stories about their poor character, unappetising food, nasty sexual practices and, above all, appalling sanitation standards. (On one trip, the traders stopped to go to the toilet in a small copse of trees on the outskirts of Mengla – one less visit to the appalling toilets in town!) These negative ethnic stereotypes play into and reinforce a widely held view in the trading community that China is a risky place to do business, a view given considerable currency when China's sudden imposition of a 200 per cent duty on car imports left stockpiles of cars stranded throughout the north-west (see page 74). Finally, while there is general agreement that many Chinese goods are cheaper than Thai goods, there is equally widespread concern about their quality. A number of traders commented that their customers were no longer willing to buy Chinese goods because they were not "beautiful." This may not be a factor when it comes to batteries, beer, cigarettes and thermos flasks, but it certainly is when it comes to clothes, toiletries, footwear and toys (GLPDR 1994e: 60).[12] In brief, north-western trading women continue to make trips to China but for many this is only an adjunct to the more lucrative and reliable trade with Thailand.

A Space of Opportunity

It would be tempting to account for the activities of these north-western Lao traders purely in terms of the rapid increases in cross-border trade and the encouragement of private sector involvement that has occurred since the late 1980s. There is no doubt that women have benefited from the commercial, social and physical mobility that Smith (1976a: 352) refers to when she writes of "trade niches" that proliferate as externally oriented commerce "penetrates the countryside." Nor is there any doubt, as Ng (1991: 179) foreshadowed, that some Lao women, in an environment of economic transition, have been able to "capitalise on their knowledge of market conditions and market networks to strengthen their economic status." Indeed, the relationship between free-market reform and new trading opportunity seems self-evident. However, an examination of the historical development of this independent trade suggests that the social and commercial processes were much more complex. The following pages will demonstrate that restrictive trading environments can be as important as more liberal trading environments in creating commercial opportunity. And, in *both* restrictive and liberalised trading environments,

---

12 A common story – a "rural myth" perhaps – is that Chinese clothes are taken to Thailand, relabelled with Thai labels and re-imported into Laos.

regulatory practices have been crucial in supporting the long-distance trading opportunities for Lao women.

From the fragmentary historical record, it seems likely that the social organisation of trade in Laos followed a typically "South-East Asian pattern" prior to the tumultuous events of the 1960s and 1970s. There was high participation of women in small-scale, localised market trade whereas long-distance wholesale trade was dominated by Chinese men. There were some exceptions – Khmu women, for example, were active in long-distance exchanges of highland rice, forest products and salt (Damrong 1994; Izikowitz 1979) – but the overall pattern was clear.[13] Chinese dominance in long-distance distribution systems had thwarted early French colonial trading enterprises and, as trading and transport systems in neighbouring Thailand developed, the Chinese mercantile penetration of Laos increased (Gunn 1990: 22; Reinach 1911: chapter 10; Stuart-Fox 1995a: 122).[14] In the 1950s, Halpern (1961: 5–7) found that 80 per cent of shops in Louangphabang were controlled by Chinese, and in the entrepôt of Oudomxai all of the shops were operated by Chinese families who had migrated from Thailand during the 1930s. Precise details are lacking, but there were also Chinese commercial communities in Muangsing, Louangnamtha and Houayxay (Halpern 1961: 14; Izikowitz 1979: 313).[15] Chinese-owned shops in the north-west were supplied by wholesalers in Louangphabang, Vientiane, Chiang Saen and Chiang Khong. Some of the wholesalers operated air services to the rough north-western airstrips (Damrong 1994: 108–114), while others used boats to bring goods along the Mekong, and packhorses and bullocks to carry them from small river ports into the hinterland (Halpern 1961: 96; Rowley 1960: 174).

Within the long-distance Chinese trading networks, men predominated. Most of the merchants – especially those in the more remote areas – arrived as single men, creating a substantial gender imbalance in the Chinese community in northern Laos (Halpern 1961: 6–7). Many married locally, and while these marriages may have provided an avenue to commercial ventures for some Lao women, it seems probable that their activities remained localised: maintaining local commercial contacts; managing the day-to-day operations of retail outlets; and, in some cases,

---

13 "Partly because of the long distances that must be travelled, men make up the majority of the mountain groups that come to trade in the Lao village." (Roberts et al. 1967: 249)

14 Halpern (1961: 1) estimates that the official Chinese population in Laos increased from only 486 in 1911 to over 30,000 in 1955, though this probably understates the number of Chinese traders in Laos in the early years of the century. See also Purcell (1965:170–172).

15 Chinese merchants in Laos came overland from Yunnan and overseas, usually via Thailand, from other southern Chinese provinces. The Yunnanese presence was strongest in the northern areas near the Chinese border. Generally it appears that the Yunnanese were involved in regional trade with hill-dwellers while other Chinese groups were involved in shopkeeping (Halpern 1961).

providing a public Lao face for the enterprise when legislative restrictions were placed on Chinese involvement in some lines of commerce (Halpern 1961: 4–7; Purcell 1965: 179, 219). Long-distance commercial networks were probably maintained by Chinese men, due to the importance of linguistic, social and cultural linkages with fellow Chinese suppliers and creditors in the major trading towns and further afield in Bangkok, Saigon and even Hong Kong (Halpern 1961; LeBar and Suddard 1960: 219). Some of the more successful merchants maintained shops – and quite possibly wives and families – in more than one location (Halpern 1961: 5, 10; Mayoury 1993: 84). In summary, it seems very likely that the situation in Laos was similar to the situation in Thailand where, in Kirsch's (1982: 29) words, "[p]rivate inter-regional trade tended to fall into non-Thai [Chinese] hands ... [and] [n]o class of women traders arose to take control of the marketing system of the entire kingdom."

The tumultuous events of war and revolution in the 1960s and 1970s brought about fundamental changes in these regional trading systems, with important implications for women's involvement in commerce. Large-scale refugee movement from the Pathet Lao zones (Muangsing, Louang-namtha, Viangphoukha, Oudomxai and, later, Pakbeng) resulted in a massive bloating of the Royal Lao Government (RLG) outposts on the Mekong (Houayxay and Louangphabang). In 1971, it was estimated that there were over 28,000 refugees receiving "food and rehabilitation" support in Houayxay alone (Whitaker et al. 1972: 26). Not only did this refugee movement give many women an unprecedented experience of mobility but it also seems to have disrupted traditional occupational structures and severely tested cultural regulation of feminine commercial activity. A significant number of women were drawn into the vibrant Mekong River commercial economies – fuelled by foreign aid, sawmilling and drug money (see page 56). In Houayxay there were numerous opportunities for cross-border commercial interaction with Thailand, many of them petty and localised but providing women with cross-border contacts and exposing them to a level of economic activity that they had never experienced before. One woman from Pakbeng, for example, made her first contacts in Thailand manufacturing and selling whisky to Chiang Khong's cross-river boat operators and traders who liked to spend clandestine evenings drinking with the Lao refugee girls. Some of her contacts, first made in the early 1970s, now provide a group of Pakbeng traders with accommodation on their regular trips to Chiang Khong. Other women worked as housekeepers for military officials, regularly flying to army bases at Xianghon and Hongsa and developing a taste for *Heineken* beer and sandwiches. And others worked on an island in the middle of the river – the island of "heaven and happiness" – serving in restaurants and gambling houses and entertaining anti-communist troops on rest and recreation. The 1960s and early 1970s in RLG Laos have been portrayed as a period of decadence, corruption and prostitution – Mayoury (1993: 53) writes that "[w]omen were reduced to dull flesh" – but there is no doubt that new social and commercial opportunities also emerged.[16] Some of these opportunities enabled Lao traders to make headway against the Chinese merchants in the localised economic booms (LeBar and Suddard 1960: 159; Purcell 1965: 219).

The large-scale refugee movements of the war years also affected traditional socio-spatial arrangements. Marriages, friendships and commercial contacts made in the crowded towns of Houayxay and Louangphabang provided a wide range of options for post-war settlement decisions. In the domestic resettlement programs after 1975, some returned to their homes, some stayed in the Mekong River towns and others moved to new locations altogether. The overall effect was a geographic dispersal of family, kinship and marriage links, a partial shift from the traditional matrilocal tendency of Lao settlement patterns, and providing some women with an unprecedented network of accommodation, information and support throughout the region.[17] What Kirsch (1985: 313–314) refers to as the traditional "grounding ... of women in their home locale" was disrupted. Som, for example, was born in Paktha. She spent the war in Louangphabang where she worked with her mother as a petty trader in the market. After 1975 they moved to Oudomxai, joining friends – originally from Pakbeng – who they had first met in Louangphabang. With one of these friends she operated a restaurant near the market and, later, through contacts in the market, they became involved in small-scale cross-border trade with China. Now – disillusioned with the China trade – she travels regularly to Chiang Khong staying with her friend's relatives in Houayxay who themselves moved there after the bombing of Pakbeng in the early 1970s. Spatially dispersed networks of contacts like this are common throughout north-western Laos and, while they have proliferated in the modern trading system, many owe their origin to the confused demography of the war and post-war resettlement.

On the face of it, the period following the Pathet Lao victory in 1975 was not a promising time for new commercial opportunity. As discussed in chapter 2 (page 60), the new regime placed a state monopoly on external trade, restricted internal trade and enforced wide-ranging price controls. Heavily subsidised stock sold in state stores also placed pressure on

16 See also Savage (1996: 282). Robbins (1988: 171–184) provides a colourful account of war-time life in Vientiane. Kibria (1993: 57) has written of women's petty trading opportunities in war-time South Vietnam: "The peculiar qualities of the South Vietnamese urban economy – the abundance of luxury consumer items and foreign goods, combined with the plentiful discretionary income of certain segments of the population – often made such trading quite lucrative."

17 Mayoury (1993: 79–80) notes the increasing popularity of "neolocality" since the war.

independent traders. Trading conditions were made worse by the Thai government's closure of the upper-Mekong border in 1976 and the Chinese government's closure of their border a few years later. Writing of this era, Ireson (1992: 8) has suggested that "[s]tate limitations on private commerce had the potential for destroying one of rural women's most important sources of power and autonomy." She writes, for example, that many village shopkeepers – "frequently Laotian women" – left Laos after 1975 or "quietly stashed their capital" until the situation improved (Ireson 1992: 14). The *Far Eastern Economic Review* (FEER 1977: 217) reported that "thousands of petty village merchants were coaxed ... to return to rice production." In a similar vein, Evans (1993: 144) has argued that "the promotion of trading cooperatives ... threatened the important role of women in trade." However, while the fortunes of rural traders and shopkeepers may have declined, there is considerable evidence that the restrictive trading conditions that followed 1975 facilitated the entry of some women into long-distance, wholesale trade. Strict state regulation of trade created opportunities for women that enabled them to build on their commercial and social experiences in the war-time era. There were a number of elements to this process.

First, restrictions on private trade, appropriation of property and personal harassment resulted in a widespread exodus of the established trading class from Laos. By one account most of the country's Chinese community – estimated to number about 30,000 – had left by 1978, leaving "dead shells of barred and shuttered shops" (Stuart Fox quoted in Vokes and Fabella 1995: 108). This exodus has not been well documented in the north but local recollection indicates that in Houayxay, for example, most of the established Chinese shopkeepers and entrepreneurs fled across the Mekong to Chiang Khong.[18] Their commercial presence in Houayxay was replaced by sparsely stocked stores operated by the provincial authorities. In the major northern towns of Oudomxai and Louangnamtha, the Chinese merchants probably fled much earlier – when the towns fell to communist forces in the late 1950s and early 1960s (Dommen 1972: 90) – and under the new administration there were no privately operated shops of any importance. With the removal of the established merchant class, the way was clear for others to take on new commercial roles, albeit initially at a relatively small scale given the restricted trading conditions. Women, who dominated local market trade, were the obvious candidates. Preecha's (1980) study in northern Thailand suggests that the reluctance of successful market women to expand the scale or range of their operations arises in part from the presence of well-established and well-connected Chinese merchants (see also Geertz 1963; Szanton 1972). In Laos, this

---

18 The Ban Tong refugee camp, just south of Chiang Khong, was the only refugee camp in the north with a significant number of Chinese (Van-es-Beeck 1982: 332).

important barrier to feminine ambition was removed by vigorous state intervention.[19]

Second, regulatory restrictions created opportunities for windfall profits in what would normally be petty and localised trade – a sector in which women dominated. With the official closure of the border, women who were experienced as cross-border traders in vegetables, fish or forest products could now make good profits by taking delivery of smuggled manufactured goods from Chiang Khong, Chiang Saen and small villages along the river. This was a risky business for Thai traders – a number were shot by Thai border police – but Lao provincial authorities took no action to prevent transactions on their side of the river. There was extraordinary demand in Laos for Thai consumer goods and, by making shrewd purchases, petty traders could quickly build up their stock of trading capital. Profits could be enhanced by transporting to towns and villages some distance from the border, supplying, for example, resettlement communities at Viangphoukha who were still heavily dependant on imported goods. In a situation of very restricted supply, women's petty trade became a lucrative business. A similar process was observed on the Thai side of the border where smuggling "contributed to better distribution of income from established traders to small local inhabitants" (Bunyaraks et al. 1977: 2).

Third, the new government created new avenues of influence and petty patronage. Some of the early entrepreneurs were the wives, daughters or relatives of provincial officials. These connections provided them with access to education, employment or assets that could form the basis for trading careers. Air, the daughter of a well-connected official, explicitly linked her skill as a long-distance trader with her state-sponsored education in Hanoi and Moscow. Dam, after marrying into a powerful family in the new administration, left her noodle stall behind and became one of the largest wholesale traders in the north-west, eventually establishing a shop and small warehouse on government land. Other women who had acquired state jobs in the new administration used their non-traditional employment as a stepping stone into commercial enterprise (Ng 1991: 179). Indeed, Mayoury (1993: 133–134) has suggested that women were encouraged to resign from the state sector and pursue other careers as a result of fiscal constraints in the 1980s. Panh's employment in the Post Office provided her with the contacts and confidence to resign and pursue a wholesale trading career. When Noi was employed as a customs officer, she saw that

---

19 Dewey's (1962b: 188) observations on trade in Java are particularly interesting in this context: "These *makelar* [Javanese traders] emerged when the Chinese shopkeepers had to leave the rural villages during the Japanese war and the subsequent disturbances at the time of the Revolution. The vacuum created by the departure of the Chinese was filled by Javanese who wished to become traders on a fairly large scale."

she could make much more money from trade and soon developed a lucrative business carrying goods from Chiang Khong to Oudomxai. Her customs contacts were the envy of many. Other women were encouraged to become involved in trade by their husbands who sought to supplement meagre state incomes with private economic activity (Evans 1995: xvi; Mayoury 1993: 134). A good number of the north-western traders are the wives of petty bureaucrats, teachers, policeman and soldiers and it is possible that the wives of local officials were more able to manipulate government restrictions on trade. Finally, some women were introduced to trade through connections with the state trading enterprises. Tan, for example, first got involved in trade by travelling with her husband who drove a state-owned cargo boat. There was often spare capacity in the boat and she and other private traders used it to carry their goods as far downstream as Pakbeng and Louangphabang. Ireson (1992: 14) reports that some women were employed in state trading stores, another possible avenue of entry into independent trade.

By the early 1980s, these intersecting socio-economic developments had come together in the establishment of the twice-monthly border market at Muangmom, on the Lao-Burma border, just north of the Golden Triangle (Map 1.2). As discussed in chapter 2 (page 61), this market was frequented by Thai shopkeepers from Chiang Saen and Mae Sai who travelled through Burma to avoid the closed Thai-Lao border. Despite the formal regulatory regime of trade restriction, Lao authorities in Houayxay did not oppose the market and, in fact, extended the rough riverside road to link the new market village with the provincial capital. Explicit state support for the market was probably motivated by the need to supply its trading stores in Houayxay and Louangphabang but, as noted in chapter 2, state marketing networks were poorly developed and a new class of independent traders gradually emerged to facilitate the exchange of imported consumer goods for agricultural products. Many women began their long-distance trading careers in the informal and opportunistic frontier atmosphere at Muangmom. Early trading expeditions were financed with profits from smuggling, income from noodle stalls, the sale of gold jewellery, loans or gifts from relatives or money they received upon marriage. "On market days Houayxay was very quiet," one recalled, "everyone went to Muangmom." They travelled in small boats, in old trucks abandoned by Thai sawmillers, by bicycle, on horseback and even on foot. Localised and small-scale cross-border trade was gradually transformed as distribution networks for the highly sought-after Thai imports extended from Houayxay and Louangphabang to Viangphoukha and Hongsa and then to Louangnamtha and Oudomxai. The taxes levied by the Lao customs officers who camped at the market were heavy but, in the riverside atmosphere of sociality, whisky and young women away from home, there was often room for compromise.

The border market at Muangmom operated until the reopening of the upper-Mekong Thai-Lao border in 1988. In the intervening years, many of the domestic restrictions had also been relaxed and those that remained continued to be loosely enforced in the north-west. With the re-establishment of a convenient, permanent and well supplied trade route through Chiang Khong, the overall level of trade increased dramatically (page 71). It was not uncommon for some of the more successful traders to increase the scale of their operations tenfold, in the space of only a few years. When the Chinese border reopened in the early 1990s, there were even more opportunities. Suddenly, petty traders living near the border were making day-trips to Mengla to buy cartons of beer and tape-recorders, and larger-scale traders supplying the market in Oudomxai and Louangnamtha could add a Chinese side-trip to their trading itineraries. The level of trade has continued to increase until the present day but there is still substantial excess demand – as the frantic scenes at the Oudomxai market show – and opportunities for new entrants remain. With good contacts and shrewd buying, windfall profits are still possible. Long-distance trading is now well recognised as an occupational option for women and new traders are still entering the market inspired, and often assisted, by friends and relatives. The widespread practice of trading in groups facilitates market entry. An aspiring trader can travel with friends – buying very little and incurring few costs – while she makes contacts with suppliers and customers, increases her product and price knowledge and learns how to negotiate with port labourers, transport operators and state officials. The emergence and consolidation of a class of Lao transport operators – not infrequently the husbands or relatives of traders – has also helped maintain accessibility for women in the long-distance trading system. Alvarez and Collier (1994: 623), for example, have written of the role of local truckers in "expanding the territorial boundaries of 'community' within which ... women can move about, seek redress for wrongs, and be reasonably assured of security and appropriate social and sexual conduct."

In this more liberalised trading regime, state regulatory action still plays an important role in supporting trading women in the north-west. Though they regularly complain about the predations of the customs officers, the negotiability of customs payments at Houayxay gives north-western traders an important competitive advantage over those who have to deal with the more rigorous customs procedures at Vientiane. At present, the north-western penetration of Thai goods coming through Vientiane is very limited – partly due to poor transport connections but also due to the much higher customs payments that are paid there. "Here we only pay tax on two or three boxes in ten" one Houayxay-based trader told me. "In Vientiane it's eight or nine out of ten." The competitive advantage of Houayxay's customs payments may become even more important as transport connections between Louangphabang and Vientiane improve. The intricate negotiation of payments at Houayxay also assists existing traders by preventing the market being flooded by new and inexperienced entrants. Experienced traders possess an important element of market power in their ability to negotiate successfully with the customs officers and some appear to limit the extent to which they assist others in these crucial dealings. Payment of prohibitive import duty is a common cause of failure of new entrants who do not have the assistance of established traders.

Finally, the state also assists the north-western trading community by restricting the involvement of Thai traders. Traders and shopkeepers in Chiang Khong are relatively free to conduct cross-border trade with Houayxay but to travel further into Laos they would require a passport – which very few have – and a business visa – which would require a long and probably unsuccessful trip to the Lao embassy in Bangkok. Even if Thai traders did succeed in obtaining visas, they would probably encounter further difficulties in obtaining the appropriate import paperwork and permits in Houayxay. As a result, the wholesalers in Chiang Khong must rely on Lao traders to distribute their goods throughout the north-west. This distribution is usually funded by the extension of large amounts of credit to the Lao traders – a situation that many of Chiang Khong's shopkeepers resent, but over which they have little control. It is has been widely observed that credit for merchant capital typically "flows upon the foundations laid by consanguinity and territoriality" (Gregory 1994: 936) but the constraints placed on Chiang Khong's shopkeepers encourages credit to follow more spatially and ethnically dispersed paths. Commercial relationships based on credit are, then, partly a product of a Lao regulatory regime that enforces differential access to mobility.[20]

This regulated credit relationship between spatially constrained Thai shopkeepers and mobile Lao traders is problematic and creates inequalities in the Lao trading community itself. Most credit is provided with considerable and understandable reluctance – the debts are unsecured, the shopkeepers have no legal redress in Laos and a limited network of "enforcers" to call upon in the case of bad debts. The traders who have succeeded in gaining credit are those who have demonstrated their reliability by making regular trading trips to Chiang Khong and, more importantly, those who have been able to establish trusting and friendly relations with the shopkeepers. As with patron-client relations throughout the region (Hanks 1962; 1975; Scott 1972), these relationships emphasise extra-economic sociality such as the sharing of meals and, less often, the

---

20 Dewey (1962b: 189) reports a comparable situation in Java: "Immediately after the [Second World] war there were no Chinese traders left in the rural villages. The town Chinese were forced to advance capital to Javanese buyers if they wished to engaged in this trade."

provision of accommodation by the shopkeepers when the traders come to Chiang Khong. Some shopkeepers also make social visits to the traders' homes in Laos, especially those in Houayxay across the river, but occasionally also those in Louangphabang. In establishing these relationships, married women, especially those who trade with their husbands, appear to be at a substantial advantage. In Chiang Khong, they are perceived as more stable, reliable and respectable credit risks than unmarried women, many of whom have difficulty getting credit despite a history of regular trading journeys to Chiang Khong. Unmarried women can demonstrate themselves to be good and reliable traders but they have difficulty establishing socially respectable relationships with the shopkeepers. Some of the male shopkeepers quietly entertain hopes of sexual access but the semi-formal and domesticated relationships that surround the provision of substantial credit are highly problematic. There are also spatial factors that influence access to credit. Some of the shops in Chiang Khong have an explicit policy of only lending to traders in Houayxay, traders whom they have visited and whose house, land and other assets they have informally inspected. This has placed Houayxay-based traders in a highly advantageous position and they appear to be disproportionately represented among the most affluent and largest-scale traders.

To summarise, the experiences of long-distance trading women illustrate the complex intertwining of liberalising and regulatory practices, and the social benefits that flow from them. Many trading women gained invaluable mobile and commercial experience in the bloated and open trading economies of the 1960s and early 1970s; however many established their position as long-distance traders in the restrictive economy of the late 1970s and early 1980s. This new class of traders has consolidated its position in the more liberalised late 1980s and 1990s, but continues to benefit from a range of state regulatory practices. These regulatory benefits are uneven, advantaging those best in a position to negotiate effectively with customs officers and those who can best gain access to the credit which the spatially constrained shopkeepers in Chiang Khong are forced to provide if they want to sell large volumes in Laos. To conclude, I would like to explore some of the ways in which trading women also benefit by manipulating some of the more "cultural" forms of regulation.

Conclusion: Travelling Identities

The highly mobile and usually successful lives of long-distance traders in north-western Laos suggest that there may be positive and valued "travelling identities" available to women that are not constrained by the negative stereotypes of feminine mobility referred to at the outset of this chapter. While further research is required – especially of traders "at home" rather than "on the road" – I would like to suggest that there are

159

opportunities for women to manipulate and profit from cultural forms of regulation just as there are opportunities to benefit from the more formal regulatory practices of the state. This is not done without some tension, pain and anguish but it does suggest that gender identities may be more malleable and problematic than some interpretations of supposedly "fundamental ideals" (Keyes 1984: 223) may suggest.

Clearly, there are tensions between the roles of long-distance trader and mother. It is not uncommon for traders to spend more time on trading journeys than they do at home and they rely heavily on friends and relatives for assistance in child rearing. Trading women often comment that the regular absence from their children is one of the main difficulties of a trading lifestyle and some of the women try to minimise their absence by, for example, travelling in expensive speedboats rather than accompanying the cargo boats for trips along the Mekong. Yet the role of mother is closely intertwined with the role of nurturer and provider (Keyes 1984), and in this respect most trading women are quite successful. Their houses are almost universally modest, but increasingly their domestic lives are stocked with washing machines, stereo systems, televisions, satellite dishes, battery-operated toys and glass-fronted cupboards displaying Chinese nic-nacs. Most women traders probably contribute substantially more to household finances than husbands who are in salaried employment, and a number of men have joined their wives in trade in recognition of this. Moreover, when both husband and wife are traders, there is often grudging masculine recognition that the women are better operators because they are less likely to be distracted, impoverished or, indeed, infected by whisky, gambling and girls along the way. The household finances are safer in feminine hands. As Ng (1991: 179) wrote of Laos in 1991, "[s]ome women are beginning to be aware of their economic edge over their husbands, and are utilising it subtly to improve their standing within the family." An identity as long-distance trader is not, then, inconsistent with an identity of nurturer and provider and, for some women, it reinforces a longstanding feminine role of household economic manager (Muecke 1984: 464).

There are also cultural tensions and opportunities in the experience of travel itself. Many of the women complain of the rigours of travel – sleeping on boats, travelling all night crammed in the cabins of trucks with chain-smoking truck drivers and spending days in the burning sun at the muddy Mekong ports. Added to this is the stress of managing the transport of large quantities of goods through difficult – and sometime treacherous – terrain. The women rarely express concerns about their personal security, but the effects of this rugged lifestyle, stress and sleep deprivation on their feminine beauty and charm are common preoccupations. "It's a bad life for a woman," one of the more successful traders told me. Yet, once again, there is a positive side. Many of the women value the adventure and excitement of travel very highly, especially when it is shared with their friends in trading groups. In Chiang Khong, for example, some of the women are literally wide-eyed with amazement when they observe extravagantly funded Thai public rituals. They enjoy browsing in Chiang Khong's well-stocked shops, buying clothes or occasionally a gold chain, eating in Chiang Khong's many restaurants or just sitting around in the houses of friends eating one *baht* satay sticks and watching television. In China – their cultural prejudices notwithstanding – there are even more shops and restaurants and electronic goods and cheap cosmetics and fake fur coats and hotels with televisions in the room. Even the stories of horrific experiences in Chinese toilets gain something in the telling. While it is masculine travel and adventure that is usually celebrated in Lao and Thai culture, it seems, as Kirsch (1985: 313–314) has noted, that mobile women have been able to tap into a strong cultural valorisation of travel itself, building a travelling identity that is more open and accessible to them. Moreover, while the rigours of travel may undermine some aspects of femininity, the cosmetics, clothes and jewellery that are obtained in Chiang Khong and Mengla contribute to its distinctive refashioning.

Long-distance trade and travel also creates opportunities for sexual freedoms, though the travelling sexualities of women traders seem to be much more restrained that those of the men (Walker 1995). Some of the women traders have taken the opportunity to enter into sexual relationships with officials, boat operators or even other (male) traders. For others, participation in trading groups – while providing a measure of respectability denied to women trading alone – also allows relaxed and relatively unsupervised interaction with male traders. Evening meals in boats and restaurants along the route are often accompanied by prolonged and ribald discussions of extra-marital liaisons, prostitution, homosexuality and the sexual desperation of some of their male companions. Some of the women are renowned for their whisky drinking in these sessions. Of course, this relative sexual freedom has its consequence and, among the trading and transport community I worked with, there was speculation about the promiscuity, willingness to engage in prostitution or the AIDS status of some women traders. Others were more gentle in their criticisms, merely suggesting that some of the women were "not polite," "not respectful" or simply just "not good." But, once again, there are cultural opportunities here. Women's mobile sexuality may be dangerous but it is also powerful, relatively disciplined and, as long-standing cultural motifs recognise, it can be deployed for material gain (Keyes 1984: 232–233). While some trading women experience difficulties in obtaining credit, there is recognition that feminine sexuality can help negotiate passage and access in a trading system that is full of petty barriers and regulation. Nowhere is this more evident that in the negotiations between the traders and the tight-trousered officials at Houayxay's port. Here, customs officials are often locked in long, confidential conversations with young and attractive traders and it is

161

not uncommon for traders to attribute their low rate of taxation to the charms of one member of their group. One woman was particularly successful. During the final inspection of the boat, her husband, also a trader, would always busy himself tying down the load while his wife talked (almost in whispers) with the customs officers and the immigration police in the crowded front cabin – standing just a little too close, making squeals of protest at the amounts they demanded, subtly drawing attention to the money tucked away in her brassiere and handing them little gifts of fruit or sweets as they left the boat. As Kirsch (1985: 313) has indicated, longstanding sexualised practices can now be profitably deployed on a broader and more mobile stage.

How, then, are we to interpret the lives of these mobile women? Their experiences suggest that, in the right circumstances, there may be room for manoeuvre in the cultural regulation of Lao gender categories. Manoeuvre seems to be a more apt description of the social and cultural strategies of these mobile women than either the "unmoor[ing] from ... Buddhist values" (Keyes, 1984: 236) that some seem to regret or the "play[ing] havoc with gender ideologies" (Ong and Peletz 1995: 4) that others applaud and encourage. The long-distance trading women of north-western Laos have created innovative travelling identities which resonate with – rather than abandon or subvert – some of the common cultural regulatory practices in their communities. They have succeeded in a careful intertwining of motherhood, money, travel and sex. While the emergence of women as long-distance traders is the product of very specific historical and geo-political circumstances, their successful moulding of gender categories suggests that there may have been other innovative opportunities in the past. And, in the future, if independent traders are sidelined by ten-wheel trucks, import-export companies and supermarkets, new cultural and geographic niches will probably emerge, allowing enterprising Lao women new opportunities for profit and pleasure.

CHAPTER SEVEN

Entrepreneurs, Bureaucrats and the Army

Sawmills and the Timber Trade

Introduction: Incident at Sin Udom

One grey morning in early August 1994, I stood chatting with truck drivers at Houayxay's main cargo port. They had come across the river from Chiang Khong on the vehicular ferry, a circuitous route around sandbanks and rocky outcrops. There were eight trucks, all of them owned by Chiang Khong Transport, an affiliate of the *Sin Udom Sawmill Company* which ran a timber yard a few kilometres along the road to Chiang Rai. They had come across to Laos, as they did almost every week, to collect a load of sawn timber from Sin Udom's sawmill, just downstream from Houayxay on the banks of the Mekong. I was keen to visit the mill and, when one of the truck drivers asked if I wanted to go along for the trip, I readily accepted. It was little more than ten kilometres along the rough road built in the 1960s to reinforce RLG control on a narrow riverside strip of non-communist territory (Map 2.3) but, in the midst of the rainy season, the road was reduced to a quagmire. It was over three hours before we arrived in the muddy and oil-soaked log-yard beside the mill – a huge ancient-looking wooden building in a clearing on the southern side of a ramshackle and squalid village. A mountain of sawdust dominated the river-bank, gently trickling into the river as it was fed by women and young girls pushing rough wooden hand-trolleys. A tangle of bicycles, seemingly abandoned outside the mill, indicated a substantial work force inside. Dotted along the steep river-bank, charcoal pits smoked, adding to the melancholy and misty air. "If there is such a thing as primitive accumulation," I thought, "this is surely it."

The two-storey company office, like many Lao offices, seemed to be full of empty rooms with the occasional large desk for work and out-of-date Lao Beer calendars – featuring modestly dressed Lao girls – for decoration. The local manager welcomed me warmly, sitting me down with a can of *Sprite* and some tinned fish curry with rice. As I ate, I tried to take in the

163

maps on the wall. They seemed to have logging concessions and cubic metres marked on them but I couldn't get my bearings and the village names were meaningless to me. I asked my host where the timber for the mill came from. "From the forest" he said.

I did not get much more than this. We chatted for a while and I spent some time wandering around the unfriendly village before heading down to the river to wave down a passing boat for the trip back to Houayxay. But the boats were infrequent, mostly full, and they mainly took the narrow channel on the far side of the river, several hundred yards away. The torrential afternoon rain defeated me and I retreated to the company office where things had started to warm up. Two girls from Houayxay's favourite *karaoke* hall had arrived, prompting the preparation of greasy chunks of turkey and the production of bottles of Thai whisky. Soon after, we were joined by two *Department of Forestry* officers from Houayxay who had come to supervise the export of the timber being loaded onto the trucks, to reconcile the amount loaded with the export paperwork. We sat and ate and drank and smoked and got silly. One of the girls disappeared upstairs, her friend was having second thoughts. The Sin Udom office workers were interested. The minds of the forestry officers turned from regulation to sex. One of them asked me how many times a day a *faraŋ* (a westerner) could do it. Ten, I told him. It was a good joke. Outside the monsoon rain was pounding down. The single whisky glass we all shared now had a liberal coating of turkey fat. In the middle of the smoky mayhem the paperwork for the timber was produced, figures rapidly recited and official signatures easily obtained. Eventually the rain cleared, a speedboat was summoned with a two-way radio and in no time at all we were skidding along the river towards Houayxay. Anthropologist, *karaoke* workers, company official and the forestry officers nursing bottles of whisky and packets of cigarettes beneath their coats.

This, then, is a muddy and smoky corner of the Economic Quadrangle. The era of the Quadrangle in north-western Laos has witnessed a spate of Thai investment in sawmilling and rapid increases in the export of sawn timber. Nationally, timber is now the largest export item for Laos, the bulk of it heading across the Mekong to Thailand. According to Hirsch (1995: 235–236), this is part of a "new geopolitics of resource development" in mainland South-East Asia, a geopolitics dominated by Thailand whose "regional agenda" is now focused on the "development and exploitation of neighbouring countries' resources." This, he argues, has arisen out of political and practical limits on natural resource exploitation within Thailand, typified by the national logging ban of 1989 (Hirsch 1995: 238–240; see also Pinkaew and Rajesh 1992). Laos, he suggests, is increasingly becoming a "resource periphery for the rapidly industrialising Thai economy" (Hirsch 1995: 254).

Hirsch's notion of a newly emerging centre-periphery relationship is popular in analyses of the timber industry in Laos. In their overview of environmental change in South-East Asia, Bryant and Parnwell (1996: 15–16) refer to the negative consequences of the "Lao PDR's relatively recent arrival on the fringes of the global capitalist system, following the partial dismantling of its command economy." In the same volume, Rigg and Jerndal (1996) develop the argument further, suggesting that a poorly developed Lao state has little control over powerful logging interests in neighbouring Thailand. With a rudimentary legal framework and weak bureaucratic institutions, the Lao government is forced into "policy-making on the run" and "seems to be powerless to halt" widespread deforestation (Rigg and Jerndal 1996: 159, 161). They conclude that "Thailand will be the main winner" in the resource economies of the Economic Quadrangle (Rigg and Jerndal 1996: 162).

In this chapter, my final case study of the Economic Quadrangle, I examine recent developments in the timber industry in north-western Laos. The centre-periphery analyses of Hirsch and others are, undoubtedly, supported by the predominance of Thai investment in north-western sawmilling. The two main waves of Thai investment since 1988 are examined in the first section of the chapter. Yet, as the previous chapters have argued, regulatory regimes *within* Laos have had a strong impact on patterns of trade and commercial activity. Local contours of regulatory power are influential and tend to be overlooked in analyses of central power and peripheral passivity. In the second section, I examine the changing regimes of Lao forestry regulation and the opportunities *and* constraints these regulations have created for Thai sawmillers. While the writers cited above emphasise the vulnerability of an increasingly open Lao economy, recent Thai investment in sawmilling has, in fact, taken place in a context of tighter regulation of the timber industry. The most dramatic change occurred in late 1994, when Lao military companies were given a monopoly on logging and sales of timber to sawmills. The dramatic effects of this most recent exercise of "peripheral power" are examined in the third section. I conclude by proposing two qualifications to Hirsch's (1995: 236) concept of a "new regional resource economy." First, returning to the historical theme that has run through this work, I suggest that the current geopolitics of timber exploitation in north-western Laos is far from new but, in many respects, represents a revival of the cross-border economic relations that were briefly disrupted after the change of government in 1975. Second, geopolitical images of Thai resource domination – and the centre-periphery models that inform such images – should not obscure the extent to which regimes of regulation in the era of the Economic Quadrangle are increasingly constraining Thai investment strategies. Of particular importance in this respect is the role of the Lao army and its corporate off-shoots.

Entrepreneurs: Thai Investment in Sawmilling

In the late 1980s, the Lao government moved to revitalise its capital-starved industrial sector by introducing a more liberal policy on foreign investment. A new law permitted foreign participation in most sectors of the economy, providing for joint ventures – including ventures with Lao state enterprises – and for wholly foreign-owned enterprises (GLPDR 1989a). The law has been assessed by the Lao government to be "successful far beyond estimation" (BP 21 February 1995) despite the relatively small size of most projects (BP 22 February 1994). By mid-1994, foreign commitments had been made to over 430 projects, mainly in the tourism, transport, mining, manufacturing and agribusiness sectors (BP 21 February 1995; Vokes and Fabella 1995: Table 21). Thailand is by far the largest investor, with over 37 per cent of projects and over 60 per cent of investment capital (BP 21 February 1995). A new foreign investment law, which streamlined administrative procedures and lowered some taxes, was adopted in 1994 (GLPDR 1994d).

The north-western Lao sawmilling industry exemplified the need for foreign capital. In the late 1980s it was in a parlous state. Of the ten or so sawmills that had been built around Houayxay during the 1960s and early 1970s, only two survived the withdrawal of investment and the severing of border trade that followed the Pathet Lao victory in 1975. But even for these two – Sin Udom and Bandan (Map 1.2) – shortages of fuel and spare parts were chronic problems and their output amounted to only a few hundred cubic metres of sawn timber per year (GLPDR 1990b). Two other north-western mills – built by provincial authorities in Oudomxai and Louangnamtha with Chinese assistance and machinery confiscated from Thai mills near Houayxay – were also operating, but they too had an output amounting to only a few per cent of their capacity (GLPDR 1990b). Assessments of the Lao sawmilling industry undertaken during the 1980s indicate that the technology was basic, the quality of processed wood was low and log wastage was high (Khambay and Frederiksen 1989: 22). One study found that less than half of the logs cut in the forest ever reached the mills (Keating 1989). Nationally, an annual average of only 6,000 cubic metres of sawn timber was exported in the first half of the 1980s (GLPDR 1986: 3).

The first wave

In the late 1980s, a number of Thai entrepreneurs were invited by Lao provincial authorities to invest – under leasing arrangements – in the refurbishment and upgrading of sawmills.[1] The mills at Sin Udom and

---

1 Bunyaraks et al. (1977: 37) suggest that some Thai investment in sawmilling may have been sought by Lao authorities around Vientiane as early as 1977. I obtained some sketchy information about a Bangkok-based timber trading company that was involved in the mill at Bandan in the early 1980s, but it was impossible to gain further details.

Bandan had been "nationalised" after they were abandoned by their Thai owners in 1976, but the provincial government – though keen to secure the revenue that would flow from a revived trade in sawn timber – had extremely limited funds to invest. Under the new cooperative arrangements with Thai entrepreneurs, well over two million *baht* was invested at Bandan, close to one million at Sin Udom and almost two million at Louangnamtha (GLPDR 1990b: Appendix 1/4).[2] Reinvestment in sawmilling in the north-west was consistent with trends elsewhere in Laos, whereby 36 mills were bought into production between 1988 and 1990, increasing national milling capacity by almost 60 per cent (GLPDR 1990b: 6–8).

The Sin Udom sawmill was initially leased out by provincial authorities for 100,000 *baht* per year. The lease was held by two Thai businessmen – Visit and Sompong – who formed the *Sin Udom Sawmill Company* and established a substantial timber yard just to the south of Chiang Khong. This was Sompong's first involvement in timber, but Visit had been active in the timber trade in Vientiane and Houayxay during the 1960s and 1970s and he claimed to have maintained official contacts in Laos, despite the change of government in 1975.[3] Initially, their sawmilling efforts were hampered by a shortage of logs but, by the early 1990s, they had built a network of forest tracks and invested in trucks and elephants to secure their supply. However, the partnership did not last long and Visit transferred his investment to the mill at Louangnamtha. Nevertheless, Sin Udom prospered and by 1993 its timber exports at Chiang Khong accounted for almost 70 per cent of the mill's rated capacity. The company emerged as a substantial business force in Chiang Khong. In 1995, it owned the town's main trucking company, a new housing estate opposite the timber yard, extensive tracts of rural land, the local supermarket and the cross-river ferry between Chiang Khong and Houayxay, privatised by Lao authorities several years before. None of this, however, generates as much local discussion as the fact that Sompong is said to have two wives.

In Louangnamtha, Visit – also locally renowned for his polygamy – has invested heavily in upgrading the mill, and has succeeded in poaching a number of skilled mill operators, truck drivers and elephant handlers from Sin Udom. It is now the most technologically advanced of the original north-western mills, and also boasts a modern furniture factory, built in recognition of the increasing encouragement of domestic timber processing (see page 172). The sawmill is also diversifying into road construction, using the equipment and expertise acquired for building forest access roads

---

2 The 1989 *Sawmill Survey* (GLPDR 1990b) also indicates that a small mill was built at Paktha, but I could not obtain any local information on this. Nor could I obtain any information on the fate of the mill at Oudomxai, except that it had closed some time before I undertook my fieldwork due to exhaustion of local timber supplies.

3 Hirsch (1995: 239) also refers to the importance of pre-1975 timber experience amongst current investors.

around Louangnamtha. Visit's sawmilling company has succeeded in winning road building contracts in both Louangnamtha and Phongsali provinces.

Details on the Thai investment at Bandan are sketchy. The initial investor was said to be a Bangkok-based timber trading company, with military connections that enabled it to export some sawn timber prior to the official reopening of the border. By the early 1990s, the lease for the mill had been obtained by a timber trading company based in Nong Khai (Map 1.1) that had also been involved in the timber trade in Vientiane in the 1970s. The mill at Bandan now has the highest output of any mill in north-western Laos, obtaining a generous supply of logs from the Special Region (Map 1.3).

Most of the output of these mills – at least 70 per cent from Louangnamtha, close to 90 per cent from Sin Udom and Bandan – is exported to Thailand through the port of Chiang Khong. Sawn timber from Sin Udom and Bandan is carried upstream on privately owned Lao cargo boats, while the timber from Louangnamtha is trucked to Pakbeng and then transferred to boats for the journey up river. The level of export timber traffic has risen substantially since 1988, with the Lao-Thai balance of trade at Chiang Khong actually favouring Laos in 1992 and 1993 (Table 3.1) – largely as a result of timber exports. I estimate that timber now makes up almost 60 per cent of the Lao export trade at Chiang Khong and a string of riverside timber yards has sprouted in the village of Hua Wiang, on the northern outskirts of the town (Map 4.1). Each of the mills has at least one timber trading company in Chiang Khong which coordinates payment of Thai import duties and the dispatch of timber to buyers throughout Thailand and, in some cases, abroad. There are also a number of independent timber trading companies in Chiang Khong which buy small lots of sawn timber from some of the north-western mills as well as large volumes from the mill in the far northern province of Phongsali.[4] Several of these trading companies have "parent" companies in north-east Thailand that are also heavily involved in the Thai-Lao timber trade.

The second wave

The second wave of Thai investment took place between 1993 and 1995, with three new, modern mills being constructed. Two of the new mills are located on the Mekong itself, one at the small market village of Pakkhop and the other just downstream from Pakbeng (Map 1.2). The third mill is located near Muanghun, about 30 kilometres north-east of Pakbeng on the road to Oudomxai (Map 1.2). The mill at Muanghun began full-scale production in late 1994, while the mills at Pakbeng and Pakkhop were

---

4 Timber from Phongsali is trucked to Pakbeng via Mengla district in China.

opened in mid-1995. The effect of this second wave of investment – approaching 20 million *baht* – is more than a doubling of capacity in the north-west and a significant increase in sawmilling's regional coverage.

The mill at Pakbeng is owned by Anuwat Wongwan, currently one of the most entrepreneurial members of Thailand's famous Wongwan family. The family, originally from the timber-rich province of Phrae (Map 1.1), has had a long involvement in timber ventures in northern Thailand, dating from a teak concession subcontracted from the *East Asiatic Company* in the nineteenth century. Narong, the current family head, has been involved in sawmilling since the 1950s, but made most of his fortune through tobacco cultivation and processing. He has also been involved in politics since the 1940s, rising to Minister of Agriculture in 1990. In 1992, he was set to become Prime Minister of Thailand until American allegations of involvement in the drug trade surfaced (Pasuk and Sungsidh 1994: 72–73). The Wongwan's have been involved in Laos for several years, with investments in tobacco cultivation and curing at Louang-namtha, a cigarette factory in Vientiane and a substantial interest in Vientiane's *Lane Xang Hotel*. To my knowledge the mill at Pakbeng is their first non-domestic timber venture. The mill is strategically placed to secure timber both from Oudomxai province and from the Special Region and, in late 1994, had already stockpiled large quantities of logs while the mill was still under construction. Their investment suffered an expensive but temporary setback when a boat carrying the milling equipment from Chiang Khong struck rocks in the Mekong and sank.

The owner of the mill at Pakkhop is from a northern Thai province bordering Burma and was previously a senior police officer and later a member of parliament. As one of his friends told me, "he made his money

Table 7.1 North-western Lao sawmills, 1995

	Built	*Investment*	*Capacity*	*Main Timber Source*
Sin Udom	1968	Thai	9,000	Bokeo
Bandan	1968	Thai	10,000	Bokeo, Special Region
Louangnamtha	1976	Thai	7,500	Louangnamtha
Pakkhop	1994	Thai	11,000	Special Region
Muanghun	1994	Thai/Lao	12,000	Oudomxai
Pakbeng	1995	Thai	11,000	Oudomxai, Special Region

Source: Fieldwork 1994–1995 and GLPDR (1990b).
Notes: Construction dates for Sin Udom and Bandan are approximate. 'Capacity' is an estimate of the annual volume (cubic metres) of logs that can be processed. The figures vary somewhat depending on the mix of hard-wood and soft-wood. There is also a very small mill operating at Hongsa and several small 'furniture factories' throughout the region.

169

first, now he's going into business." I am uncertain, but suspect that he may have had some involvement in logging in Burma – several of the skilled workers at the mill said they had worked in Burma – but this is his first venture in Laos. I could obtain no information on the Thai investors in the mill at Muanghun except that they have entered into a joint venture with a prominent northern Lao trading company – *Huakhong* – and that their investment in the mill was preceded by involvement in the export of unprocessed logs from Oudomxai province.[5]

Bureaucrats: Regulating the Timber Industry

As argued in the previous chapters, the intertwining of state liberalising and regulating practices creates a complex environment of opportunities and constraints. This is equally true of the re-emerging sawmilling industry in the north-west. Liberalising measures have certainly created opportunities for Thai investors. In 1988, the border crossing at Chiang Khong-Houayxay was reopened, enabling the official recommencement of sawn timber exports which had been suspended since late 1976. It also enabled the importation of machinery, spare parts, vehicles, fuel and elephants, all of which were essential for the revival of sawmilling. As noted above, the Lao foreign investment law also permitted joint ventures between provincial timber enterprises and foreign investors (Carnegie 1993: 40; GLPDR 1989a). The law provided for a substantial strengthening of the "informal" relationships that had already developed between Thai timber traders and provincial governments in Laos. In the late 1980s, there was also a policy emphasis on the privatisation of state assets as part of the move towards a more market-oriented economy. The sawmills at Sin Udom, Bandan and Louangnamtha were leased, rather than sold outright, in what was a common form of "collaborative privatisation" throughout Laos. Leasing of sawmills was favoured both by provincial authorities – who were keen to maintain some control over what were likely to be lucrative enterprises – and by the Thai investors – who were cautious about the investment climate in Laos and who appreciated the low leasing charges set by the capital-hungry provinces.[6]

Nevertheless, while liberalising measures have created important opportunities, both phases of Thai investment have taken place in the context of increasing forestry regulation within Laos. Images of external penetration of an increasingly open industry are a little misleading. For the Thai sawmillers there have been important tensions and contradictions within this process. On the one hand, a key thrust of the new regulatory

---

5 *Huakhong's* main activity in the north-west is the distribution of fuel under contract to the *Lao State Fuel Company*. It also operates several petrol stations.
6 For a general discussion of privatisation and leasing, see Vokes and Fabella (1995: 80).

environment has been to encourage the domestic processing of timber rather than the export of unprocessed logs. This has clearly contributed to a favourable policy and administrative environment for Thai investment in Lao sawmilling. On the other hand, the regulatory environment has also been characterised by centralisation of forestry power, most clearly expressed in Vientiane's imposition of provincial logging quotas. Until about late 1994, Thai sawmillers appeared to be successful in undermining many aspects of central regulation, but this evasion – and the obvious financial success it has generated – has recently prompted a dramatic change in Lao government strategy. The tensions of investment in an environment of increasing forestry regulation have now started to take their toll. In the following sections I trace this intriguing history.

Centralisation, quotas and evasion

In the first half of the 1980s, the emphasis in the forestry industry was on provincial autonomy, with only broad policy guidelines set by the central government. Provinces were authorised to conduct logging, sawmilling and timber export (Stuart-Fox 1986: 118; WB 1992; Young and Hyde 1988: 21). In the north-west the level of sawmilling activity was low, but there were some unprocessed log exports through Houayxay-Chiang Khong and at other less supervised points along the border. Some logs came from as far downstream as Louangphabang (Stuart-Fox 1986: 118). Officially, the border was closed until 1989, but Lao provincial authorities were keen to exchange timber for manufactured goods and Thai currency. On the Thai side of the border, well-connected timber merchants could ensure that Thai army units and border police turned a blind eye to the cross-border consignments.[7] Thai buyers often secured very favourable deals as a result of Lao provincial officials' ignorance of international market conditions (Evans 1991a; Young and Hyde 1988). In a crucially important development in 1985, the Lao Army was also permitted to establish timber extraction and marketing enterprises (GLPDR 1990c: 76; Stuart-Fox 1986: 118). Military involvement in forestry activities in the north-west was limited, though they were very active in nearby Xaignabouli province (Map 1.3), from which they would later extend their influence.

By the late 1980s, serious concerns had emerged about the degree of provincial independence in the timber trade. In part, these concerns were financial. The provinces relied heavily on timber sales for provincial revenue but they received poor prices for timber and had a poor record in

---

7 Most of this trade was "unofficial" though both the Thai army and Lao provincial authorities were heavily involved. Official Chiang Khong customs figures for 1979 record no imports of sawn timber or logs from Houayxay, while the figures for 1980 and 1984 are a tiny 340 tonnes and 50 tonnes respectively (IMC 1987: B.04).

the collection of resource and trading taxes (Douglas 1989; Evans 1991a: 112; Khambay and Frederiksen 1989: 22). However, the main stated concern was the environmental impact of what was seen as unsustainable and indiscriminate felling (GLPDR 1990c: 21). Log exports were increasing rapidly and new sawmills were being approved with little regard to planning a sustainable supply of timber (GLPDR 1990b: 17). As the *World Bank* reported:

> Since the mid-1980s the rate of deforestation has become unsustainable as local governments relied on timber sales to raise revenues and the Thai logging ban created more lucrative export opportunities. (WB 1994: 271)

Rates of logging were relatively low in the north but environmental impacts there were compounded by a higher level – and longer history – of forest-depleting shifting cultivation (Douglas 1989: 2; FAO 1980; Hirsch and Cheong 1996: 48). In 1989, the *First National Conference on Forestry* recognised the need for more developed forest policy and legislation and, over the following years, an array of – sometimes inconsistent – regulatory measures were put in place to increase central government control over the flow of timber out of the country (Table 7.2). These included: bans on the export of logs; bans on logging altogether to encourage clear-up of old logs; increased resource and export taxes; forest inventories; and the development of forest management plans. A driving force was the *World Bank*-sponsored *Tropical Forest Action Plan* (TFAP) (GLPDR 1990c). A central goal was to encourage local processing of timber. The goal set by the TFAP was that only ten per cent of felled timber would be exported as logs (GLPDR 1990c: 88). Restrictions on log exports in central and southern Laos have been relatively unsuccessful but, in the north-west, timber traders report that log exports at Houayxay-Chiang Khong were almost entirely replaced by exports of sawn timber in the first half of the 1990s.[8]

Regulatory restrictions on log exports and an emphasis on domestic processing undoubtedly encouraged Thai investment in sawmilling. These *regulatory* initiatives in the forestry sector resonated favourably with *liberalising* policies relating to foreign investment and privatisation. However, less favourable was the attempt to restrict the rate of timber extraction through the imposition of a series of provincial quotas (Table 7.3). In 1990, their first year of operation, the quotas came to a national total of 280,000 cubic metres. This was the level of sustainable cut that had been recommended in the TFAP (GLPDR 1990c; WB 1992: 4). In 1991, they were increased to well over 400,000 cubic metres, substantially higher than the TFAP had advised, but still a far cry from the two million cubic metres recommended at one stage by a number of international agencies

---

8 My observations in Chiang Khong during 1994 and 1995 confirm this.

Table 7.2 Regulation of the timber industry in Laos, 1981–1994

1981	Provinces granted autonomy on forestry exploitation.
1985	Army permitted to establish forestry exploitation and marketing enterprises.
1988	Central government condemns provincial over-exploitation in the Sixth Resolution. Ban on log exports to encourage local processing.
1989	*First National Conference on Forestry* calls for centralised forest policy, legislation and regulation (GLPDR 1990c: 22; see also GLPDR 1989b). Timber resource taxes introduced and export taxes increased "drastically" (GLPDR 1990c: 16). Taxes encouraged the clear up of old logs (Keating 1989: 11) but the system of taxes and royalties is considered to be inadequate by international standards (Carnegie 1993: 75). *Decree 117 (Management of Forests and Forested Land)* establishes regulatory framework.
1990	Publication of *Tropical Forestry Action Plan* (GLPDR 1990c). Sets aim that log exports be only ten per cent of the total log cut. Provincial logging quotas introduced.
1991	*Decree 67/PM* places temporary suspension on logging while a country-wide audit is undertaken and guidelines are developed for further exploitation (GLPDR 1991a). Decree condemns widespread violation of 1989 forestry decree (*Decree 117*). Stricter controls placed on timber exports across the land border between Xaignabouli province and Thailand (Stuart-Fox 1991: 3).
1992	Timber exports temporarily suspended.
1993	"Log export volume reached all-time high despite the prevailing ban" (GLPDR 1994b). *Prime Minister's Decree 169 on Management and Use of Forests and Forest Land* replaces *Decree 117* of 1989 (GLPDR 1994c). It provides for detailed regulation of forestry activities. Tree felling is forbidden unless in accordance with forest management plans. Logging companies are made responsible for reforestation (Carnegie 1993: 77).
1994	Logging concessions for sawmills revoked. National logging and timber marketing rights granted to three state (military) enterprises.

Table 7.3 North-western Lao timber quotas: 1991–1996

	1991/1992	1992/1993	1993/1994	1994/1995	1995/1996
National	443,800	553, 670	564, 300	489,000	637,000
Bokeo	10,050	7,000	2,000	1,700	3,000
Louangnamtha	4,800	3,000	2,000	1,000	2,000
Oudomxai	13,350	7,000	1,000	1,200	4,000
Special Region	n.a.	5,200	3,000	1,200	5,000
North-west total	28,200	22,200	8,000	5,100	14,000

Source: Lao PDR *Ministry of Agriculture and Forestry* and *World Bank* (1992).
Notes: Figures are in cubic metres. The quota figures for each 'year' refer to the dry-season cutting period which runs from about November to June in the following year. In 1991/1992 the districts making up the Special Region were part of Oudomxai province. By 1995/1996 they had been incorporated into Xaignabouli province and I have estimated the amount for the Special Region districts from the provincial total for Xaignabouli.

(FEER 1982; UNDP 1991). In the years since, quotas have increased further, reaching a total of 637,000 cubic metres in the 1995/1996 cutting season.

As a result of the rethinking that followed the 1991 logging ban, there has been a dramatic increase in the percentage of quota derived from "project areas" – mostly areas to be flooded as a result of hydro-electric schemes (mainly in southern and central Laos). In 1995/1996, for example, it is planned that almost half of the national quota will be extracted from the reservoir for the proposed Nam Theun 2 dam in southern Laos. In many other provinces, substantial portions of the quotas will be derived from road-way and electricity line clearance. The decline in quotas from non-project areas is reflected in the north-west where the four province quota was reduced from over 20,000 cubic metres in 1991/1992 and 1992/1993 to only 5,100 cubic metres in 1994/1995. However in 1995/1996 it was increased to about 14,000 cubic metres, no doubt reflecting the expansion in sawmilling capacity.

It is not easy to assess the impact of the quota regime in the north-west. What initially appears to be a simple system is clouded at the provincial level by a series of "additional approved quotas," "province approved quotas" and "quotas carried over from previous years." Undoubtedly, this ambiguity and provincial flexibility points to weaknesses in the system and recently the government has moved to revoke powers to issue permits for quota extensions. There also appear to be substantial problems in relation to the status of the quota figures. In 1994/1995, for example, quotas substantially higher than the central government figures were widely discussed in the north-west, with a high degree of consistency between sawmillers, provincial regulators and timber traders. These totalled 18,000 cubic metres for the north-western provinces, more than three times the official quota set for that cutting season.

Timber export figures indicate that logging and milling well in excess of official quotas is taking place. During 1994, over 11,000 cubic metres of sawn timber was exported – through Houayxay-Chiang Khong – by north-western Lao sawmills, the vast majority of it from the three mills in the first wave of Thai investment. By local industry standards, this represents over 22,000 cubic metres of logs processed,[9] almost three times the official quota for the prior felling season (1993/1994). The discrepancies are highlighted if the performances of the three mills that were fully operational during this period are examined. Sin Udom, in only nine months of operation prior to its closure in October 1994, exported over 3,200 cubic metres of sawn timber representing well over 6,000 cubic metres of logs. This is more than three times higher than the 1993/1994 quota for Bokeo,

---

9 This is based on a recovery rate of 50 per cent which is the average industry standard in Laos. See, for example, GLPDR (1990b: 11) and WB (1992).

the province from which Sin Udom gets almost all its timber. Most of this excess appears to have been approved provincially as a carry-over of an unused portion of the 1992/1993 provincial quota, though the export of over 3,400 cubic metres in 1993 would have accounted for almost all of this. It must also be noted that the Bokeo quota is shared with the mill at Bandan. During 1994, Bandan exported sawn timber accounting for almost 10,000 cubic metres of logs, close to full capacity for the mill. No wonder the owner's daughter told me that Bokeo's quota – 2,000 cubic metres! – was insufficient, forcing the mill to ship large numbers of logs upstream from the Special Region. But the Special Region's quota for 1993/1994 was only 3,000 cubic metres and this was also being drawn on by the new mills at Pakbeng and Pakkhop who were building up log-stockpiles even before their milling machinery had arrived from Thailand. The third operating mill – at Louangnamtha – exported timber accounting for 4,000 cubic metres of logs from a province where the official logging quota was only 2,000 cubic metres.

All of these comments are based on exports to Thailand only, and do not take into consideration timber used for domestic consumption (perhaps an additional ten or 20 per cent) or exports to China and Vietnam (albeit at a low level). Also, while there were no unprocessed log exports at Houayxay-Chiang Khong during 1994 or 1995 – a success for central government regulation – it is possible that illegal log exports take place across the land border between the Special Region and remote parts of northern Thailand. It is also possible that the export figures – provided by Thai customs – are understated, given collaborative evasion of Thai import duties and other charges. All in all, my research lends strong support to the claim in the *Vientiane Times* that "over quota logging [is] prevalent in [the] provinces" (VT 18–24 November 1994).

The most ominous sign for the quota system is the dramatic increase in sawmilling capacity. The annual capacity of the six sawmills in the north-west is now over 60,000 cubic metres of logs. This is well beyond the 1995/1996 quota of 14,000 cubic metres and even substantially exceeds estimates of sustainable logging levels for all of northern Laos, not just the north-west (GLPDR 1990c: 77). With the installation of new capacity, the north-west has been brought into line with provinces in central and southern Laos where milling capacity typically exceeds quotas by a factor of at least three (WB 1992: 5). Talking to new mill operators, it seems that the investment has gone ahead in the belief that the quotas would not be strictly enforced and, as the figures above indicate, they had good reason to believe this.

The sociology of this confidence is fascinating and requires further – and possibly foolhardy – investigation. At one level, as Rigg and Jerndal (1996: 158–162) have suggested, it is based on the poor resourcing, the low salaries, and low level of education of regulatory staff. Provincial and district offices are chronically understaffed and there are shortages of vehicles and basic office and field equipment. Supervision of logging and sawmilling operations is often undertaken by young men working and living in isolated environments alongside the management and staff of the sawmilling companies. They are clearly vulnerable to social, sexual and financial favours and what the Lao government itself has called the "corruption of cadres" (GLPDR 1991a). Moreover, the collection of resource and export taxes at a provincial level provides regulatory staff with the opportunity to accept under-reporting of timber in return for a share of the taxes that are avoided. Perhaps this accounts for the fact that recorded 1994 timber exports at Houayxay were less than two thirds the level of imports on the other side of the river in Chiang Khong. As the new mills at Pakkhop and Pakbeng develop road links direct into Thailand, the opportunities for even more blatant under-reporting at isolated border posts will proliferate.

It is also likely that there has been active collaboration between sawmillers and senior figures in the government administration. In the north-western provinces, where there is still a very poorly developed commercial class, the sawmillers are a major business force and a number indicated to me that they enjoy close personal relations with senior officers in provincial governments. Observers elsewhere in Laos have noted that the practice of semi-privatisation through leasing and licensing has provided avenues for enrichment for members of the administrative elite (Evans 1995: xvi) and it is likely that this is the case in the sawmilling sector, especially in the light of what appear to be extraordinarily low official leasing charges. Several sawmilling investors are also involved in activities extending beyond sawmilling – road-building, transportation, fuel trading and tobacco processing – increasing their influence in investment-hungry provinces and providing diverse opportunities for favours and kick-backs. Their powerful position is comparable to that of the provincial *caw phɔɔ* ("godfathers") in Thailand who also rose to power in times of economic transformation, benefiting from their "informal influence" in local, regional and national political arenas (Pasuk and Sungsidh 1994: 74–86). As Pasuk and Sungsidh (1994: 76) have argued, location is also important and "it is significant that many of the most notorious *caw phɔɔ* centres emerged either on the coasts or borders which offered opportunities for smuggling, or close to the forests, which, with the right kind of protection, provided massive opportunities for illegal logging." North-western Laos provides an ideal combination of both these factors. Narong Wongwan, whose son, Anuwat, owns the mill at Pakbeng, is one of the more prominent *caw phɔɔ* in Thailand (Pasuk and Sungsidh 1994: 72–73) and is clearly in a position to exercise influence at even the highest levels in Laos.

These bureaucratic-business collaborations are one aspect of the persistent autonomy of Lao provinces. While the overarching presence of the highly centralised communist party in Laos may have inhibited the widespread development of Thai-style *caw phɔɔ* (Evans pers. comm.), it seems likely that the entrepreneurial activities of provincial administrations have drawn party officials into unlikely alliances with commercial interests. In the case of the timber industry this has even involved the resumption of provincial alliances with Thai entrepreneurs that were first cultivated by Royal Lao Government elites in the 1960s and 1970s. Whether or not these commercial alliances will lead to a diminution in central party power is unclear, but what is clear in the timber industry – as it is in the transport and trading sectors discussed previously – is that "the party and the state [are] no longer the exclusive source of social mobility in the new Laos" (Evans 1995: xvi). What is also clear is that communist party structures at a provincial level have been relatively incapable or unwilling to effectively implement some of the main regulatory strategies of the central government. This failure has opened the way for a dramatic regulatory intervention by the army "the one possible nation wide organization which could substitute itself for the party if necessary" (Evans 1995: xvii).

To summarise the argument so far: there is no doubt that Thai investors are heavily involved in the extraction, milling and export of timber in north-western Laos and that their "penetration" of the Lao "periphery" has been facilitated by the liberalisation of the Economic Quadrangle. Yet this "penetration" has also been *managed* – to some extent – by Lao regulation. Leasing arrangements for sawmills, policies encouraging the domestic processing of timber and provincial quotas are all part of a regulatory regime that has provided opportunities and constraints for Thai sawmillers. Thai companies have been relatively successful in evading quotas, but this success is not due merely to the weakness of Lao administration but also to collaboration between external investors and domestic officials. In brief, the deliberate and active participation of Lao interests in the timber industry should not be understated.

The Army: Changing the Rules

> ... for many years, the Party and the Government have laid down many strategic plans and made sizeable investment for the forest protection and development, aiming to have this rich national heritage effectively and sustainably utilised. However, there are remaining some public servants, businessmen and inhabitants who do not profoundly understand and appreciate the immense utility and strategic implication of forest resource. ... [T]here is a tendency to see the Government continue to permit the private companies to cut the trees in the forests and operate the logging activities in the competitive manner as in the past without considering the serious negative effects which are multifaceted

177

and intractable. . . . Therefore, the Prime Minister issues Additional Order as follows: 1. For the logging and export oriented wood-processing, the Government has authorised only the State Enterprises which have received the permission to carry out the logging and to build downstream integrated wood industries such as: Agriculture Forestry Development and Service Company [AFD], Phoudoi [Mountainous Area] Development Company [MAD], and Integrated Agriculture Forestry Development Company [DAFI] on the basis of annual quotas from the Government and in specific operation areas for each company. (GLPDR 1994a)

In October 1994, the central government, concerned about continued logging in excess of quotas, acted to disrupt some of the unhealthy borderlands alliances between sawmillers and provincial officials. Logging concessions throughout Laos were revoked, removing from sawmills the right to cut their own timber. Logging rights were transferred to three state enterprises who were allocated roughly one third of the country each. The three enterprises were made responsible for logging within provincial quotas and in strictly limited and inventoried forest areas. They were also made responsible for the sale of logs to sawmills on a competitive basis, for forest rehabilitation and for cooperation with provincial, district and village authorities on forest management. The wording of the decree is very unclear, but it was also widely reported that the enterprises had taken control of the management of exports of sawn timber, previously the domain of the sawmills through their Thailand-based trading companies. While international agencies were applauding the Lao government's move towards a market economy, significant sections of the timber industry were all but nationalised. The *World Bank* (1994) coyly described the new regime as a "program of forestry conservation."

The three state enterprises are the *Mountainous Area Development Company* (MAD), the *Integrated Agriculture Forestry Development Company* (usually referred to as DAFI) and the *Agriculture and Forestry Development Import Export and General Services Company* (AFD). North-western Laos fell within the eight-province domain of AFD. The three companies are all state enterprises with very close ties to the military. They were quarantined from the privatisation of state enterprises that took place in the late 1980s and early 1990s (Vokes and Fabella 1995: 71). Both MAD and DAFI have relatively high profiles in Laos. MAD was founded by the military in the mid-1980s to operate a timber business in central Laos (VT 18–24 October 1994) and is now involved in massive logging operations in the reservoir for the proposed Nam Theun 2 dam (Sluiter 1992: 18). In 1994/ 1995 it was allocated over 80 per cent of the national logging quota (BP/ RT 6 June 1995). The company has many other business ventures including road and river transportation, construction, machinery and tourism (BP 7 March 1995; MAD 1996). It has also been reported to be involved in the drug trade in Laos (Thayer 1993). The second company, DAFI, was established "under the wing of the military" (BP/RT 6 June 1995) in the late 1980s to operate as a logging broker in southern Laos. It has since expanded into mining, construction and fuel distribution and runs a high profile national tour company.

AFD has a much lower profile than either of its counterparts. In Vientiane, its head-office is in a pair of nondescript villas on the suburban outskirts of town, a striking contrast with MAD's grand headquarters in its "company town" near the Vietnamese border (BP 7 March 1995; MAD 1996). In Houayxay, the branch office is in a modest shop, featuring a single desk where most of my inquiries were politely ignored. In Oudomxai, AFD's office is a rough bamboo building behind a service station. But the public face is deceptive and AFD is probably the most powerful enterprise – Lao or foreign-owned – in northern Laos. It too was founded in the 1980s by military interests keen to secure a share of the re-emerging timber trade. Like its counterparts, it is closely allied with the military, and senior officials in the company are said to have very close links with the Prime Minister, a former commander-in-chief of the Lao army. Until recently its northern Lao activities were focused in the province of Xaignabouli where it owns at least one sawmill and operates a network of timber trucks, elephants and cargo boats. Xaignabouli has a long, rugged and isolated land border with Thailand and is rumoured to be a northern Lao heartland for military involvement in illegal timber trade (Sesser 1993: 112; Stuart-Fox 1991: 3). AFD has also diversified and is involved in import-export trade, road construction, cement production and mining, including a remarkable 25 per cent share in the massive Thai-Lao lignite project at Hongsa (Surasit n.d.). As one of their senior officials in Vientiane told me, "we do different things in different places."

The October 1994 decree has bought about a dramatic change in the regulatory environment of the timber trade in north-western Laos. Most important is AFD's role in selling timber to the sawmills. Officially, the company is responsible for timber felling, but it has limited equipment in the north-west, and most logging continues to be undertaken by the sawmills themselves, though with close supervision from AFD and the provincial forestry office. What, in fact, AFD sells is the timber quota, with mills competing to buy quota allocations on a supposedly competitive basis. With dramatic increases in capacity coming on line, there are widespread concerns among sawmillers and timber traders that competition between the mills for timber is driving up prices.[10] AFD is exploiting

---

10 A sawmiller in southern Laos was quoted in the Bangkok Post: "There is no commitment as to how soon you will get the logs [despite payment of a substantial deposit]. If logs happen to rise in price the brokers may sell them to a trader prepared to pay more." (BP/RT 6 June 1995)

the fear of further price increases and, in late 1996, I heard reports of a meeting of sawmillers in Louangnamtha where AFD extracted a multi-million *baht* payment in return for a guarantee of price stability in the coming year. Quotas can be sold across provincial boundaries and some sawmillers are said to be deeply resentful of timber quotas being "stolen" by sawmillers in neighbouring provinces. As a result, several established sawmills no longer have a secure supply of timber.

In addition to selling logs to sawmills within Laos, AFD is also active in managing log exports, despite the official policy emphasis on domestic processing. High quality log sales are being made to China, with truck and boat operators reporting consignments of several hundred cubic metres at a time. There are also reports of substantial log sales to Vietnam and there are now some log exports being made to Thai buyers in Chiang Khong. Officially the logs being sold to Thai buyers are plantation timber, though from one consignment I saw stacked in a timber yard at Chiang Khong it was clear that some forest logs are being exported. Huge tree stumps are also being unloaded at Chiang Khong. Finally, there are strong reports that AFD is managing the sale of Burmese timber to Thai buyers. The timber is said to be purchased in remote areas bordering the Mekong and is transported by a number of routes through north-western Laos to buyers in Chiang Saen and Chiang Khong.[11] All of these log sales are bypassing the sawmills in the north-west, most of which are desperate for timber.

Finally, AFD acts as a "broker" in the sale of sawn timber to buyers in Thailand. There is little need for this brokerage service, because sawmills and their affiliated trading companies have no problems locating buyers and coordinating the transport of timber from the mills. Indeed, AFD's brokerage role seems to be limited to processing and approving export paperwork, in conjunction with provincial forestry and customs staff. For this regulatory intervention they are said to receive an extraordinary nine per cent of the sale value of the timber. As one resentful timber trader complained, "they just sleep and collect money."

The response of the Thai sawmillers to AFD's entry into the industry has been understandably negative and, between late 1994 when the decree was issued and late 1996 when I last visited the area, there appeared to have been a series of important changes in the industry. The owner of the sawmill at Sin Udom sold the mill in 1995. He told me that he was tired of doing business in Laos and of the constant payments he had to make "under the table." Local rumour suggests that the mill made windfall profits from logging above quotas and avoiding government royalties and taxes. It was said that AFD had restricted the supply of logs to the mill and insisted on back-payment of a substantial amount of tax. The new owner of the Sin

---

11 This parallels the situation in southern Laos, where Cambodian timber is said to be illegally exported to Thailand via Laos.

Udom sawmill – a businessman with a long history of involvement in sawmilling in northern Thailand and in pre-1975 Laos – is also having problems securing sufficient timber for the mill and is reportedly having difficulties with Chiang Khong customs over the evasion of Thai timber import taxes. The mill at Louangnamtha has also greatly cut back its output – apparently operating only a few months each year – because it has had little success in bidding for timber allocations. Its Chiang Khong-based trading companies now have a very low profile. The investor in the new mill at Pakkhop has reportedly withdrawn from Laos having lost heavily on his investment, and the operators of the Pakbeng and Muanghun mills are also struggling to secure sufficient timber for their new, higher capacity, mills. Among timber merchants in Chiang Khong, there is now a strong feeling that Lao sawmilling is a very risky proposition and that timber trading – which requires little up-front investment – is a much more viable proposition. Despite the increases in timber prices and taxes, Lao timber is still highly valued in Thailand and substantial, though reduced, trading profits are still being made by some trading companies.

Nevertheless, at least two new mills are being constructed in what appears to be a third wave of Thai investment in north-western Lao sawmilling. There are reports of a new mill under construction near Oudomxai and another on the Mekong, a short distance downstream from Bandan. Given the widely discussed problems in the industry, there is some incredulity at this new investment. When I mentioned the new mills to one successful Lao trader and transport operator, he told me that Thai businessmen were "crazy about spending money" and "couldn't sleep at night unless they had spent some during the day." But these latest investments are probably not so easily dismissed. I could not obtain any information on the new investors at Oudomxai, but the main Thai investor in the new riverside mill near Bandan was previously involved in the mills at both Sin Udom and Louangnamtha and seemed well aware of the current realities of doing business in Laos.[12] It is said that he has succeeded in cultivating close connections with the Lao military and has been able to negotiate good supplies of logs for his new mill. It appears that the mill is, in fact, a joint venture with AFD and supplies of logs – above quota if necessary – are guaranteed. The name of the investing company – the *Thai-Lao Cooperation Company* – is revealing and reflects some of the shift in the balance of power that has taken place in the sawmilling industry. Pasuk and Sungsidh (1994: 82–84) have written of the importance of military connections in the rise of many *caw phɔɔ* in Thailand and it appears likely that this will be a basis for future success in the timber industry in north-western Laos. Whether or not other Thai sawmillers succeed in forging these mutually beneficial connections remains to be seen.

---

12 His original sawmilling experience was in Phrae province in Thailand (Map 1.1).

There is one final factor that must be mentioned. For some time there have been proposals to build a hydro-electric dam on the Tha River, some distance upstream from Paktha (Map 1.2) (ADB 1996c). Feasibility studies are currently being undertaken. Given the nationwide shift to logging in areas to be flooded by dams, this may represent a huge new timber source for the north-western sawmilling industry. In the case of the proposed Nam Theun 2 dam, massive logging commenced while there was still considerable uncertainty about the dam going ahead (Hirsch and Cheong 1996: 81; Lintner 1994: 71). The military company MAD is heavily involved in this large-scale timber extraction. If the valley of the Tha River is handed over to AFD in the same way, it will greatly enhance their power in the north-western resource economy. It may prove to be a fertile location for future collaboration between the Lao military and Thai sawmillers.

Conclusion: A New Regional Resource Economy?

> Teak is destined to disappear from Siam in the near future: it will
> be necessary then, we are told, to seek it on the Mekong, in the
> vicinity of Pak-Lay and of Nan. (Orléans 1894: 523–524)

To what extent, then, do developments in north-western Lao sawmilling, in the era of the Economic Quadrangle, support Hirsch's (1995) contention that we are witnessing the emergence of a "new regional resource economy" whereby resource management in Indochina is increasingly determined by Thailand's resource constraints and demands. Clearly, there is some support for this argument in the material I have presented: Thai businessmen have dominated investment in sawmilling and the vast majority of the region's sawn timber output has been exported to buyers in Thailand. Nevertheless, there are two important qualifications that I would make to Hirsch's argument. These relate to the two central concerns of this book – history and regulation.

First, what we are witnessing now in north-western Laos is, to a large extent, the re-emergence of an *old* regional resource economy. Lowland Thai states have long depended on the products of Lao forests and, as Pasuk and Baker (1995: 7) have written, "[c]ontrolling the trade in forest products was the key to economic and political power in the region."[13] Trade in forest labour was also crucially important, and Khmu timber workers from north-western Laos provided a substantial proportion of the labour force for logging operations in northern Siam.[14] French logging firms, which were active on both sides of the Mekong, provided some

---

13 For some details of this trade out of Laos, see Picanon (1901: 274–296); and Reinach (1911: 281–296).
14 See, for example, Bock (1884: 363); and McGilvary (1912: 141, 192).

competition for the Siamese in the Lao forests, but they failed to halt the flow of Lao forest products to Uttaradit and Bangkok or, despite some initial success, the flow of Khmu labourers to the logging camps around Chiang Mai.[15]

It was during the 1960s that the resource economy of upper-Mekong forestry started to take its present shape. During this period there was significant growth in forestry output in Laos, reflected in a ten-fold increase in exports in the latter years of the decade (CAID 1969: 17; USAID 1970: 42). By 1969, timber accounted for almost 40 per cent of total exports from Laos, supplying the expanding Thai economy and the construction of American military bases. The industry was supported by Thai investment, foreign aid and foreign technical support (USAID 1970). The primary areas for forestry development were in central and southern Laos, but the narrow strip of RLG territory around Houayxay was also caught up in the boom (Rantala 1994: 130). A series of sawmills were established in villages along the river-bank, from Bandan to Bankhwan in the north (Map 1.2). Road construction around Houayxay, to support refugee settlements and to encourage rural pacification, opened up large areas of forest for the new mills. According to USAID (1970: 60), there were five mills in this area with a processing capacity of some 30,000 cubic metres of logs per year. Local recollection is that there were even more mills – at least ten – and by the early 1970s Thai boats were reported to be carrying close to 20,000 cubic metres of sawn timber – representing well over 40,000 cubic metres of logs given the primitive operating conditions – for export at Chiang Saen and Chiang Khong (IMC 1976: 3).[16] The sawmills were operated by an unholy borderlands alliance of Thai and Lao entrepreneurs, heroin manufacturers and RLG army officers.[17] In a prescient assessment made in the early 1970s, USAID lamented that:

---

15 There are numerous fragmentary references to the French interest and involvement in the upper-Mekong timber industry. See, for example, Carné (1872: 250); Orléans (1894: 470–471); Lefèvre-Pontalis (1902:128); Pavie (1903: 43–45); Thompson (1941: xxix); and Robequain (1944: 273). For French actions on the Khmu, see Smyth (1898a: 107); Lefèvre-Pontalis (1902: 113); Le May (1926: 252); and Halpern (1964b: 119). For the use of the Mekong for the transport of logs, see Smyth (1898a: 102); Coolidge (1933: 205); 'Ath (1992: 52); and Stuart-Fox (1995a: 135).

16 In 1974, official timber imports at Chiang Khong alone were reported to be almost 23,000 tonnes, representing in the order of 20,000 cubic metres.

17 Locals recall that a number of the region's famous heroin refineries were located at sawmills. This is confirmed by the work of McCoy (1972). The mill at Ban Khwan was owned by the *Royal Lao Army* Commander in Chief, General Ouane Rattikone, who was actively involved in the heroin trade. His sawmill was the site of the famous battle between forces of Shan "warlord" Khun Sa and Kuomintang forces for control of the opium trade (McCoy 1972: 322–328). The Yao military leader Chao La was also involved in the opium trade and heroin production (McCoy 1972: 248, 301) and had interests in at least one of the riverside mills. Another senior military figure – possibly Colonel Khampay, a close follower of General Ouane and also involved in the drug trade (McCoy 1972: 450, footnote 327) – was, by local accounts, the original investor in the mill at Sin Udom.

> Military commanders' interests in logging and sawmilling are a
> real threat to Laos' long range potential forestry operations.
> Correction will be extremely difficult but should be attempted.
> (USAID 1970: 27)

What is important to note is that this large-scale development of Lao
sawmilling took place in a period when there was rampant logging and
sawmilling in Thailand itself. As such, current interest in the Lao timber
industry may be less a reflection of the Thai national logging ban – though
it is obviously important – than a resumption of the economic connections
that were in place prior to 1975. A number of the current Thai
entrepreneurs have experience dating from this period, though now they
have to deal with Lao army officers from the other side. As I have argued a
number of times throughout this book, there are important continuities in
the era of the Economic Quadrangle. Emphasis on the recent "penetration" of a "peripheral" Laos obscures the extent to which Laos has had
longstanding experience in managing interconnections with the neighbouring economies of the region.

My second comment, taking up issues that Hirsch (1995: 249, 251–252,
254) himself alludes to, is that an emphasis on Thai economic domination
can obscure the extent to which Thai entrepreneurs confront – with varying
degrees of success – local contours of power and influence. The Lao army's
move on the timber industry, through its company AFD, clearly shows that
Thai interests can come off second-best in the cross-border resource
economy. Indeed there is some evidence that, regionally, Thai timber
companies are facing increasing resistance. Extensive logging concessions
issued in Burma in the late 1980s have been revoked and, in Cambodia, Thai
companies have had enormous problems dealing with the highly volatile
political and military mix of the borderlands.[18] In Laos itself, a major forest
contract was signed with a Malaysian company in late 1994 giving it access to
timber in Xaignabouli province – the heartland of AFD power (VT 25
November 1994; see also Hirsch 1995: 254–255). Representatives from AFD
have also been active in courting Chinese buyers for Lao timber and
exploring possibilities for Chinese involvement in sawmilling. For the central
Lao government, Malaysian, Taiwanese and Chinese firms may be a more
attractive prospect, given the greater cultural distance between them and
provincial regulators. Certainly, there is a widespread view that Lao officials
and entrepreneurs are keen to temper the level of Thai influence in the
economy and that other nations in the region are keen to expand their own
Mekong influence (Vatikiotis 1996a: 279–281). These issues will be explored
further in the following, concluding, chapter.

---

18 TN 15 February 1994; BP 19 July 1994; BP 28 December 1994; BP 31 December 1994;
   BP 7 January 1995; BP 4 March 1995; BP/RT 27 June 1995; TN 15 December 1996.

The image of a plentiful, vulnerable and available Laos is central to the geopolitical fantasies of certain sections of the Thai elite and of numerous mobile phone-bearing businessmen who cross the Mekong between Chiang Khong and Houayxay every day. I agree that many aspects of the timber industry in Laos provide substantial nourishment for these fantasies. What I seek to highlight is the active facilitating and resisting roles that Laos has played – and has always played – in regional resource regulation. The trade in timber is a clear illustration of the borderlands irony that as cross-border trading and investment systems become more liberalised and integrated, the opportunities and incentives for profitable regulation flourish.

CHAPTER EIGHT

Conclusion

Regulation and Liberalisation

In popular, journalistic and academic writing, a clear-cut distinction is often drawn between regulation and liberalisation. Around this distinction, a series of ideas and concepts are clustered. Regulation, almost inevitably, is associated with the public sector; liberalisation with the private sector. Regulation invokes a centrally managed, controlled and often isolated economy while liberalisation calls forth a decentralised free market, in which products, labour and capital can freely cross national boundaries. In the historical narratives of mainland South-East Asia, regulation is the past – ideological orthodoxy, cold-war tension and tense borders – while liberalisation is a present and future of globalisation, cooperation and trans-border regional economies. As Reyes (1997: 50) has argued in his recent assessment of economic management in Laos, the transition from a "central command" to a "market based" economic system can be imagined as a gradual movement "from left to right along the continuum."

This book has argued that economic, social and spatial processes in the upper-Mekong borderlands of Laos are not so easily, nor comfortably, categorised. The seeming naturalness of the association between regulation and the state, the controlled economy and the past has been challenged. The smoothness of the free-market reform continuum has been called into question. Indeed, the central argument of the book has been that forms of regulation are flourishing in the era of the Economic Quadrangle, an era which is said – with some justification – to be characterised by an increasingly active private sector taking advantage of more open border-lands markets. I have argued that there are three key elements to this seemingly contradictory efflorescence of both regulation and liberalisation.

First, the *subtleties of state regulatory power* must be recognised. There is no denying that regulation is central to the activities of the state. This book has explored some of the ways in which the Lao and Thai states are

186

involved in the micro-regulation of border passage, the national regulation of trade and transport, and the macro-regulation of trans-border infrastructure projects. States are actively involved in managing the interconnections between places in the borderlands. What this book has emphasised, however, is the extent to which these "public sector" practices are collaboratively intertwined with the activities of the "private sector." This is strikingly evident in the localised mix of state and non-state regulation of the Mekong River border between Chiang Khong and Houayxay (chapter 4). There are tensions and changes in this collaborative mix, but Chiang Khong's cross-river boat operators consistently depend on state power to reinforce their own local sources of authority. State regulatory support for the enterprises of "independent" long-distance truck and boat operators is also a feature of the borderlands trading system (chapter 5). Like the cross-river boat operators, these long-distance transport operators have prospered in the liberalised environment of the Economic Quadrangle but their profitable itineraries are dependant on ongoing state protection. The regulatory activities of these long-distance operators are much less enthusiastic than those of the cross-river operators in Chiang Khong, suggesting that collaborative regulation may be more elaborate and intricate where the state is relatively less intrusive. Lao women traders are also the beneficiaries of state regulation. Many established their trading careers in the restrictive environment of the late 1970s and early 1980s, a period which is usually associated with the suppression of commercial opportunity (chapter 6). In the more liberalised environment of the Economic Quadrangle, trading women in the north-west continue to manipulate various forms of regulation to maintain their trading niche. Even in the timber industry, where relations between state and entrepreneurs have been relatively volatile, there has been ongoing collaboration between state officials and sawmillers (chapter 7). Thai investment, while dependant on some liberalising reforms, has also been facilitated by the regulatory encouragement of domestic processing. Relations between the private and public sectors have soured in recent years but there are signs that new forms of collaborative control of the timber trade are emerging. In brief, each of the Economic Quadrangle case studies has shown that both the public and private sector have an active stake in the development and maintenance of regulatory practices.

Second, the *regulatory opportunities and incentives afforded by a liberalised market* need to be recognised. As paradoxical as this may seem, it is central to an understanding of contemporary processes in the borderlands. It was best explained to me by a customs officer in Houayxay who told me how easy his job was in the early 1980s – when closed borders greatly restricted formal trade – and how busy it had become in the open-border 1990s. When there is no trade or passage, there is not much to regulate. Throughout this book, I have shown how liberalised border trading conditions have provided a windfall for state and non-state regulators: road building companies with plans for a string of toll stations; customs officers filling provincial coffers (and back pockets) with tariff revenue; local transport associations managing the allocation of cargo; and traders developing collaborative arrangements for the payment and evasion of customs duties. An increasingly open and market-oriented economy has provided opportunities for officials, traders, transport operators and entrepreneurs to create, consolidate and reinforce their micro-monopolies. Perhaps the most dramatic regulatory interventions have been in the timber trade, where the re-establishment of cross-border trade and investment has been accompanied by an ever increasing array of regulatory policies, culminating in the forestry "coup" staged by the Lao army's corporate off-shoots. It is a more liberalised market environment that has made all this regulatory intervention both possible, profitable and, in some cases, necessary. To re-emphasise a recurring theme, open borders can be more regulated than the closed borders that preceded them.

This, of course, suggests that the *assignment of regulation to the past –* and liberalisation to the present and future *– is simplistic and misleading.* There is no doubt that from the mid-1970s to the mid-1980s, Laos was *relatively* isolated and that the particular forms of internal and external regulation restricted trans-border passage. But this was only one – fairly short – phase in the history of borderlands regulation. Places in north-western Laos have a long history of managed interconnection with other places (chapter 2). Controlling, directing and taxing the passages through the borderlands has been a longstanding strategy for the exercise of power. While the contrast between the closed borders of the immediate past and the open borders of the present may appear striking, this longer historical perspective suggests that the Economic Quadrangle is the latest phase in the reorganisation of borderlands connections: it is the latest regime of regulation (chapter 3). Forecasts that the development of transborder economies will undermine the state – and liberate the borderlands from state constraint – seem overly preoccupied with states as bounding and restricting entities (as they sometimes are) and neglect the longstanding role of states in collaboratively managing cross-border flows.

In brief, the approach I have taken in this book is not to contrast regulation with liberalisation but to highlight the intertwining of regulatory and liberalising practices and document some of the social and economic implications for borderlands communities of this dynamic relationship. This perspective has been facilitated by an emphasis on regulation as the management of flow and interconnections. If regulation is simplistically associated with restriction, boundary and the dead hand of centralised bureaucratic power, its relevance in a world of increasingly regionalised and globlalised flows does indeed appear tenuous, and the arguments suggesting a decline of state power appear compelling. But, these are no more than stereotypes of regulatory power and – as compelling as they may be for free market economists and post-modern theorists alike – they do little justice to the reality of persistent state and non-state collaboration in the management of external connections.

The Future of the Economic Quadrangle

> A return to old-style socialism [in Laos] seems out of the question but recent government attempts to assert control are chilling reminders of a past most businessmen thought was gone for good. (Lintner 1997: 71)

What, then, of the future? Does this intertwining of liberalisation and regulation merely reflect the immaturity of the Economic Quadrangle's development? As infrastructure projects proceed, will Laos become the "truck stop of Asia," serving cheap meals and girls to the deregulated drivers of foreign ten-wheelers? Is the persistence, even growth, of government regulation the defensive reaction of a state under pressure (Hall 1991: 36–39)? Will the Lao government – seeking enhanced regional credibility – be persuaded to embrace the free market more eagerly and rein in its entrepreneurial military? Will Lao traders be sidelined by container-loads of thongs, televisions and washing powder trucked into supermarkets in Louangnamtha and Oudomxai? Will north-western Laos lose its regulatory control of the connections it has with other places?

There are some factors that may encourage an affirmative answer to these various questions. Most important is the admission of Laos to ASEAN in 1997. Under the terms of its membership, Laos will be required to adhere to the *ASEAN Free Trade Area Agreement*, which requires all members to impose wide-ranging tariff reductions by 2003. Though a three-year extension, at least, will be granted for Laos, the eventual effect on state finances and regulatory power may be substantial. Moreover, with official tariffs drastically lowered, the ability of borderline regulators to extract unofficial payments will be greatly reduced. As a full member of ASEAN, Laos is also likely to face increasing pressure to lift visa restrictions and to reduce the barriers to trading companies and transport operators from fellow ASEAN countries. Pressures will be particularly intense if ASEAN members are the main investors in large-scale infrastructure projects.

In north-western Laos there are some signs of more immediate threats to Lao regulatory control. In chapter 5, I outlined some of the threats to Lao long-distance transport operators: a new supply of cheap trucks imported by road construction firms; calls for more open participation by trucking enterprises in Thailand and China; road-building projects that may make existing operations redundant; limits on the domestic construction of timber boats; and strong Chinese interest in developing

189

large-scale upper-Mekong navigation. The long-distance traders discussed in chapter 6 may also face some threats. Examining border trade between Burma and China, Porter (1995: 82) has shown how improvements in transport infrastructure and trading conditions have encouraged the emergence of "powerful trading/transport alliances which exert great influence over market prices and commodity volumes." Trading volumes are much greater in northern Burma, but his analysis suggests a scenario where, with improved roads, Thai, Chinese or even Lao trading enterprises could transport large volumes of goods to the major townships of north-western Laos, achieving economies of scale that threaten the viability of independent Lao traders and transport operators. Already, one north-western trading company, in cooperation with the Chiang Khong office of a Thai trading company, has imported several container loads of goods – purchased at favourable prices in Bangkok – to stock its retail shop in Houayxay. In early 1995, a Thai/Lao trading company opened an office in Houayxay and commenced construction of a large warehouse near the main cargo port. It was rumoured that the warehouse would be stocked with Thai goods for sale throughout northern Laos and in bordering regions of China and Burma. In brief, there are some indications that Laos may be moving closer to the situation described by Smith (1976c: 338) where local populations "play no entrepreneurial roles in an economy where the exchange system is controlled by external metropoles."

However, there are equally strong indications that such a path to loss of local control over external connections is far from inevitable. At the most general level, there are doubts about the viability of the upper-Mekong Quadrangle concept itself. The concept draws much of its strength from superficial comparisons with transborder economic regions elsewhere in Asia. As McGovern (1996) has argued, successful transborder growth regions have relied on their proximity to highly advanced and prosperous economies such as Singapore. This spatial precondition is notably absent in the upper-Mekong. Without such proximity, Mekong infrastructure investment will probably be slow and, as noted in chapter 3, may well be drawn to the relatively more populous and developed areas in the lower-Mekong basin. With over 40 billion dollars of Mekong "priority projects" on the table, this southward shift could be fatal for infrastructure development in the Quadrangle. No amount of talk about regional cooperation can hide the intense competition for scarce investment capital amongst the "[m]ass of competing and unruly interests" in the Mekong region (Hinton 1996a: 6). Widespread concerns in Thailand about cheap Chinese goods flooding the domestic market may make upper-Mekong investment an even less attractive prospect: "the unfettered flow of goods could be economically and politically explosive" (TN 15 December 1993).

Reservations about the viability and desirability of trans-border integration are also evident within Laos itself. Recent action to restrict the use of foreign currency within Laos, though immediately motivated by a desire to protect the value of the *kip*, seems to be symptomatic of a more assertive management of external economic connections. There are a number of indications that Thai entrepreneurs, in particular, are coming under increasing pressure. In part, this reflects the Lao government's desire to broaden the sources of foreign investment in response to fears of Thai economic domination and negative perceptions of Thai business practices (McGovern 1996: 65). This policy has been welcomed elsewhere in Asia, with Singapore and Malaysia, in particular, using the ASEAN forum to push for wider participation in the Mekong region (McGovern 1996; Vatikiotis 1996a). "In the wake of the 1995 ASEAN summit," Vatikiotis (1996a) writes, "Thailand looked less like a regional centre, and more like a regional competitor." With this diversification of interest, opportunities are likely to emerge for playing potential investors off against each other. As critics of "dependency theory" have pointed out, Third-World states have enjoyed considerable success in "shaping the pattern of investment by international capital" (Rodan 1988: 42). This "bargaining" role is already evident in the Lao state's recent intervention in the timber industry, and its courting of non-Thai forestry investment. Regional competition seems an ideal environment for domestic regulation.

Pressure on Thai investors is also coming from the increasingly entrepreneurial role of the Lao state. Recent developments – whereby military companies have taken control of the timber trade – have been discussed in detail in chapter 7. There are indications that this government action against Thai sawmillers is part of a broader policy thrust. In early 1996, the central government announced that the tobacco concession held by the Wongwan family – the owners of the sawmill at Pakbeng – would be revoked and that the government would take over its processing plant in Vientiane (*Than Setthakit* 17 January 1996). In a similar vein, a major upper-Mekong river-cruise service – established by a prominent Thai politician and businessman and a central motif in Economic Quadrangle promotions – was acquired by the Lao government after longstanding regulatory resistance to its operation in Lao waters. A press report of this transaction clearly demonstrates how liberalised cross-border relations can be profitably regulated:

> Never before has Laos held 100 percent of a company. MP World Travel is now owned by the *state-run* Darpli Travel; Phu Doi District Development [MAD] Travel; and National Travelling. Moreover, it is the first consortium to use *state money* since Laos embraced the market economy in the mid-1980s. ... To be sure, the deal did not happen by chance, but it is part of *Vientiane's vision for an industry of high potential.* The operation, which has six boats, not only facilitates tourism but demonstrates that Laos is

> conforming with the Asian Development Bank's grand scheme for sub-regional economic cooperation. ... *Control of key sectors* will provide the country with considerable profits to match revenue from hydro power export to Thailand. (BP/RT 11 February 1996, my emphasis)

The presence of the military company MAD in this consortium is not surprising, given the army's penetration of numerous sectors of the Lao polity, economy and society. A significant increase in military representation at the highest levels of government (Bourdet 1997; Dommen 1995); an increasing military role in social policy (such as the resettlement of upland communities in lowland areas to reduce resource competition); and the planned resumption of barter trade as a means of obtaining Russian military hardware all indicate that the army's move on the timber industry is far from an isolated development. No doubt the entrepreneurial role of the military does "further guarantee the irreversibility of the transition to capitalism in Laos," as Evans (1995: xvii) has argued, but it is a brand of capitalism in which the state is a willing and active participant.

The role of the drug trade in the Lao economy has received relatively little attention. Hinton (1996b), however, has written about the continuing massive heroin trade in the region. He estimates that the value of Burma's Golden Triangle heroin exports – around $1.65 billion at Bangkok prices – outstrips the value of Thai rice exports (Hinton 1996b: 16). While it is impossible to estimate the amount of this heroin traded through Laos, there have been a number of reports that Laos is an increasingly popular conduit for the trade and that the realignments in the regional trade after the "surrender" of the Shan "warlord" Khun Sa have prompted the search for new outlets and distribution paths (RT/BP 10 June 1997; RT/BP 23 June 1997). In 1996, a heroin and amphetamine refinery was closed down in the Lao village of Muangmom (Map 1.2) and there were also local reports of other factories and cross-border trading points upstream and downstream from Houayxay. In raising this issue, my aim is not to revive the old Golden Triangle myths of lawless frontiers, but to suggest, following Hinton (1996b: 15–17), that there may be substantial sources of economic power that are being left out of the Quadrangle equation. Control of parts of the drug trade – to which the Lao military has been linked (Thayer 1993) – may be an important source of ongoing regulatory power, especially in an environment starved of capital for major infrastructure projects. Further investigation is clearly required.

At a local level, there are also indications that transport operators and traders are continuing to succeed in carving out operating niches. In chapter 4, I noted that a number of Chiang Khong's cross-river operators have optimistic visions of lucrative food-stalls and mini-cruise services operating from a concreted and transformed river-bank. In chapter 5, I referred to the striking affluence of some of the large boat operators, some of whom are now investing huge amounts in small fleets and gradually consolidating their hold on the river trade. Visiting in late 1996, I also found that some of the more successful long-distance traders had prospered beyond my most optimistic expectations. One trader, for example, had demolished her rustic house and, with her husband, built a small row of two-storey shop-houses. From her base in Houayxay, she was regularly using her newly acquired mobile phone to contact customers in the northern towns, and to pass instructions to her brother who was now managing a warehouse they had built in Oudomxai. She was in the process of stocking the warehouse and was planning to retail direct, undercutting the shop-keepers in the sprawling Oudomxai market. No doubt, family enterprises such as these may in turn be undercut by the economies of scale of large commercial operators, but it is relevant to note that the retail and wholesale sector across the border in Chiang Khong is still predominantly in the hands of family enterprises, despite a substantially higher level of commercial development. In Laos, close interpersonal relations with government regulators, strong networks of kinship and friendship within the trading and transport sectors, detailed local market knowledge and comparatively low levels of overall consumer demand may all contribute to the resilience of these small-scale enterprises.

To summarise, there are signs that Lao officials, transport operators, traders and entrepreneurs will play an active role in managing the future development of an increasingly regionalised Lao economy. As Laos is drawn into new phases of regional and global interconnection it is very likely that new, and not so new, opportunities for regulation will emerge. The persistence of regulation in Laos has been all too readily explained away as reflecting a lack of "competent personnel" trained, presumably, in the wonders of free market economics (Reyes 1997: 60). However, perhaps the possibility should be entertained that deliberate, alternative, regulatory choices are being made. It is now well recognised that globalisation – while homogenising at one level – also encourages regionalism and sharpens the focus on locality. The regulatory opportunities that arise out of global flows undoubtedly contribute to the piquancy of these regional and local phenomena.

The Legend of the Golden Boat

A few years ago, a Thai businessman came to Chiang Khong, a kilometre or so across the Mekong from the stupa of the golden boat. Through local talk, he heard about the treasure that lay across the river and decided to steal it. The gold would make a fine contribution to the resort hotel he was planning to build on the bank of the river. However, he was scared of the angels that guarded the stupa and, after extensive inquiries, he secured the services of a ritual specialist who assured him that he would be able to drive the protecting angels away. Soon after, the businessmen and his entourage came to the stupa and pretended to make merit, while the ritual specialist discretely recited the formulae that would facilitate their theft. The Abbot of the temple soon realised what they were trying to do and sent a young novice to summon the police from Houayxay. Realising that they had been discovered, the businessman's party fled across the Mekong empty-handed. Soon after, one of his colleagues died.

How are we to read the legend of the golden boat? At one level it encapsulates the disappointments of the Economic Quadrangle. Bureaucrats, academics, consultants, and entrepreneurs have had numerous meetings where they have sat and recited the ritual passages that may unlock the wealth of the borderlands. "A new era in cooperation" ... "subregional integration" ... "harmonisation of barriers" ... "free flow of capital and labour" ... "the Mekong corridor" ... "the Danube of the East!" But their magic has not been sufficiently powerful and the results have been disappointing. Planned international highways are now little more than seasonal tracks where, in the "space-time *de*compression" of the wet season, a one-hour journey extends into a nine-hour struggle with axle-deep mud. Transit agreements are delayed as Burmese and Lao officials refuse to surrender their taxing rights on passing traffic. The only resort hotel in Chiang Khong is a ply-wood model beneath a perspex lid. Mobile phones refuse to work in Pakbeng. And trucks laden with Lao lignite roll into ditches as newly made culverts crumble beneath their unprecedented weight. The spirits of the borderlands are at work.

The legend of the golden boat could, then, be used to reinforce popular stereotypes about Laos: isolated, impenetrable and reluctant to yield its treasures. However, I prefer to read it as a symbol of the regulatory power in the borderlands, power in which local and state practices are closely intertwined (the Abbot had faith in the angels but he had no qualms about calling the police). It is a power that derives not from isolation, peripherality or marginality but from connectedness. Its origin lies in the travels of the brothers Malawar and Malawor and of the itinerant monk who gave them the opportunity to make merit. Without these external connections, the golden boat would never have come to the upper-Mekong and the regulatory power embedded in the stupa would have little authority. The lesson of the golden boat is not, then, that isolation is persistent but that local power and non-local connections are inseparable.

Bibliography

Newspapers and databases

BP   Bangkok Post (Bangkok, Thailand)
RT   Reuters Textline
TN   The Nation (Bangkok, Thailand)
VT   Vientiane Times (Vientiane, Laos)

Articles, books, manuscripts and reports

For reissued versions of historical texts which are cited often, I have cited the date of original publication. The actual publication date of the version I have used is listed in square brackets after the publisher. Page numbers in citations refer to the reissued versions.

Abou-el-Haj, Barbara
1991   Languages and models for cultural exchange. In *Culture, globalization and the world-system: contemporary conditions for the representation of identity*, edited by Anthony D King, pp. 139–144. Macmillan, State University of New York at Binghamton.

Abu-Lughod, Janet
1991   Going beyond global babble. In *Culture, globalization and the world-system: contemporary conditions for the representation of identity*, edited by Anthony D King, pp. 131–137. Macmillan, State University of New York at Binghamton.

ADB (Asian Development Bank)
1993   *Subregional economic cooperation: initial possibilities for Cambodia, Lao PDR, Myanmar, Thailand, Viet Nam and Yunnan Province of the People's Republic of China.* ADB, Manila.
1996a   *Economic cooperation in the greater Mekong subregion: an overview.* ADB, Manila.
1996b   *Economic cooperation in the greater Mekong subregion: facing the challenges.* ADB, Manila.
1996c   *Summary of priority subregional projects in the greater Mekong subregion.* ADB, Manila.

Addus, A A
1989   Road transportation in Africa. *Transportation Quarterly* 43 (3):421–433.

Agar, Michael H
1986   *Independents declared: the dilemmas of independent trucking.* Smithsonian Institution Press, Washington, D. C.

Agnew, John
1993   Representing space: space, scale and culture in social science. In *place/culture/representation*, edited by James Duncan and David Ley, pp. 251–271. Routledge, London.

Alexander, Jennifer
1987   *Trade, traders and trading in rural Java.* Oxford University Press, Singapore.

Alexander, Jennifer, and Paul Alexander
1991   Protecting peasants from capitalism: the subordination of Javanese traders by the colonial state. *Comparative studies in society and history* 33 (2):370–394.

Alvarez, Robert R, and George A Collier
1994   The long haul in Mexican trucking: traversing the borderlands of the north and the south. *American Ethnologist* 21 (3):606–627.

Amin, Samir
1976   *Unequal development: an essay on the social formations of peripheral capitalism.* The Harvester Press, Sussex.

Anan Ganjanapan
1983   *The differentiation of the peasantry and the complex "sakdina" relationship under forced commercialization, 1900–1921.* Paper presented at Conference on Change in Northern Thailand and the Shan States, Chiang Mai, June 1983.

Anderson, Benedict
1991   *Imagined communities: reflections on the origin and spread of nationalism.* Verso, London.

Anek Laothamatas
1992   *Business associations and the new political economy of Thailand: from bureaucratic polity to liberal corporatism.* Westview Press, Boulder.

Anon
1896   Boundary treaties in Siam and Indo-China. *The Geographical Journal* 7 (3):297–299.
1966   *Twelve years of American intervention and aggression in Laos.* Neo Lao Haksat Publications.
1985   *Fact and data on Lao-Thai relations in the past ten years (1975–1985).* KPL News Agency, Vientiane.
1990   *ʔamphəə chiaŋ khɔɔŋ: ʔɛɛw chiaŋ khɔɔŋ thɔŋ dɛɛn laaw chon plaa byg.* Chiang Khong District Office, Chiang Khong.
n.d.   *prawad saphaab tɔɔngthii lɛ panhaa khɔɔŋ ʔamphəə chiaŋ khɔɔŋ caŋwad chiaŋraaj.* Chiang Khong District Office, Chiang Khong.

Appadurai, Arjun
1990   Disjuncture and difference in the global cultural economy. *Public Culture* 2 (2):1–24.
1991   Global ethnoscapes: notes and queries for a transnational anthropology. In *Recapturing anthropology: working in the present*, edited by Richard G Fox, pp. 191–210. School of American Research Press, Sant Fe.

1995   The production of locality. In *Counterworks: managing the diversity of knowledge*, edited by Richard Fardon, pp. 204–225. Routledge, London.

Appadurai, Arjun, and Carol A Breckenridge
1995   Public modernity in India. In *Consuming modernity: public culture in a south Asian world*, edited by Carol A Breckenridge, pp. 1–20. University of Minnesota Press, Minneapolis.

Archer, W J
1889   *Extracts from Mr W. J. Archer's journal of a visit to Chiengtung in May and June 1888*. British Foreign Office, London.
1896   *Report by Mr Archer on a tour to Chiangsën, Chiang Khong, and Muang Nan.* British Foreign Office, London.

Arunrat Wichiankiaw, and Narumon Ruangrangsi
1994   *ryaŋ myaŋ chiaŋtuŋ.* Suriwong Books, Chiang Mai.

Asia Watch
1993   *A modern form of slavery: trafficking of Burmese women and girls into brothels in Thailand.* Human Rights Watch, New York.

'Ath, Colin De
1992   A history of timber exports from Thailand with emphasis on the 1870–1937 period. *Natural History Bulletin of the Siam Society* 40:49–66.

Backus, Mary (editor)
1884   *Siam and Laos as seen by our American missionaries.* Presbyterian Board of Publication, Philadelphia.

Barth, Fredrik
1992   Towards greater naturalism in conceptualizing societies. In *Conceptualizing society*, edited by Adam Kuper, pp. 17–33. Routledge, London.

Bassenne, Marthe
1995   *In Laos and Siam.* White Lotus, Bangkok.

BCEOM
1994   *Strategy study on the development of upper Mekong navigation (basinwide): final report.* Mekong Secretariat, Bangkok.

Berdan, Frances F
1989   Trade and markets in precapitalist states. In *Economic anthropology*, edited by Stuart Plattner, pp. 78–107. Stanford University Press, Stanford.

Bhabha, Homi K
1994   *The location of culture.* Routledge, London.

Bo Yang
1987   *Golden Triangle: frontier and wilderness.* Joint Publishing Company, Hong Kong.

Bock, Carl
1884   *Temples and elephants: the narrative of a journey of exploration through upper Siam and Lao.* White Orchid Press [1985], Bangkok.

Boulanger, Paul le
1931   *Histoire du Laos Français: essai d'une étude chronologique des principautés Laotiennes.* Librairie Plon, Paris.

Bourdet, Yves
1994   Budget policy under transition in Lao PDR. In *Economic development in Lao PDR: horizon 2000*, edited by Do Pham Chi, pp. 72–81. Bank of the Lao People's Democratic Republic, Vientiane.
1996   Laos in 1995: reform policy, out of breath? *Asian Survey* 31 (1):89–94.
1997   Laos: the sixth Party Congress, and after? *Southeast Asian Affairs* 1997:143–160.

Bourdieu, Pierre, and Loïc J D Wacquant
1992   *An invitation to reflexive sociology*. Polity Press, Cambridge.

Bowie, Katherine A
1992   Unravelling the myth of the subsistence economy: textile production in nineteenth-century northern Thailand. *The Journal of Asian Studies* 51 (4):797–823.

Brenier, Henri
1914   *Essai d'atlas statistique d'Indochine Française*. Imprimerie d'Extrême-Orient, Hanoi.

Boyer, Robert
1990   *The regulation school: a critical introduction*. Columbia University Press, New York.

Brimble, Peter
1994   *Promoting subregional cooperation among Cambodia, the People's Republic of China, Lao People's Democratic Republic, Myanmar, Thailand, and Viet Nam: trade and investment (interim report)*. ADB, Manila.

Brown, MacAlister, and Joseph J Zasloff
1986   *Apprentice revolutionaries: the communist movement in Laos, 1930–1985*. Hoover Institution Press, Stanford.

Brumfiel, Elizabeth M
1994   The economic anthropology of the state: an introduction. In *The economic anthropology of the state*, edited by Elizabeth M. Brumfiel, pp 1–16. University Press of America, Lanham.

Bryant, Raymond L, and Michael J G Parnwell
1996   Introduction: politics, sustainable development and environmental change in South-East Asia. In *Environmental change in South-East Asia: people, politics and sustainable development*, edited by Michael J G Parnwell and Raymond L Bryant, pp. 1–20. Routledge, London.

Bunyaraks Ninsananda, Kasem Snidvongse, Sumet Tantivejkul, Phayap Phayo-myond, Santi Bang-Or, and Kitti Itiwitya
1977   *Thai-Laos economic relations: a new perspective*, Bangkok.

Burling, Robbins
1965   *Hill farms and padi fields: life in mainland Southeast Asia*. Prentice-Hall, Englewood Cliffs, New Jersey.

CAID (Canadian Agency for International Development)
1969   *Reconnaissance survey of lowland forests: Laos*. Canadian Agency for International Development, Vientiane.

Carné, Louis de
1872   *Voyage en Indo-Chine et dans l'empire Chinois*. E Dentu, Paris.

Carnegie, Georgina
1993   *Investment guide to the Lao PDR*. Vientiane International Consultants, Vientiane.

Chai-Anan Samudavanija
1995   Bypassing the state in Asia. *New Perspectives Quarterly* 12 (1):9–14.

Chaiyan Rajchagool
1994   *The rise and fall of the Thai absolute monarchy: foundations of the modern Thai state from feudalism to peripheral capitalism*. White Lotus, Bangkok.

Chambers, Iain, and Lidia Curti
1996   Preface. In *The post-colonial question: common skies, divided horizons*, edited by Iain Chambers and Lidia Curti, pp. xi-xii. Routledge, London.

Chandler, Glen
1984   *Market trade in rural Java*. Centre of Southeast Asian Studies, Monash University, Clayton, Victoria.

Chandran Jeshurun
1971   *The Burma-Yunnan railway: Anglo-French rivalry in mainland Southeast Asia and south China, 1895–1902*. Ohio University Center for International Studies, Athens, Ohio.
1977   *The contest for Siam 1889–1902: a study in diplomatic rivalry*. Penerbit Universiti Kebangsaan Malaysia, Kuala Lumpur.

Chapman, E C
1995   Plans and realities in the development of trans-Mekong transport corridors: reflections from recent fieldwork in the upper Mekong corridor. *Thai-Yunnan Project Newsletter* 29:10–17.

Chapman, E C, and Peter Hinton
1993   The emerging Mekong corridor: a note on recent developments (to May 1993). *Thai-Yunnan Project Newsletter* 21:12–16.
1994   *The Mekong Corridor/"Economic Quadrangle": who benefits?* Paper presented at Conference on Asia's New Growth Circles, Chiang Mai Orchid Hotel, 3–6 March 1994.

Chapman, E C, Peter Hinton, and Jingrong Tan
1992   Cross-border trade between Yunnan and Burma, and the emerging Mekong corridor. *Thai-Yunnan Project Newsletter* 19:15–19.

Charivat Santaputra
1985   *Thai foreign policy 1932–1946*. Thammasat University, Bangkok.

Chazee, Laurent
1990   *La province d'Oudomsay: monographie provinciale et étude de districts et villages*. UNDP, Vientiane.
1991   *La province de Luang Namtha: monographie provinciale et étude de districts et villages*. UNDP, Vientiane.

Chiou, C L
1982   China's policy towards Laos: politics of neutralization. In *Contemporary Laos: studies in the politics and society of the Lao People's Democratic Republic*, edited by Martin Stuart-Fox, pp. 291–305. University of Queensland Press, St Lucia.

Chiranan Prasertkul
1989   *Yunnan trade in the nineteenth century: southwest China's cross-boundaries functional system*. Institute of Asian Studies, Chulalongkorn University, Bangkok.

Choung Phanrajsavong
1996   *Hydropower development in the lower Mekong basin*. Paper presented at Workshop on Development Dilemmas in the Mekong Subregion, Monash Asia Institute, Monash University, Melbourne, 1–2 October 1996.

Christaller, Walter
1966   *Central places in southern Germany*. Prentice-Hall, Englewood Cliffs, New Jersey.

Clifford, Hugh
1905   *Further India: being the story of exploration from the earliest time in Burma, Malaya, Siam, and Indo-China*. Alston Rivers, London.

Coedès, G
1968   *The Indianized states of Southeast Asia*. Australian National University Press, Canberra.

Cohen, Erik
1987   Thailand, Burma and Laos - an outline of the comparative social dynamics of three Theravada Buddhist societies in the modern era. In *Patterns of modernity volume II: beyond the West*, edited by S N Eisenstadt, pp. 192–216. Frances Pinter, London.

Cohen, Paul
1996   *Lue across borders: pilgrimage and the Muang Sing reliquary in northern Laos*. Paper presented at Conference on South China and Mainland Southeast Asia: Cross Border Relations in the Post-Socialist Age, The University of Hong Kong, 4–6 December 1996.

Colquhoun, Archibald Ross
1885   *Amongst the Shans*. Field and Tuer; Simpkin, Marshall and Company, London.

Compagnie Nationale du Rhône
1994   *Mekong mainstream run-of-river hydropower: main report*. Mekong Secretariat, Bangkok.

Condominas, Georges
1990   *From Lawa to Mon, from Saa' to Thai: historical and anthropological aspects of Southeast Asian social spaces*. Department of Anthropology, Research School of Pacific Studies, The Australian National University, Canberra.

Coolidge, Harold J, and Theodore Roosevelt
1933   *Three kingdoms of Indo-China*. Thomas Y Crowell Company, New York.

Cornish, Andrew
1988   Two meetings: contrasting use of space by Malay villagers and Thai officials in southern Thailand. *Mankind* 18 (2):90–100.

Credner, Wilhelm
1966   *Siam: das land der tai*. Otto Zeller, Osnabrück.

Crèvecoeur, Jean Boucher de
1985   *La liberation du Laos: 1945–1946*. Service Historique de l'Armée de Terre, Château de Vincennes.

Crosby, Sir Josiah
1945   *Siam: the crossroads.* Hollis and Carter Ltd., London.

Cross, J P
1992   *First in, last out: an unconventional British officer in Indo-China (1945–46 and 1972–76).* Brassey's, London.

Cushman, Jennifer Wayne
1975   *Fields from the sea: Chinese junk trade with Siam during the late eighteenth and early nineteenth centuries.* University Microfilms International, Ann Arbor, Michigan.

Damrong Tayanin
1994   *Being Kammu: my village, my life.* Cornell University, Southeast Asia Program, Ithaca.

Daniel, James
1994   Progress in the privatization program in Lao PDR. In *Economic development in Lao PDR: horizon 2000*, edited by Chi Do Pham, pp. 72–81. Bank of the Lao People's Democratic Republic, Vientiane.

Davis, Richard B
1984   *Muang metaphysics: a study of northern Thai myth and ritual.* Pandora, Bangkok.

Decoux, Amiral
1950   *A la barre de l'Indochine: histoire de mon Gouvernement Général (1940–1945).* Librairie Plon, Paris.

Deuve, Jean
1984   *Le royaume du Laos 1949–1965.* École Française d'Extrême Orient, Paris.
1992   *Le Laos 1945–1949: contribution a l'histoire du mouvement Lao Issala.* Universite Paul Valery, Montpellier.

Devillers, Philippe, and Jean Lacouture
1969   *End of a war: Indochina, 1954.* Frederick A Praeger, New York.

Dewey, Alice G
1962a   *Peasant marketing in Java.* Free Press, Glencoe.
1962b   Trade and social control in Java. *The Journal of the Royal Anthropological Institute of Great Britain and Ireland* 92:177–190

Direk Chaiyanam
1966   *thaj kab soŋkhraam loog khraŋ thii sɔɔŋ: lem nyŋ.* Thai Watthana Phanit, Bangkok.

Dommen, Arthur J
1964   *Conflict in Laos: the politics of neutralization.* Pall Mall Press, London.
1972   Lao politics under Prince Souvanna Phouma. In *Indochina in conflict: a political assessment*, edited by J J Zasloff and A E Goodman, pp. 81–97. Lexington Books, Lexington.
1995   Laos in 1994: among generals, among friends. *Asian Survey* 35 (1):84–91.

Donner, Wolf
1978   *The five faces of Thailand: an economic geography.* University of Queensland Press, St Lucia.

Dooley, Thomas A
1959   *Doctor in the Asian beyond: the edge of tomorrow.* Victor Gollancz Ltd, London.

1963   *The night they burned the mountain.* The World's Work (1913) Ltd, Kingswood.

Douglas, J J
1989   *Discussion paper: economic policy and organizational aspects of forestry development in Laos.* Unpublished paper, Vientiane.

Duangjan Chareunmuang
1992   *bodbaad myaŋ khanaad klaaŋ nay kaan phadthanaa phuumiphaag: karanii sygsaa myaŋ chiaŋraaj.* Social Research Institute, Chiang Mai University, Chiang Mai.

Eade, John
1997   Introduction. In *Living the global city: globalization as a local process*, edited by John Eade, pp. 1–19. Routledge, London.

Ellis, Cynthia
1960   *Mango summer.* Hodder and Stoughton, London.

Embree, John F
1949   Ethnology: a visit to Laos, French Indochina. *Journal of the Washington Academy of Sciences* 39 (5):149–157.

Evans, Grant
1988   *Agrarian change in communist Laos.* Institute of Southeast Asian Studies, Singapore.
1990   *Lao peasants under socialism.* Yale University Press, New Haven.
1991a Planning problems in peripheral socialism: the case of Laos. In *Laos: beyond the revolution*, edited by Joseph J Zasloff and Leonard Unger, pp. 84–130. Macmillan, Basingstoke.
1991b Review of Le Laos: stratégies d'un état-tampon. *Sojourn* 6 (1):157–159.
1993   Buddhism and economic action in socialist Laos. In *Socialism: ideals, ideologies, and local practice*, edited by C M Hann, pp. 132–147. Routledge, London.
1995   *Lao peasants under socialism and post-socialism.* Silkworm Books, Chiang Mai.
1996   *Transformation of Jinghong, Xishuangbanna, P.R.C.* Paper presented at Conference on South China and Mainland Southeast Asia: Cross Border Relations in the Post-Socialist Age, The University of Hong Kong, 4–6 December 1996.

Evans, Grant, and Kelvin Rowley
1990   *Red brotherhood at war: Vietnam, Cambodia and Laos since 1975.* Verso, London.

Evers, Hans-Dieter, Ruediger Korff, and Suparb Pas-Ong
1987   Trade and state formation: Siam in the early Bangkok period. *Modern Asian Studies* 21 (4):751–771.

Fall, Bernard B
1961   *Street without joy: Indochina at war, 1946–1956.* The Stackpole Company, Harrisburg.
1967   *Hell in a very small place: the siege of Dien Bien Phu.* J. B. Lippincott, Philadelphia.
1969   *Anatomy of a crisis: the Laotian crisis of 1960–1961.* Doubleday and Company, New York.

FAO (Food and Agriculture Organisation of the United Nations)
1980   *Reports of the Lao PDR Champassak/Attopeu forestry project identification mission.* FAO, Rome.

Fardon, Richard
1995   Introduction: counterworks. In *Counterworks: managing the diversity of knowledge,* edited by Richard Fardon, pp. 1–22. Routledge, London.

FEER, Far Eastern Economic Review
1975   *Asia Year Book.*
1976   *Asia Year Book.*
1977   *Asia Year Book.*
1978   *Asia Year Book.*
1979   *Asia Year Book.*
1981   *Asia Year Book.*
1982   *Asia Year Book.*

Feingold, David A
1996   *The hell of good intentions: opium in the political economy of the trade in girls and women.* Paper presented at South China and Mainland Southeast Asia: Cross Border Relations in the Post-Socialist Age, The University of Hong Kong, 4–6 December 1996.

Feng Yuan Lun
1993   *Promote friendship, strengthen cooperation and seek common development on a mutually beneficial basis.* Yunnan Provincial Border Economic Relations and Trade Administration, Kunming.

Firth, Raymond
1966   *Malay fishermen: their peasant economy.* Routledge and Kegan Paul Ltd, London.

Fisher, R J
1996   Shifting cultivation in Laos: is the government's policy realistic? In *Development dilemmas in the Mekong subregion, 1–2 October 1996: workshop proceedings,* edited by Bob Stensholt, pp. 24–30. Monash Asia Institute, Monash University, Melbourne.

Flood, Chadin, and E Thadeus Flood (editors)
1965   *The dynastic chronicles Bangkok era: the fourth reign, volume one.* The Centre for East Asian Cultural Studies, Tokyo.

Flood, E Thadeus
1969   The 1940 Franco-Thai border dispute and Phibuun Sonkhraam's commitment to Japan. *Journal of Southeast Asian History* 10 (2):304–325.

Flood, E Thadeus, and Chadin Flood (editors)
1978   *The dynastic chronicles Bangkok era: the first reign, volume one.* The Centre for East Asian Cultural Studies, Tokyo.

Forbes, Andrew D W
1987   The "Cin-Ho" (Yunnanese Chinese) caravan trade with north Thailand during the late nineteenth and early twentieth centuries. *Journal of Asian History* 21 (2):1–47.

Foucault, Michel
1980   *Power/knowledge: selected interviews and other writings, 1972–1977.* Harvester Press, Brighton.

Franck, Harry A
1926   *East of Siam: ramblings in the five divisions of French Indo-China.* The
       Century Co., New York.

Freeman, Rev. John H
1910   *An oriental land of the free.* The Westminster Press, Philadelphia.

Friedman, Jonathon
1994   *Cultural identity and global process.* Sage Publications, London.

Garnier, Francis
1885   *Further travels in Laos and Yunnan: The Mekong Exploration Commission
       report (1866–1868), volume 2.* White Lotus [1996], Bangkok.

Gaudel, André
1947   *L'Indochine Française en face du Japon.* J Susse, Paris.

Geertz, Clifford
1963   *Peddlers and princes: social change and economic modernization in two
       Indonesian towns.* The University of Chicago Press, Chicago.

Giddens, Anthony
1985   Time, space and regionalisation. In *Social relations and spatial structures*,
       edited by Derek Gregory and John Urry, pp. 265–295. Macmillan, London.

GLPDR (Government of the Lao People's Democratic Republic)
1986   *Lao wood export: seminar held in Vientiane 14–15 May 1986.* Ministry of
       Industry, Handicraft and Forestry, Vientiane.
1988a *Decree no. 12 of the Council of Ministers on directives and measures to increase the
       circulation of commodities and currencies.* Vientiane International Consultants,
       Vientiane.
1988b *Decree no. 13 of the Council of Ministers on state monopoly of import-export
       management.* Vientiane International Consultants, Vientiane.
1988c *Decree no. 14 of the Council of Ministers on state price policy.* Vientiane
       International Consultants, Vientiane.
1988d *Decree no. 18 of the Council of Ministers on the state monopoly of strategic goods
       import-export.* Vientiane International Consultants, Vientiane.
1989a *Law on foreign investment in the Lao People's Democratic Republic.* Foreign
       Investment Management Committee, Vientiane.
1989b *Resolution of the first national conference on forestry.* Vientiane International
       Consultants, Vientiane.
1990a *Decree no. 17 of the Council of Ministers on the conversion of state enterprise units
       to other forms of ownership.* Vientiane International Consultants, Vientiane.
1990b *Sawmill survey 1989.* Ministry of Agriculture and Forestry, Vientiane.
1990c *Tropical forestry action plan (first phase).* Ministry of Agriculture and
       Forestry, Vientiane.
1991a *Decree on logging ban (No. 67/PM) and recommendations on the organisation for
       the implementation of the Prime Minister's decree on national logging ban.*
       Vientiane International Consultants, Vientiane.
1991b *Trade statistics for 1986–1990.* Ministry of Commerce and Tourism, Statistics
       Division, Vientiane.
1993   *Basic statistics about the socio-economic development in the Lao PDR.*
       Committee for Planning and Co-operation, Vientiane.
1994a *Additional order of the Prime Minister on the adjustment of management
       system for logging throughout the country.* Cabinet of the Prime Minister,
       Vientiane.

1994b *Forest Marketing News, June 1994.* Marketing Information System, Department of Forestry, Vientiane.

1994c *Institutional strengthening to the Department of Forestry Lao PDR: decree of the Prime Minister on the management and use of forests and forest land, No 169/ PM, working paper number 2.* Department of Forestry, Vientiane.

1994d *kotmaay va duay kaan song sɔɔm lɛ kaan khum khɔɔng kaan long thyn khɔɔng tang pathet.* Foreign Investment Management Committee, Vientiane.

1994e *lyang banhaa kaan khaa saay dɛɛn laao-thay.* Bank of the Lao PDR, Vientiane.

1995 *sathiti kaan khaa 1986–1990.* Department of Trade, Vientiane.

Godley, G McMurtrie, and Jinny St Goar
1991 The Chinese road in northwest Laos 1961–73: an American perspective. In *Laos: beyond the revolution,* edited by Joseph J Zasloff and Leonard Unger, pp. 285–314. Macmillan, Basingstoke.

Goldman, Minton F
1972 Franco-British rivalry over Siam, 1896–1904. *Journal of Southeast Asian Studies* 3 (2):210–228.

Golomb, Louis
1976 The origin, spread and persistence of glutinous rice as a staple crop in mainland Southeast Asia. *Journal of Southeast Asian Studies* 7 (1):1–15.

GOT (Government of Thailand)
1977 *prakaad samnag naajog radthamontrii ryaŋ kaan khian chyy caŋwad kheed ʔamphəə lɛ kiŋ ʔamphəə.* Office of the Prime Minister, Bangkok.

1989 *kaan kha daan sunlakaakɔɔn chiaŋ sɛɛn.* Chiang Rai Office of Commerce, Chiang Rai.

1989 *kaan kha daan sunlakaakɔɔn chiaŋ khɔɔŋ.* Chiang Rai Office of Commerce, Chiang Rai.

1992 *kaan khaa chaajdɛɛn khɔɔŋ phaag nya kab taaŋpratheed.* Department of Trade, Chiang Mai.

1993a *kodmaaj sunlakaakɔɔn.* Thai Customs Department, Bangkok.

1993b *phaawa kaan khaa chaajdɛɛn caŋwad chiaŋraaj pii 2535.* Chiang Rai Office of Commerce, Chiang Rai.

1994 *khrooŋkaan prasaan ruam myy thaang seedthakid rawaaŋ pratheed naj ʔanuphuumiphaag lum mɛɛnaam khooŋ* National Economic and Social Development Board, Chiang Mai.

1995a *phaawa kaan khaa chaajdɛɛn daan caŋwad chiaŋraaj pii 2537.* Chiang Rai Office of Commerce, Chiang Rai.

1995b *raajŋaan sathiti kaan khaa chaajdɛɛn jɔɔnlaŋ 5 pii thaang daan caŋwad chiaŋraaj.* Chiang Rai Office of Commerce, Chiang Rai.

1995c *sathiti sinkhaa khaakhaw - sinkhaa soŋɔɔg lɛ sinkhaa phaandɛɛn.* Chiang Khong Customs Office, Chiang Khong.

Grewal, Inderpal, and Caren Kaplan
1994 Introduction: transnational feminist practices and questions of postmodernity. In *Scattered hegemonies: postmodernity and transnational feminist practices,* edited by Inderpal Grewal and Caren Kaplan, pp. 1–33. University of Minnesota Press, Minneapolis.

Grundy-Warr, Carl
1993 Coexistent borderlands and intra-state conflicts in mainland southeast Asia. *Singapore Journal of Tropical Geography* 14 (1):42–57.

Gunn, Geoffrey, C
1988   *Political struggles in Laos (1930–1954): Vietnamese communist power and the Lao struggle for independence.* Editions Duang Kamol, Bangkok.
1990   *Rebellion in Laos: peasants and politics in a colonial backwater.* Westview Press, Boulder.

Gupta, Akhil
1992   The song of the nonaligned world: transnational identities and the reinscription of space in late capitalism. *Cultural Anthropology* 7 (1):63–79.

Gupta, Akhil, and James Ferguson
1992   Beyond "culture": space, identity, and the politics of difference. *Cultural Anthropology* 7 (1):6–23.

Haas, Mary R
1964   *Thai-English student's dictionary.* Stanford University Press, Stanford.

Hägerstrand, T
1970   What about people in regional science? *Papers and Proceedings of the Regional Science Association* 24:7–21.
1978   Survival and arena: on the life history of individuals in relation to their geographical environment. In *Timing space and spacing time: volume 2,* edited by Tommy Carlstein, Don Parkes, and Nigel Thrift, pp. 122–145. Edward Arnold, London.

Hall, Catherine
1996   Histories, empires and the post-colonial movement. In *The post-colonial question: common skies, divided horizons,* edited by Iain Chambers and Lidia Curti, pp. 65–77. Routledge, London.

Hall, Stuart
1991   The local and the global: globalization and ethnicity. In *Culture, globalization and the world-system: contemporary conditions for the representation of identity,* edited by Anthony D King, pp. 19–39. Macmillan, State University of New York at Binghamton.
1996   When was "the post-colonial"? Thinking at the limit. In *The post-colonial question: common skies, divided horizons,* edited by Iain Chambers and Lidia Curti, pp. 242–260. Routledge, London.

Hallet, Holt S
1890   *A thousand miles on an elephant in the Shan states.* White Lotus [1988], Bangkok.

Halpern, Joel Martin
1959   Trade patterns in northern Laos. *The Eastern Anthropologist* 12 (1):119–124.
1961   *The role of the Chinese in Lao society: Laos project paper number 1.* Department of Anthropology, University of California, Los Angeles.
1964a   Capital, savings and credit among Lao peasants. In *Capital, saving and credit in peasant societies: studies from Asia, Oceania, the Caribbean and middle America,* edited by Raymond Firth and B S Yamey, pp. 82–103. George Allen and Unwin Ltd, London.
1964b   *Economy and society of Laos: a brief survey.* Southeast Asia Studies, Yale University, New Haven.
1964c   *Government, politics and social structure in Laos: a study of tradition and innovation.* Southeast Asia Studies, Yale University, New Haven.

Hammer, Ellen J
1966   *The struggle for Indochina 1940–1955.* Stanford University Press, Stanford.

Hanks, Lucien M
1962   Merit and power in the Thai social order. *American Anthropologist* 64 (6):1247–1261.
1975   The Thai social order as entourage and circle. In *Change and persistence in Thai society: essays in honor of Lauriston Sharp,* edited by G William Skinner and A Thomas Kirsch, pp. 197–218. Cornell University Press, Ithaca.

Hannerz, Ulf
1991   Scenarios for peripheral cultures. In *Culture, globalization and the world-system: contemporary conditions for the representation of identity,* edited by Anthony D King, pp. 107–128. Macmillan, State University of New York at Binghamton.
1992   The global ecumene as a network of networks. In *Conceptualizing society,* edited by Adam Kuper, pp. 34–56. Routledge, London.

Harvey, David
1989   *The condition of post-modernity: an enquiry into the origins of cultural change.* Basil Blackwell, Oxford.
1993   From space to place and back again: reflections on the condition of postmodernity. In *Mapping the futures: local cultures, global change,* edited by Jon Bird, Barry Curtis, Tim Putnam, George Robertson, and Lisa Tickner, pp. 3–29. Routledge, London.

Hasnah Ali
1996   *Growth triangles in the ASEAN region: issues, challenges and prospects.* Paper presented at Asian Studies Association of Australia Conference on Communications with/in Asia, La Trobe University, 8–11 July 1996.

Héduy, Philippe
1981   *La guerre d'Indochine: 1945–1954.* Société de Production Littéraire, Paris.

Hesse d'Alzon, Claude
1985   *La presence militaire Française en Indochine (1940–1945).* Service Historique de l'Armée de Terre, Château de Vincennes.

Hewison, Kevin
1995   Emerging social forces in Thailand: new political and economic roles. In *The new rich in Asia: mobile phones, McDonalds and middle class revolution,* edited by Richard Robison and David S G Goodman, pp. 137–160. Routledge, London.

High, Jack (editor)
1991   *Regulation: economic theory and history.* The University of Michigan Press, Ann Arbor.

Hill, Ann Maxwell
1982   Familiar strangers: the Yunnanese Chinese in northern Thailand. University Microfilms International, Urbana, Illinois.

Hindess, Barry
1996   *Discourses of power: from Hobbes to Foucault.* Blackwell, Oxford.

Hinton, Peter
1992   Meetings as ritual: Thai officials, western consultants and development planning in northern Thailand. In *Patterns and illusions: Thai history and*

thought, edited by Gehan Wijeyewardene and E. C. Chapman, pp. 105–124. The Australian National University, Canberra.

1995   Growth triangles, quadrangles and circles: interpreting some macro-models for regional trade. *Thai-Yunnan Project Newsletter* 28:2–7.

1996a   *Is it possible to 'manage' a river? Reflections from the Mekong.* Paper presented at Sixth International Conference on Thai Studies, Chiang Mai, 14–17 October 1996.

1996b   *Where nothing is as it seems: between south China and mainland Southeast Asia in the "post socialist" era.* Paper presented at Conference on South China and Mainland Southeast Asia: Cross Border Relations in the Post-Socialist Age, The University of Hong Kong, 4–6 December 1996.

Hirsch, Philip
1989   The state in the village: interpreting rural development in Thailand. *Development and Change* 20 (1):35–56.

1990   *Development dilemmas in rural Thailand.* Oxford University Press, Singapore.

1995   Thailand and the new geopolitics of southeast Asia: resource and environmental issues. In *Counting the costs: economic growth and environmental change in Thailand*, edited by Jonathan Rigg, pp. 235–259. Institute of Southeast Asian Studies, Singapore.

Hirsch, Philip, and Gerard Cheong
1996   *Natural resource management in the Mekong River basin: perspectives for Australian development cooperation.* AusAID, Canberra.

Hirshfield, Claire
1968   The struggle for the Mekong banks: 1892–1896. *Journal of Southeast Asian History* 9 (1):25–52.

Holm, David F
1991   Thailand's railways and informal imperialism. In *Railway imperialism*, edited by Clarence B Davis and Kenneth E Wilburn, pp. 121–135. Greenwood Press, New York.

Hong Lysa
1984   *Thailand in the nineteenth century: evolution of the economy and society.* Institute of Southeast Asian Studies, Singapore.

Howell, Signe
1995   Whose knowledge and whose power? A new perspective on cultural diffusion. In *Counterworks: managing the diversity of knowledge*, edited by Richard Fardon, pp. 164–181. Routledge, London.

IBRD (International Bank for Reconstruction and Development)
1975   *Some findings relative to the reconstruction and economic development of Laos, volume 3: transportation.* IBRD, Washington D.C.

IMC (Interim Mekong Committee)
1976   *Aids to navigation required on the Mekong river.* IMC, Bangkok.

1987   *Statistics on inland water-borne transport (Lao People's Democratic Republic and Thailand).* Mekong Secretariat, Bangkok.

Ireson, Carol J
1992   Changes in field, forest, and family: rural women's work and status in post-revolutionary Laos. *Bulletin of Concerned Asian Scholars* 24 (4):3–18.

1996   *Field, forest, and family: women's work and power in rural Laos.* Westview, Boulder.

209

Ireson, Randall W
1996   Invisible walls: village identity and the maintenance of cooperation in Laos. *Journal of Southeast Asian Studies* 27 (2):219–244.

Ispahani, Mahnaz Z
1989   *Roads and rivals: the political uses of access in the borderlands of Asia.* Cornell University Press, Ithaca.

Izikowitz, Karl Gustav
1979   *Lamet: hill peasants in French Indochina.* AMS Press, New York.
1985   *Compass for fields afar: essays in social anthropology.* ACTA Universitatis Gothoburgensis, Gothenburg.

Jessop, Bob
1990   *State theory: putting the capitalist state in its place.* Polity Press, Cambridge.

Jumsai, Manich M L
1971   *History of Laos.* Chalermnit, Bangkok.

Junko Koizumi
1992   The commutation of *suai* from northeast Siam to Bangkok in the middle of the nineteenth century. *Journal of Southeast Asian Studies* 23 (2):276–307.

Keating, J E
1989   *Tropical forestry action plan: development strategies, policies and projects for Lao PDR's wood processing industry.* Unpublished paper, Vientiane.

Kemp, Jeremy
1991   The dialectics of village and state in modern Thailand. *Journal of Southeast Asian Studies* 22 (2):312–326.

Kerr, Allen D
1979   *Lao-English dictionary.* Consortium Press, Washington.

Keyes, Charles F
1984   Mother or mistress but never a monk: Buddhist notions of female gender in rural Thailand. *American Ethnologist* 11 (2):223–241.
1993   *Who are the Lue? Revisited ethnic identity in Lao, Thailand, and China.* Paper presented at Conference on the State of Thai Cultural Studies, Office of the National Commission on Culture, Bangkok, 10–12 September 1993.

Khambay Khamsana, and Dan E Frederiksen
1989   *Tropical forestry action plan for Lao PDR: draft discussion paper on institutional aspects.* Photocopy, Vientiane.

Khamphaeng Thipmuntali
1996   *The economic, cultural and social consequences of opening of the Lao-Chinese border.* Paper presented at Conference on South China and Mainland Southeast Asia: Cross Border Relations in the Post-Socialist Age, The University of Hong Kong, 4–6 December 1996.

Kibria, Nazli
1993   *Family tightrope: the changing lives of Vietnamese Americans.* Princeton University Press, Princeton, New Jersey.

King, Anthony D
1991   Introduction: spaces of culture, spaces of knowledge. In *Culture, globalization and the world-system: contemporary conditions for the representation*

of identity, edited by Anthony D King, pp. 1–18. Macmillan, State University of New York at Binghamton.

Kingshill, Konrad
1991   *Ku Daeng - thirty years later: a village study in northern Thailand 1954–1984.* Centre for Southeast Asian Studies, Northern Illinois University, Illinois.

Kirsch, A Thomas
1982   Buddhism, sex-roles and the Thai economy. In *Women of Southeast Asia,* edited by Penny van Esterik, pp. 16–41. Center for Southeast Asian Studies, Northern Illinois University, Illinois.
1985   Text and context: Buddhist sex roles/culture of gender revisited. *American Ethnologist* 12 (2):302–320.

Kreutzmann, Hermann
1991   The Karakoram Highway: the impact of road construction on mountain societies. *Modern Asian Studies* 25 (4):711–736.

Krishna, Sankaran
1996   Cartographic anxiety: mapping the body politic in India. In *Challenging boundaries: global flows, territorial identities,* edited by Michael J Shapiro and Hayward R Alker, pp. 193–214. University of Minnesota Press, Minneapolis.

Kristof, Ladis K D
1959   The nature of frontiers and boundaries. *Annals, Association of American Geographers* 49:269–282.

Lamington, Lord
1891   Journey through the trans-Salwin Shan states to Tong-King. *Proceedings of the Royal Geographical Society* 12 (December 1891):701–719.

Lancaster, Donald
1961   *The emancipation of French Indochina.* Oxford University Press, London.

Langer, Paul F, and Joseph J Zasloff
1970   *North Vietnam and the Pathet Lao: partners in the struggle for Laos.* Harvard University Press, Cambridge, Massachusetts.

Le May, Reginald
1926   *An Asian arcady: the land and peoples of northern Siam.* White Lotus [1986], Bangkok.

Leach, E R
1960   The frontiers of "Burma." *Comparative Studies in Society and History* 3 (1):49–68.
1977   *Political systems of highland Burma: a study of Kachin social structure.* The Athlone Press, London.

LeBar, Frank M, Gerald C Hickey, and John K Musgrave
1964   *Ethnic groups of mainland Southeast Asia.* Human Relations Area Files Press, New Haven.

LeBar, Frank M, and Adrienne Suddard
1960   *Laos: its people, its society, its culture.* Human Relations Area File Press, New Haven.

Lefèvre, E
1898   *Travels in Laos: the fate of Sip Song Panna and Muong Sing (1894–1896).*
        White Lotus [1995], Bangkok.

Lefèvre-Pontalis, Pierre
1902   *Voyages dans le haut Laos et sur les frontières de Chine et de Birmanie, volume 5 of
        Mission Pavie Indo-Chine 1879–1895, géographie et voyages.* Ernest Leroux, Paris.

Legendre, Sidney J
1936   *Land of the white parasol and the million elephants: a journey through the jungles
        of Indo-China.* Dodd, Mead and Company, Binghamton, New York.

Lemoine, Jacques
1972   *Un village hmong vert du haut Laos.* Editions du Centre National de la
        Recherche Scientifique, Paris.

Lévy, Banyen Phimmasone
1963   Yesterday and today in Laos: a girl's autobiographical notes. In *Women in the
        new Asia: the changing social roles of men and women in South and South-East
        Asia,* edited by Barbara E Ward, pp. 244–265. UNESCO, Paris.

Levy, Roger, Guy Lacam, and Andrew Roth
1941   *French interests and politics in the far east.* Institute of Pacific Relations, New
        York.

Lewis, Norman
1982   *A dragon apparent: travels in Cambodia, Laos and Vietnam.* Eland Books,
        London.

Lintner, Bertil
1994   Add water: Laos' hydroelectric plans seem overambitious. *Far Eastern
        Economic Review* 13 October 1994:70–71.
1997   Old habits die hard. *Far Eastern Economic Review* 27 November 1997:71.

Ljunggren, Carl Börje
1992   *Market economies under communist regimes: reform in Vietnam, Laos and
        Cambodia.* University Microfilms International, Ann Arbor.

Lok, Renata
1989   *Mission report: socio-economic aspects of Bokeo and Luang Namtha provinces
        and recommendations for future UNDP assistance.* UNDP, Vientiane.

MAD   (Mountainous Area Development Company)
1996   *bɔɔlisat tɔɔng thiaav patthanaa khet phuu dɔɔy.* MAD, Vientiane.

Maana Maalaphet
1994   kaan khaa chaajdɛɛn thaj-laaw: panhaa lɛ thid thaaŋ. In *kaan khaa
        chaajdɛɛn,* edited by Wittaya Sujaritnarag and Chapaa Jitpratum, pp. 37–44.
        Chulalongkorn University, Bangkok.

Mangrai, Sao Saimong
1965   *The Shan states and the British annexation.* Department of Asian Studies,
        Cornell University, Ithaca, New York.

Mann, Michael
1996   Nation-states in Europe and other continents: diversifying, developing, not
        dying. In *Mapping the nation,* edited by Gopal Balakrishnan, pp. 295–316.
        Verso, London.

Maspero, Georges
1929   *Un empire colonial Français, l'Indochine: volume 1.* G Van Oest, Paris.

Massey, Doreen
1993a   Power-geometry and a progressive sense of place. In *Mapping the futures: local cultures, global change,* edited by Jon Bird, Barry Curtis, Tim Putnam, George Robertson, and Lisa Tickner, pp. 59–69. Routledge, London.
1993b   Questions of locality. *Geography* 78 (2):142–149.
1994   *Space, place and gender.* Polity Press, Cambridge.

Mayoury Ngaosyvathn
1993   *Lao women yesterday and today.* Lao State Publishing Enterprise, Vientiane.

Mayoury Ngaosyvathn, and Pheuiphanh Ngaosyvathn
1989   Lao historiography and historians: case study of the war between Bangkok and the Lao in 1827. *Journal of Southeast Asian Studies* 20 (1):55–69.
1994   *Kith and kin politics: the relationship between Laos and Thailand.* Journal of Contemporary Asia Publishers, Manila.

McCarthy, James
1900   *Surveying and exploring in Siam with descriptions of Lao dependencies and of battles against the Chinese Haws.* White Lotus [1994], Bangkok.

McCoy, Alfred W
1970   French colonialism in Laos, 1893–1945. In *Laos: war and revolution,* edited by Nina S Adams and Alfred W McCoy, pp. 67–98. Harper and Row, New York.
1972   *The politics of heroin in Southeast Asia.* Harper and Row, Singapore.

McGilvary, Daniel
1912   *A half century among the Siamese and the Lao: an autobiography.* Fleming H. Revell Company, New York.

McGovern, Ian
1996   Regional development in the Mekong basin. In *Development dilemmas in the Mekong subregion, 1–2 October 1996: workshop proceedings,* edited by Bob Stensholt, pp. 61–68. Monash Asia Institute, Monash University, Melbourne.

McLeod, W C
1867   *A journal kept by Captain W. C. McLeod, Assistant to the Commissioner in the Tenasserim Provinces, during his mission from Moulmein to the frontiers of China.* Parliamentary Accounts and Papers, London.

McVey, Ruth
1984   Separatism and the paradoxes of the nation-state in perspective. In *Armed separatism in Southeast Asia,* edited by Lim Joo-Jock and S Vani, pp. 3–29. Institute of Southeast Asian Studies, Singapore.

Meeker, Oden
1959   *The little world of Laos.* Charles Scribner's Sons, New York.

Miles, Douglas
1973   Some demographic implications of regional commerce: the case of north Thailand's Yao minority. In *Studies in Contemporary Thailand,* edited by R Ho and E Chapman, pp. 253–257. Australian National University Press, Canberra.

Mills, Mary Beth
1995 Attack of the widow ghosts: gender, death, and modernity in Northeast Thailand. In *Bewitching women, pious men: gender and body politics in Southeast Asia*, edited by Aihwa Ong and Michael G Peletz, pp. 244–273. University of California Press, Berkeley.

Mintz, Sidney
1967 Pratik: Haitian personal economic relationships. In *Peasant society: a reader*, edited by J. M. Potter, M. N. Dias and G. M. Foster. Little, Brown and Company, Boston.

Mitchell, Katharyne
1997 Transnational discourse: bringing geography back in. *Antipode* 29 (2): 101–114.

Mitton, G E (editor)
1936 Scott of the Shan hills: orders and impressions. John Murray, London.

Moerman, Michael
1968 *Agricultural change and peasant choice in a Thai village*. University of California Press, Berkeley.
1975 Chiangkham's trade in the "old days." In *Change and persistence in Thai society: essays in honor of Lauriston Sharp*, edited by G William Skinner and A Thomas Kirsch, pp. 151–171. Cornell University Press, Ithaca.

Muecke, Marjorie A
1984 Make money not babies: changing status markers of northern Thai women. *Asian Survey* 24 (4):459–470.

Murray, Martin J
1980 *The development of capitalism in colonial Indochina (1870–1940)*. University of California Press, Berkely.

Neis, Paul
1885 Voyage dans le haut Laos. *Journal of the Société de Géographie* 3rd quarter 1885:372–393.

Newman, Bernard
1953 *Report on Indo-China*. Robert Hale Limited, London.

Ng, Shui Meng
1991 Social development in the Lao People's Democratic Republic: problems and prospects. In *Laos: beyond the revolution*, edited by Joseph J Zasloff and Leonard Unger, pp. 159–183. Macmillan, Basingstoke.

Nonis, Eustace A
1994 *Economic linkages through new highways: implications of different land routes*. Paper presented at Conference on Asia's New Growth Circles, Chiang Mai Orchid Hotel, 3–6 March, 1994.

Ogus, Anthony I
1994 *Regulation: legal form and economic theory*. Clarendon Press, Oxford.

O'Harrow, Stephen
1995 Vietnamese women and Confucianism: creating spaces from patriarchy. In *'Male' and 'female' in developing southeast Asia*, edited by Wazir Jahan Karim. Berg Publishers, Oxford.

Ohmae, Kenichi
1995   *The end of the nation state: the rise of regional economies.* The Free Press, New York.

Ong, Aihwa, and Michael G Peletz
1995   Introduction. In *Bewitching women, pious men: gender and body politics in Southeast Asia,* edited by Aihwa Ong and Michael G Peletz, pp. 1–18. University of California Press, Berkeley.

Orléans, Henri-Ph de
1894   *Autour du Tonkin.* Calmann Lévy, Paris.

Osborne, Milton
1975   *River road to China: the Mekong River Expedition 1866–1873.* George Allen and Unwin, London.

PADECO, Co. Ltd
1994   *Transport (interim report): promoting subregional cooperation among Cambodia, the People's Republic of China, Lao People's Democratic Republic, Myanmar, Thailand and Viet Nam.* ADB, Manila.

Parsonage, James
1997   Trans-state developments in south-east Asia: subregional growth zones. In *The political economy of South-East Asia: an introduction,* edited by Gary Rodan, Kevin Hewison and Richard Robison. Oxford University Press, Melbourne.

Pasuk Phongpaichit, and Chris Baker
1995   *Thailand: economy and politics.* Oxford University Press, Kuala Lumpur.

Pasuk Phongpaichit, and Sungsidh Piriyarangsan
1994   *Corruption and democracy in Thailand.* Chulalongkorn University, Bangkok.

Pavie, Auguste
1901   *Exposé des travaux de la mission, volume 1 of Mission Pavie Indo-Chine 1879–1895: géographie et voyages.* Ernest Leroux, Paris.
1903   *Mission Pavie Indo-Chine atlas: notices et cartes.* Augustin Challamel, Paris.
1906   *Exposé des travaux de la mission, volume 2 of Mission Pavie Indo-Chine 1879–1895: géographie et voyages.* Ernest Leroux, Paris.

Penth, Hans
1994   *A brief history of Lan Na: civilizations of north Thailand.* Silkworm Books, Chiang Mai.

Pham, Chi Do
1994a   *Economic development in Lao PDR: horizon 2000.* Bank of the Lao People's Democratic Republic, Vientiane.
1994b   Economic reforms in Laos: an unforgettable experience in a "forgotten" land. In *Economic development in Lao PDR: horizon 2000,* edited by Chi Do Pham, pp. 14–28. Bank of the Lao People's Democratic Republic, Vientiane.

Phillips, Herbert P.
1965   *Thai peasant personality: the patterning of interpersonal behavior in the village of Bang Chan.* University of California Press, Berkeley.

Phornphimol Trichot, and Saykeew Chusaph
1994   kaan khaa chaajdɛɛn thaj-phamaa. In *kaan khaa chaajdɛɛn,* edited by Wittaya Sujaritnarag and Chapaa Jitpratum, pp. 21–36. Chulalongkorn University, Bangkok.

Picanon, Eugène
1901   *Le Laos Français.* Augustin Challamel, Paris.

Pinkaew Leungaramsri, and Noel Rajesh (editors)
1992   *The future of people and forests in Thailand after the logging ban.* Project for Ecological Recovery, Thailand, Bangkok.

Polanyi, Karl
1944   *The great transformation.* Rinehart and Company, Inc., New York.

Porter, Doug J
1995   *Wheeling and dealing: HIV/AIDS and development on the Shan State borders.* UNDP, manuscript.
1997   A plague on the borders: HIV, development, and travelling identities in the Golden Triangle. In *Sites of desire, economies of pleasure: sexualities in Asia and the Pacific,* edited by Lenore Manderson and Margaret Jolly, pp. 212–232. University of Chicago Press, Chicago.

Prachan Rakpong
1994a   *bɛɛb sanəə hua khɔɔ khroon raan kaan wicaj: kaansygsaa saphaab seedthakid lɛ wadthanatham chumchon nay kheed senthan seedthakid thaj-laaw-ciin.* Rajabhat Chiangmai Institute Training Center for Tourism Industry, Chiang Mai.
1994b   *wadthanatham chumchon nay kheed senthan seedthakid thaj-laaw.* Paper presented at Conference on Art and Culture in the Five "Chiang," Rimkok Resort Hotel, Chiang Rai, 1–6 March 1994.

Prattis, J Iain
1987   Alternative views of economy in economic anthropology. In *Beyond the new economic anthropology,* edited by J. Clammer, pp. 8–44. St. Martin's Press, New York.

Pred, Allan
1985   The social becomes the spatial, the spatial becomes the social: enclosures, social change and the becoming of places in Skane. In *Social relations and spatial structures,* edited by Derek Gregory and John Urry, pp. 337–365. Macmillan, London.
1990   *Making histories and constructing human geographies: the local transformation of practice, power relations, and consciousness.* Westview Press, Boulder.

Preecha Kuwinpant
1980   *Marketing in north-central Thailand: a study of socio-economic organization in a Thai market town.* Chulalongkorn University, Bangkok.

Prescott, J R V
1975   *Map of mainland Asia by treaty.* Melbourne University Press, Melbourne.

Purcell, Victor
1965   *The Chinese in Southeast Asia.* Oxford University Press, Oxford.

Ramsay, James Ansil
1976   Modernization and centralization in northern Thailand: 1875–1910. *Journal of Southeast Asian Studies* 7 (1):16–32.

Rantala, Judy Austin
1994   *Laos: a personal portrait from the mid-1970s.* McFarland and Company, Jefferson, North Carolina.

Regini, Marino
1995 *Uncertain boundaries: the social and political construction of European economies.* Cambridge University Press, Cambridge.

Reinach, Lucien de
1911 *Le Laos.* E. Guilmoto, Paris.

Reyes, Romeo A
1997 The role of the state in Laos' economic management. In *Laos' dilemmas and options: the challenge of economic transition in the 1990s*, edited by Mya Than and J. L. H. Tan, pp. 48–60. St Martins Press, New York.

Reynolds, Craig J
1991 Introduction: national identity and its defenders. In *National identity and its defenders: Thailand, 1939–1989*, edited by Craig J Reynolds, pp. 1–39. Silkworm Books, Chiang Mai.
1998 Globalisation and cultural nationalism in modern Thailand. In *Southeast Asian identities: culture and the politics of representation in Indonesia, Malaysia, Singapore, and Thailand*, edited by Joel S Kahn, pp. 115–145. Institute of Southeast Asian Studies, Singapore.

Rigg, Jonathan
1995 Managing dependency in a reforming economy: the Lao PDR. *Contemporary Southeast Asia* 17 (2):147–172.

Rigg, Jonathan, and Randi Jerndal
1996 Plenty in the context of scarcity: forest management in Laos. In *Environmental change in South-East Asia: people, politics and sustainable development*, edited by Michael J G Parnwell and Raymond L Bryant, pp. 145–162. Routledge, London.

Riggs, Fred Warren
1967 *Thailand: the modernization of a bureaucratic polity.* East-West Center Press, Honolulu.

Rimmer, Peter J
1974 Government influence on transport decision-making in Thailand. In *Transportation geography: comments and reading*, edited by Michael E Eliot Hurst, pp. 292–313. McGraw-Hill Book Company, New York.

Robbins, Christopher
1988 *Air America.* Corgi Books, London.

Robequain, Charles
1944 *The economic development of French Indo-China.* Oxford University Press, London.

Roberts, T D, Mary Elizabeth Carroll, Irving Kaplan, Jan M Matthews, David S McMorris, and Charles Townsend
1967 *Area handbook for Laos.* United States Government Printing Office, Washington.

Robertson, Roland
1992 *Globalization: social theory and global culture.* Sage Publications, London.

Rodan, Garry
1988 State, capital and industrialisation in the NICs: implications for industry policy in Australia. *Australian Outlook* 42 (1):37–48.

Rodan, Garry, Kevin Hewison, and Richard Robison (editors)
1997   *The political economy of South-East Asia: an introduction*. Oxford University Press, Melbourne.

Rodman, Margaret C
1992   Empowering place: multilocality and multivocality. *American Anthropologist* 94 (3):640–656.

Rowley, C D
1960   *The lotus and the dynamo: a traveller in changing South-East Asia*. Angus and Robertson, Sydney.

Rumley, Dennis
1991   Society, state and peripherality: the case of the Thai-Malaysian border landscape. In *The geography of border landscapes*, edited by Dennis Rumley and Julian V Minghi, pp. 129–151. Routledge, London.

Sabattier, Général G
1952   *Le destin de l'Indochine: souvenirs et documents 1941–1951*. Librairie Plon, Paris.

Saowapha Phaythayawat
1994   *saŋkhom lɛ wadthanatham chiaŋ thɔɔŋ*. Paper presented at Conference on Art and Culture in the Five "Chiang," Rimkok Resort Hotel, Chiang Rai, 1–6 March 1994.

Sarasin Viraphol
1977   *Tribute and profit: Sino-Siamese trade, 1652–1853*. Harvard University, Cambridge, Massachusetts.

Sasorith, Katay D
1953   *Le Laos: son évolution politique, sa place dans l'Union Française*. Editions Berger-Levrault, Paris.

Savage, Angela
1996   "Vectors" and "protectors": women and HIV/AIDS in the Lao People's Democratic Republic. In *Maternity and reproductive health in Asian societies*, edited by Pranee Liamputtong Rice and Lenore Manderson, pp. 277–299. Harwood Academic Publishers, Amsterdam.

Scott, James C
1972   Patron-client politics and political change in Southeast Asia. *American Political Science Review* 66:91–113.

Scott, J. George
1901   *Gazetteer of Upper Burma and the Shan States*. Superintendent, Government Printing, Burma, Rangoon.

Sesser, Stan
1993   *The lands of charm and cruelty: travels in Southeast Asia*. Alfred A. Knopf, New York.

Shapiro, Michael J
1994   Moral geographies and the ethics of post-sovereignty. *Public Culture* 6:479–502.
1996   Introduction. In *Challenging boundaries: global flows, territorial identities*, edited by Michael J Shapiro and Hayward R Alker, pp. xv-xxiii. University of Minnesota Press, Minneapolis.

Shapiro, Michael J, and Hayward R Alker (editors)
1996   *Challenging boundaries: global flows, territorial identities.* University of Minnesota Press, Minneapolis.

Singhanetra-Renard, A
1981   Mobility in north Thailand: a view from within. In *Population mobility and development: Southeast Asia and the Pacific,* edited by G W Jones and H V Richter, pp. 137–166. The Australian National University, Canberra.

Sivaram, M
1941   *Mekong clash and Far East crisis.* Thai Commercial Press, Bangkok.

Skinner, G William
1964   Marketing and social structure in rural China: part 1. *Journal of Asian Studies* 24 (1):3–43.

Sluiter, Liesbeth
1992   *The Mekong currency.* Project for Ecological Recovery - TERRA, Bangkok.

Smith, Carol A
1976a   Exchange systems and the spatial distribution of elites. In *Regional analysis volume 2: social systems,* edited by Carol A Smith, pp. 309–374. Academic Press, New York.

Smith, Carol A (editor)
1976b   *Regional analysis volume 1: economic systems.* Academic Press, New York.
1976c   *Regional analysis volume 2: social systems.* Academic Press, New York.

Smyth, H Warington
1895   *Notes of a journey on the upper Mekong, Siam.* John Murray, London.
1898a   *Five years in Siam: from 1891–1896, volume 1.* White Lotus [1994], Bangkok.
1898b   *Five years in Siam: from 1891–1896, volume 2.* White Lotus [1994], Bangkok.

Soguk, Nevzat
1996   Transnational/transborder bodies: resistance, accommodation, and exile in refugee and migration movements on the U.S.-Mexican border. In *Challenging boundaries: global flows, territorial identities,* edited by Michael J Shapiro and Hayward R Alker, pp. 285–325. University of Minnesota Press, Minneapolis.

Steinberg, Joel (editor)
1971   *In search of South-East Asia: a modern history.* Pall Mall Press, London.

Stensholt, Bob (editor)
1996   *Development dilemmas in the Mekong subregion, 1–2 October 1996: workshop proceedings.* Monash Asia Institute, Monash University, Melbourne.

Stott, Philip
1991   *Mu'ang* and *pa*: elite views of nature in a changing Thailand. In *Thai constructions of knowledge,* edited by Manas Chitakasem and Andrew Turton, pp. 142–154. School of Oriental and African Studies, London.

Strange, Heather
1981   *Rural Malay women in tradition and transition.* Praeger, New York.

Stuart-Fox, Martin
1980   Laos: the Vietnamese connection. *Southeast Asian Affairs* 1980:191–209.

219

1986   *Laos: politics, economics and society.* Frances Pinter, London.
1991   Laos at the crossroads. *Indochina Issues* 92:1–8.
1993   On the writing of Lao history: continuities and discontinuities. *Journal of Southeast Asian Studies* 24 (1):106–121.
1995a The French in Laos, 1887–1945. *Modern Asian Studies* 29 (1):111–139.
1995b Laos: towards subregional integration. *Southeast Asian Affairs* 1995: 177–195.
1997   *A history of Laos.* Cambridge University Press, Cambridge.

Sukhumband Paribatra, and Chai-Anan Samudavanija
1984   Factors behind armed separatism: a framework for analysis. In *Armed separatism in Southeast Asia*, edited by Lim Joo-Jock and S Vani, pp. 30–46. Institute of Southeast Asian Studies, Singapore.

Sundberg, Mark
1994   Trade policy and Lao development. In *Economic development in Lao PDR: horizon 2000*, edited by Chi Do Pham, pp. 82–92. Bank of the Lao People's Democratic Republic, Vientiane.

Supalak Ganjanakhunda
1993   Cross-border traffic. *Manager* 58:56–59.

Suparb Pas-Ong
1989   Selling for the world market: the peasant petty trader. *Sojourn* 4 (1): 113–126.

Surasit Areesiri
n.d.   *Hongsa Lignite Co. Ltd., Thai Laos Lignite Co. Ltd., Thai Laos Power Co. Ltd.* Photocopy, Bangkok.

SWECO
1990   *National transport study: draft final report.* Ministry of Communication, Transport, Post and Construction, Vientiane.

Szanton, Maria Cristina Blanc
1972   *A right to survive: subsistence marketing in a lowland Philippine town.* The Pennsylvania State University Press, University Park.

Taillard, Christian
1989   *Le Laos: stratégies d'un état-tampon.* Groupement d'Intérêt Public Reclus, Montpellier.

Tambiah, Stanley Jeyaraja
1985   *Culture, thought, and social action: an anthropological perspective.* Harvard University Press, Cambridge, Massachusetts.

Tanet Charoenmuang
1996   *thaj-laaw-phamaa-ciin.* Khop Fai, Bangkok.

Tanyathip Sriphana, Watcharin Yongsiri, and Maana Maalaphet
1992   *kaan kha thaj ʔindoociin.* Chulalongkorn University, Bangkok.

Taplin, John H E
1993   Economic reform and transport policy in China. *Journal of Transport Economics and Policy* 27 (1):75–86.

Tapp, Nicholas
1989   *Sovereignty and rebellion: the white Hmong of northern Thailand.* Oxford University Press, Singapore.

Tatsuo Hoshino
1986 *Pour une histoire médiévale du moyan Mékong.* Duang Kamol, Bangkok.

TecnEcon Asia Pacific
1994 *ADB privatization and management of road sector institutions: transport seminar.* Ministry of Communication, Transport, Post and Construction, Vientiane.

Thalemann, Andrea
1997 Laos: between battlefield and marketplace. *Journal of Contemporary Asia* 27 (1):85–105.

Than, Mya, and Joseph L H Tan
1997 *Laos' dilemmas and options: the challenge of economic transition in the 1990s.* St. Martin's Press, New York.

Thayer, Nate
1993 Diverted traffic: Indochina supplants Thailand as conduit for Burma's drugs. *Far Eastern Economic Review* 18 March 1993:24–25.

Thee, Marek
1973 *Notes of a witness: Laos and the second Indochinese war.* Vintage Books, New York.

Thompson, Virginia
1941 *Thailand: the new Siam.* The Macmillan Company, New York.

Thompson, Vincent B
1995 The phenomenon of shifting frontiers: the Kenya-Somalia case in the horn of Africa 1880s-1970s. *Journal of African and Asian Studies* 30 (1/2):1–40

Thongchai Winichakul
1994 *Siam mapped: a history of the geo-body of a nation.* University of Hawaii Press, Honolulu.
1995 The changing landscape of the past: new histories in Thailand since 1973. *Journal of Southeast Asian Studies* 26 (1):99–120.

Thünen, Johann Heinrich von
1966 *Von Thünen's isolated state.* Pergamon Press, Oxford.

Toye, Hugh
1968 *Laos: buffer state or battleground.* Oxford University Press, London.

Trankell, Ing-Britt
1993 *On the road in Laos: an anthropological study of road construction and rural communities.* Department of Cultural Anthropology, Uppsala University, Uppsala.

Turton, Andrew
1989a Local powers and rural differentiation. In *Agrarian transformation: local processes and the state in Southeast Asia,* edited by Gillian Hart, Andrew Turton, and Benjamin White, pp. 70–79. University of California Press, Berkeley.
1989b Thailand: agrarian bases of state power. In *Agrarian transformation: local processes and the state in Southeast Asia,* edited by Gillian Hart, Andrew Turton, and Benjamin White, pp. 53–69. University of California Press, Berkeley.

221

Udorn Wongtubtim
1994   *chianraaj naj judthasaad kaan phadthanaa siiliam seedthakid*. Paper presented at Conference on Strategic Perspectives for the Manager, Inkham Hotel, Chiang Rai, 23–25 September 1994.

UNDP (United Nations Development Program)
1991   The economy of Laos: an overview. In *Laos: beyond the revolution*, edited by Joseph J Zasloff and Leonard Unger, pp. 67–83. Macmillan, Basingstoke.

USAID (United States Agency for International Development)
1970   *Forestry sector evaluation for Laos*. USAID, Vientiane.

van der Kroef, Justus M
1982   Laos and Thailand: the balancing of conflict and accommodation. In *Contemporary Laos: studies in the politics and society of the Lao People's Democratic Republic*, edited by Martin Stuart-Fox, pp. 274–290. University of Queensland Press, St Lucia.

Van-es-Beeck, Bernard J
1982   Refugees from Laos, 1975–1979. In *Contemporary Laos: studies in the politics and society of the Lao People's Democratic Republic*, edited by Martin Stuart-Fox, pp. 324–334. University of Queensland Press, St Lucia.

Vatikiotis, Michael R J
1996a   Shades of *suvanaphum*: Thailand in the new regional order 1988–1996. Paper presented at The 6th International Conference on Thai Studies, Chiang Mai, Thailand, 14–17 October 1996.
1996b   *Political change in south-east Asia: trimming the banyan tree*. Routledge, London.

Vickery, Michael
n.d.   *Two historical records of the kingdom of Vientiane*. Unpublished manuscript.

Viravong, Maha Sila
1964   *History of Laos*. Paragon Book Reprint Corp., New York.

Vokes, Richard, and Armand Fabella
1995   *Economic reform in the Lao People's Democratic Republic*. Unpublished manuscript.

Walker, Andrew
1994   The Myanmar trade fair: Tachileik 21–31 December 1993. *Thai-Yunnan Project Newsletter* 24:8–9.
1995   *Borderline sex*. Paper presented at Conference on Gender and Sexuality in Thailand, The Australian National University, Canberra, 11–12 July 1995.
1996   *New links between northern Thailand and Laos*. Paper presented at The 6th International Conference on Thai Studies, Chiang Mai, Thailand, 14–17 October 1996.

Walker, Anthony R
1992   North Thailand as geo-ethnic mosaic: an introductory essay. In *The highland heritage: collected essays on upland north Thailand*, edited by Anthony R Walker, pp. 1–93. Suvarnabhumi Books, Singapore.

Wallerstein, Immanuel
1974   *The modern world-system: capitalist agriculture and the origins of the European world-economy in the sixteenth century*. Academic Press, New York.

Warner, Denis
1964 *The last Confucian: Vietnam, South-East Asia and the west.* Angus and Robertson Ltd, Sydney.

Warr, Peter
1997 *Impacts of market reforms on agricultural development in Laos.* Unpublished paper, The Australian National University, Canberra.

Watts, Michael J
1992 Space for everything (a commentary). *Cultural Anthropology* 7 (1):115–129.

WB (World Bank)
1987 *Staff appraisal report: Lao PDR southern transport project.* World Bank, Vientiane.
1992 *Staff appraisal report: Lao PDR forest management and conservation project.* World Bank, Vientiane.
1994 *Trends in developing economies.* World Bank, Washington D.C.

Wenk, Klaus
1968 *The restoration of Thailand under Rama I 1782–1809.* The University of Arizona Press, Tucson.

Whitaker, Donald P, Helen A Barth, Sylvan M Berman, Judith M Heimann, John E MacDonald, Kenneth W Martindale, and Rinn-Sup Shinn
1972 *Area handbook for Laos.* The American University, Washington.

Whittaker, Andrea
1996 Primary health services in rural Thailand: problems of translating policy into practice. *Asian Studies Review* 20 (1):68–83.

Wijeyewardene, Gehan
1991 The frontiers of Thailand. In *National identity and its defenders: Thailand, 1939–1989,* edited by Craig J Reynolds, pp. 156–190. Silkworm Books, Chiang Mai.

Wilson, Constance M
1990 *The northeast and the middle Mekong valley in the Thai economy: 1830–1870.* Paper presented at Third International Conference of Thai Studies, The Australian National University, Canberra, 3–6 July 1987.

Wittfogel, Karl A
1957 *Oriental despotism: a comparative study of total power.* Yale University Press, New Haven.

Wolf, Eric R
1982 *Europe and the people without history.* University of California Press, Berkeley.

Wollaston, Nicholas
1960 *China in the morning: impressions of a journey through China and Indo-China.* Jonathan Cape, London.

Woodthorpe, R G
1896 The country of the Shans. *The Geographical Journal* 7 (6):577–602.

Wyatt, David K (editor)
1994 *The Nan chronicle.* Southeast Asia Program, Cornell University, Ithaca, New York.

Yeoh, Brenda S A, and Tou Chuang Chang
1995   The challenge of post-modern scholarship within geography. *Sojourn* 10 (1):116–130.

Yothin Sawaengdee, and Pimonpan Isarabhakdi
1991   *phrydtikaan romsiaŋ khɔɔŋ phanagŋaan khab rod siblɔɔ tɔɔ kaanrab lɛ phrɛɛ chya roog eeds.* Mahidol University, Nakhon Pathom.

Young, John E de
1966   *Village life in modern Thailand.* University of California Press, Berkeley.

Young, Victor, and Martin James Hyde
1988   *Southern area development master plan sectoral report: forestry.* State Planning Committee, Vientiane.

Yuan Zhou
1996   *Growth triangles: comparative analysis on development of Lancang-Mekong River sub-region and Tumen River area with mutual impacts for APEC.* Paper presented at Workshop on Development Dilemmas in the Mekong Subregion, Melbourne, 1–2 October 1996.

Zheng Peng
1993   *Xishuangbanna gai lan.* Yunnan Ethnic Publishers, Kunming.

Index